# ENCOUNTER

Issues of

Human Concern

# ENCOUNTER

## Issues of
## Human Concern

Edited by ROBERT V. GUTHRIE

*Chairman, Behavioral Sciences Department*
*San Diego Mesa College*
*San Diego, California*

CUMMINGS PUBLISHING COMPANY

Menlo Park, California

CUMMINGS PUBLISHING COMPANY
2727 Sand Hill Road
Menlo Park, California 94025

# PREFACE

Students, while demanding more and more that their studies corre-
late to the society and world in which they function, still have
questions and needs which directly relate to theoretical, experimental, and other work long under way in the many areas of psychology. This text squarely faces critical issues foremost in student
consciousness, while showing the intimate ties between the dyna-
mism of the present and the vitality of the expanding fields of
psychology. This book amply fulfills the need to link the sometimes
seemingly abstract concerns of psychology to the explosive questions
of present-day students.

Today, more than at any time before, social scientists must make
the world their laboratory. Dissent, assassination, addiction, and
displacement are the raw material for classes in human behavior,
and indeed for this book. Relevance is the byword of this generation, and relevance is the key to this book. Racial crisis, student
protest, drug addiction, and situation ethics: these are not only
symptoms of our social malaise but manifestations of psychological
principles that we as instructors have too often presented in a
vacuum. This text, at every point, illustrates the connection of
abstract principle and pressing problem—a connection which has
always been present, but frequently ignored.

The book is divided into six sections. *Section One* serves as an introduction and discusses the study of personality theory and the healthy personality. *Section Two* concentrates on the over-all question of normality; *Section Three* deals with youth and protest; *Section Four* presents case studies of mass hysteria, displacement, psychotic and neurotic reactions; *Section Five* deals with the issue of psychedelic drug usage. Finally, *Section Six* discloses some of the contemporary issues and problems yet to be solved.

I would like to acknowledge my debt to the staff of Cummings Publishing Company who aided and encouraged me through every stage of the book.

To the many authors, editors, and publishers who directly or indirectly contributed suggestions and permission to use copyrighted materials, I gratefully acknowledge my indebtedness and appreciation.

*San Diego, California*                                                    R. V. G.
*January 1970*

# CONTENTS

# PERSONALITY, BEHAVIOR, AND ATTITUDE

*. . . Men acquire a particular quality by constantly acting in a particular way.*

Aristotle

All college students regard personality, behavior, and attitude of major importance to them. Lower division courses in psychology and sociology frequently treat these topics as major subject matter areas. When you stop to realize how often the words *personality, behavior,* and *attitude* are used in discussions, you begin to understand the magnitude of their importance. The terms themselves are closely related. *Personality* is generally viewed as patterns of an individual's total behavior. *Attitude* is seen as a state of readiness to respond in a specific way to social stimuli. *Behavior* is the manner of one's conduct and carriage with respect to propriety or morals.

The selections in Section One are designed to aid in the over-all study into personality, its theory, and application to the healthy person. *The Study of Personality* by Thorpe and Schmuller introduces two conflicting and popular views of personality. Techniques in studying personality and the scientific method are discussed further in this selection. Next, Bischof's *Personality Theory: An Overview* discusses what constitutes a theory and why we study personality theory. This article also lays further groundwork by presenting various attempts to define *personality*. The third selection, Mathews' *Successful Adjustment: A Frame of Reference,* focuses on the importance of attitude and behavior in adequate adjustment to one's environment. Mathews represents the viewpoint that adjustment is the process of internalizing social values at a meaningful level. This section ends with Jourard's *Interpersonal Behavior and Healthy Personality.* Jourard delves into questions of importance to every college student: Why do we need other people? What do we need them for? This selection ends with an interesting view of role behavior and the healthy personality.

# The Study of Personality

LOUIS P. THORPE AND ALLEN M. SCHMULLER

In past eras and societies in which there was little regard for the individual, concern with personality was naturally submerged. Recent human problems and more democratic governments have produced an increasing interest in the individual and his role in society. The present trend is to regard the individual himself as a major focus of interest. This emphasis on individuality has brought with it a need for a clear understanding of the nature of personality.

Defining personality is difficult, because the concept has been so widely used in unscientific settings (and is thus impeded by an accumulation of past and present prejudices and superstitions) and because the scientific data are insufficient to yield a satisfactory definition. Inadequacies of recent research concerning personality have resulted from too narrow views of the concept. Some psychologists have endeavored to study personality primarily in terms of the environment; others have concentrated their efforts on determining the biological basis of personality. Some have viewed these factors in combination, but too few have realized that the study of human personality involves the life process itself—a consideration which calls for a broad and comprehensive approach.

An adequate definition of personality needs to emphasize the point that the individual is a human being *enmeshed in a social order*—and symbolic culture—which influences his every action. Although positions regarding the nature of personality vary from theorist to theorist, few students of the subject would deny that personality should be considered *a unified process* rather than a mere expression of the individual. The definition of personality found in the Fact-Finding Report of the Midcentury White House Conference on Children and Adults appears to be especially congruent with this position. Personality is there described as "the thinking, feeling, acting human being, who, for the most part, conceives of himself as an individual separate from other individuals and objects. The human being does not *have* a personality; he *is* a personality."[1]

An investigation of an individual's personality (psychological characteristics) must include an investigation of his home, his interests, his attitudes, and his personal involvements. Problems of personality pervade all aspects of society. Unless these components are integrated, we shall continue to struggle with partial views of personality and never really understand its nature. Every aspect of personality has significant implications for all other aspects; any one, taken alone is virtually meaningless. We must combine the findings of the different disciplines—psychology, sociology, cultural anthropology, education—so that they provide a total or holistic picture.

## POPULAR CONFLICTING VIEWS

Two conflicting and popular views of personality are the mask and the adjustment concepts.

### THE MASK CONCEPT

The word "personality" has been derived from the Latin *persona,* "mask," a term akin to the verb *personare,* "to speak through," and referring to speaking through the mask worn by an actor on the stage. Both Greek and Roman drama employed masks extensively, a theatrical stratagem which made it possible for spectators to distinguish the characters at a distance. Personality was thought of as precisely what the mask of the actor implied, a cover for the "real" person behind it.

One of the strongest influences in the preservation of the concept of personality as a mask was the philosophy of Plato. Plato's views represent the clearest expression of idealistic philosophy, a philosophy which still is very much in evidence and should not be underestimated in any consideration of the problem of personality. Some scholars still believe that personality is a mere façade for some "substance" presumably underlying it. Psychoanalysis is anchored in the belief that the ego represents the real individual and that conformity to social customs and laws covers this ego with layers of apparently protective behavior.

[1] H. L. Witmer and R. Kotinsky, eds., *Personality in the Making* (New York: Harper & Brothers, 1950), p. 3.

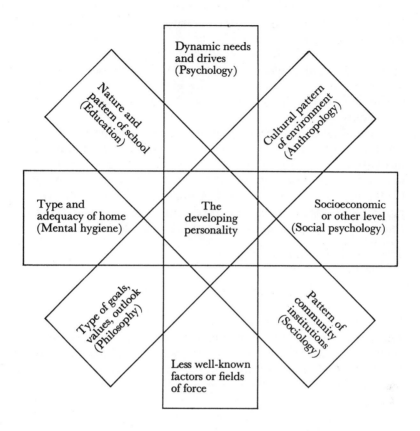

*The interlocked disciplines (Fields of Force) apparently
responsible for the formation of personality.*

PERSONALITY AS ADJUSTMENT

One of the major contemporary views of personality is that it is
molded by the individual's efforts to meet the demands of daily
living. Thus a personality is considered to be maladjusted when the
individual is unable to adapt to the requirements of the cultural
group of which he is a member. In contrast to those who hold the
mask view of personality, the advocates of this view see behavior as

the actual personality. In short, the sum of the individual's movements as he adapts himself to the environment *is* personality, or is all that can be known about the subject. Instead of being a thing in itself, personality becomes a. consensus of what can be observed about the actions of a human being.

Psychologists who favor the adjustment view consider the data of personality to be valid only to the extent that they emerge from behavior itself. Professor Clark L. Hull, for example, makes no distinction between a theory of behavior and a theory of personality.

Evaluating the different theories about personality is a major concern of this book. Three problems involved in making such an evaluation are (1) outlining the major features of a particular theory without interfering with the basic thesis of its proponents, (2) finding standards by which conflicting theories can be compared, and (3) for one who holds an eclectic view, building a framework of principles concerning which there is mutual agreement.

## A SEARCH FOR AGREEMENT

Much of the controversy which obscures the nature of personality is occasioned by a lack of agreement regarding basic features. It seems reasonable to expect that an adequate concept of personality can be formed from features of the various existing theories, especially if they are combined into a pattern sufficiently flexible for practical use. This volume attempts to present a picture of personality which might be called *patterned eclecticism.* One of the authors' goals is the ferreting out of features which are common to the several schools of personality. Heidbreder, for one, has seen that there are such areas of agreement. In her *Seven Psychologies,* she wrote:

> There is more in psychology than systems, more even than scattered facts. Running through its factual content, even as seen through the eyes of rival systems, are converging lines of evidence that point to the same conclusions. The most impressive are those marked out by workers who, starting from very different theoretical bases, meet on common ground in the discovery of common facts—or rather, of facts that call for a common interpretation. There is nothing in psychology more promising than the trends of agreement in independent pieces of research that different systems have inspired, trends which

may be the beginnings of a solid groundwork on which a factual science of psychology will be founded.[2]

The chapters to follow will indicate the extent to which theoretical views of personality vary among themselves and in some instances even within themselves. Although considerable disagreement exists, the fact that there is some degree of consensus is a hopeful indication of possible future progress.

## SCIENCE AND THE STUDY OF PERSONALITY

A hopeful sign is the recently developed fund of experimental data regarding the nature of personality. This has opened the way to insight hardly considered possible even a few years ago. Not the least of the advantages of having this collection of empirical data is the dispelling of some common but false assumptions concerning personality.

### THE METHOD OF SCIENCE

With the advent of the scientific method, the study of personality received a new and powerful impetus. To points of view on personality dominated by dogma and opinion, the scientific method brought an objective and quantitative approach. The unscientific investigator tends to favor his own a priori views; that is, he searches for such facts as will bolster his original opinions. The scientific investigator presents his materials as impartial evidence.

The soundness of any theory depends upon the method used to supply the data on which the theory is based. In general, research concerning personality has progressed from naive, subjective, and unverified approaches to the more precise and impartial methods of the natural sciences. Pearson described the method as follows:

> Now this is the peculiarity of scientific method, that when once it has become a habit of mind, that mind converts *all* facts whatsoever into science. The field of science is unlimited; its material is endless, every group of natural phenomena, every phase of social life, every stage of past or present development is material for science. *The unity of all science consists alone in its method, not in its material.* The man who classifies facts of any kind whatever, who sees their mutual relation and

[2] Edna Heidbreder, *Seven Psychologies* (New York: Appleton-Century-Crofts, Inc., 1933), p. 414.

describes their sequences, is applying the scientific method and is a man of science.[3]

In an effort to insure the general validity of its observations, science has established certain controls. First, the scientist endeavors to rid himself of personal bias. He does not proselytize, neither does he defend a viewpoint which is not fully substantiated by such facts as can be agreed upon. Scientific analysis is precise and exacting. It employs the most accurate instruments it is possible to secure, and is based upon a foundation of statistical verification and controlled experimental procedures. The data are gathered in an organized procedure: facts are collected in accordance with a tentative hypothesis, which itself is subject to verification or disproof. Instead of being isolated, facts come to have a relationship to other facts and to the hypothesis which has led to their observation. Finally, the facts are verified by an experiment which can be repeated with equivalent results by another investigator working under like circumstances.

TECHNIQUES IN STUDYING PERSONALITY

Objectively designed tests and inventories have made it possible for a subject, through his own replies, to reveal certain of his "inner" feelings and attitudes. Projective devices have been constructed for the specific purpose of penetrating the "outer layers" of behavior, induced by conformity to the folkways and mores of society, and assessing latent as well as covert aspects of personality. Case studies conducted by trained investigators have brought together much relevant information concerning individual personality patterns. All of these techniques constitute the means by which the most complete objective information concerning a given individual is gathered.

Largely because of such developments as these, the scientific method of inquiry has made possible a broader and more thoroughly objective point of view regarding the nature and development of personality. The basis of personality is no longer assumed to be "innately" formed and unmodifiable. Tests have shown that personality is subject to change and that certain experiences can do much to bring about particular types of personality patterns.

There is general agreement today that personality formation is

[3] Karl Pearson, *The Grammar of Science* (London: Adam & Charles Black, Ltd., 1911), p. 12.

most effectively studied in its primary setting, which includes the society in which the individual is reared.

## THE NEED FOR CAUTION

It should perhaps be pointed out that science, although the most effective method yet devised for exploring both the physical world and man, still is primarily a method and not an absolute answer to questions relating to personality. Theories concerning the nature of personality, like other theories in the social sciences, cannot be regarded as wholly objective constructions. Although the scientist attempts to be impartial and unemotional, human beings by virtue of their fallible senses are always involved in the interpretation of that which is being measured. Furthermore, as Guilford cautions us, "Every measurement that we make is, in a sense, an error, for it deviates from the true value that we want to find, and it deviates even from the average. Only in very rare cases does any one measurement actually coincide with the average. *And whether or not the average itself even coincides with the true value, we can never know.*[4]

Still another flaw in scientific procedure which some students of personality have noted is its apparent slighting of the individual. It must be admitted that science is concerned with the establishment of general principles based upon a representative number of specific instances or individuals. For example, certain writers on the subject hold that objective testing has resulted in too great emphasis on norms, figures which they maintain do not apply accurately to any given individuals. Gordon Allport, a leader in the field of personality study, takes issue with the method of science so far as concern for the individual is involved. He writes as follows:

> Why is it that science and common sense part company over the fact of human individuality? The answer is that science is an arbitrary creed. It defines itself as a systematic attempt to trace order in nature through the discovery of regularities and uniformative *characteristics of a whole class* of objects. By choice, therefore, scientists have preoccupied themselves with generalized truth, with occurrences that are common to events of one class. A "class," to be sure, is a question-begging concept, for it in turn is an abstraction designed to cover common occurrences. So it turns out that the

[4] J. P. Guilford, *Psychometric Methods* (New York: McGraw-Hill Book Company, Inc., 1936), p. 23. Italics are the author's.

"order in nature" which the scientist seeks is after all quite a circular matter.[5]

Allport, among others, proposes to meet the weakness which he imputes to science. There is, of course, great need for examining the dimensions of personality which characterize the uniqueness of a given person. Individual differences are the basis of personality study but, as Kluckhohn and Murray have declared in a recent authoritative text, ". . . for general scientific purposes the observation of uniformities, uniformities of elements and uniformities of patterns, is of first importance. This is so because without the discovery of uniformities there can be no concepts, no classifications, no formulations, no principles, no laws; and without these no science can exist."[6]

In this volume we will review and evaluate some of the propositions on the foundations and determinants of personality in an attempt to discover the principles and laws governing personality formation and development, and point to the more fruitful lines of study designed to fill in the gaps in our knowledge.

## BIBLIOGRAPHY

Anastasi, A., and J. P. Foley, *Differential Psychology* (New York: The Macmillan Company, 1958), Chap. 1.

Brand, H., ed., *The Study of Personality* (New York: John Wiley & Sons, Inc., 1954).

Dennis, W. R. D., *Readings in General Psychology* (New York: Prentice-Hall, Inc., 1949), Chap. 10.

Eysenck, H. J., *The Scientific Study of Personality* (London: Routledge & Kegan Paul, Ltd., 1952), Chap. 1.

Fairbairn, W., and D. Ronald, *An Object-Relations Theory of Personality* (New York: Basic Books, Inc., 1954), Chap. 1.

Flugel, J. C., *A Hundred Years of Psychology* (London: Gerald Duckworth & Co., Ltd., 1951), Chaps. 1, 2.

Kluckhohn, C., and H. A. Murray, eds., *Personality: In Nature, Society, and Culture* (New York: Alfred A. Knopf, Inc., 1954), Part I.

McClelland, D. C., *Personality* (New York: The Dryden Press, Inc., 1951), Chap. 1.

[5] Gordon W. Allport, *Personality: A Psychological Interpretation* (New York: Henry Holt and Company, Inc., 1937), pp. 3–4.

[6] Clyde Kluckhohn and Henry A. Murray, eds., *Personality: In Nature, Society, and Culture* (New York: Alfred A. Knopf, Inc., 1954), pp. 37–38.

Maslow, A. H., *Motivation and Personality* (New York: Harper & Brothers, 1954), Chap. 1.

Murphy, G., *An Historical Introduction to Modern Psychology* (New York: Harcourt, Brace and Company, Inc., 1949).

Murray, H. A., *et al.*, *Explorations in Personality* (New York: Oxford University Press, 1938), Chap. 2.

Schrödinger, E., *Science and Humanism* (New York: Cambridge University Press, 1951).

Snygg, D., and A. W. Combs, *Individual Behavior* (New York: Harper & Brothers, 1949), Part I.

Spearman, C., and L. L. Wynn Jones, *Human Ability* (London: Macmillan & Co., Ltd., 1950), Chap. 1.

Stagner, R., *Psychology of Personality* (New York: McGraw-Hill Book Company, Inc., 1948), Chaps. 1–3.

Thorpe, L. P., *Personality and Life* (New York: Longmans, Green & Co., Inc., 1941).

White, R. W., *Lives in Progress: A Study of the Natural Growth of Personality* (New York: The Dryden Press, Inc., 1952).

# Personality Theory: An Overview

LEDFORD J. BISCHOF

*Know then thyself, presume not God to scan*
*The proper study of mankind is man.*

Alexander Pope—*Essays on Man,*
*Epistle II, line 1*

## WHY STUDY PERSONALITY THEORY?

Plato in *The Apology* paraphrases Socrates when he says, "The unexamined life is not worth living." This interesting thought from the ancient Greeks has been carried down through the ages and even today is the rationale for much of man's self-analysis. Personality theories fit within the picture of examining life, because they concern themselves with the general theories of behavior as man lives his life.

Personality theories are functional. By this we mean they are ongoing processes, that they are active and not inactive. "Functional" further means a useful activity, designed to maintain balance between variable parts of a system. Progressing from this we find that personality theories are concerned with the very basis of man's behavior. What we are about to examine, then, are theories which concern themselves with the deepest, innermost determinants of human behavior.

Personality theories are integrative. They attempt to bring together the many facets of man's behavior and to weld these into a meaningful statement which will help to clarify the question of why man behaves as he does. Rather than fractionize man's behavior, personality theorists are interested in unifying the multitude of activities and binding them together into a functioning whole.

The most casual observer of the human scene can find overwhelming evidence that everyone is interested in human behavior.

Though not all of us are societally oriented, at least we are extremely interested in ourselves. As outmoded as introspection may be on the current psychological scene, all of us indulge in the phenomenon of self-examination, for we are always held within the walls of our own selves no matter what we do. Personality theorists try to further man's interest in human behavior and to refine the limited knowledge we possess concerning the human animal.

The "What am I?" question is not a new one. Philosophy and religion have for many centuries examined it. Novelists and poets have created literary works directed toward exploring the answers to the question. Personality theory is the psychological attempt to bring more scientific evidence into play in resolving the timeless question of "What am I?"

At times the entire area of personality theory may seem to be best approached from a plain, good, old-fashioned, common-sense point of view. Any student of human behavior, even in the traditional basic psychology class, soon finds that common sense may be indeed common, or general, but its sense is surrounded by prejudice, superstition, and acres of wishful thinking. For example, the common-sense, or popular idea that love will conquer all is neatly handled in Bettelheim's *Love Is Not Enough.* You may love a person with every fiber of your body, but that cannot repair a broken leg or a psychotic ego. Again, personality theory tries to bring fresh insight, and, eventually, predictable patterns into the study of human behavior, strengthened by a growing concern to examine behavior in a research-oriented situation.

One of the universal questions current is that of survival in an age of atomic warfare. Gradually we are beginning to realize the enormity of retaliation leading to annihilation. Out of this framework of fear have come some approaches which suggest possibilities for understanding not hitherto tried. One such approach suggests that modern man must first try to learn to understand himself. With this background of understanding, he may then be better able to understand others, and he will be much better able to cooperate on a more realistic and meaningful level with all peoples. Such an attempt to reanalyze the current international scene was brilliantly made by Jerome Frank (see J. D. Frank, The Great Antagonism: The U.S. versus the U.S.S.R., *Atlantic*, 202, No. 5, 58–63). Personality theory, then, can be a first step toward the foregoing approach to bettering human relationships on the international scene. It would be intellectual dishonesty to maintain that studying personality theories can bring world peace, but it would also be intellectual evasion to deny the right of self-examination as an avenue toward bettering human relationships on all fronts. If a theory concerning human behavior is universal for all cultures and ethnic groups, it must then be held that to study the theory is to understand all peoples better than has been possible in the past.

Although the reader will realize after some time that this is a book about himself, his personality, his dynamics of behavior, it can never be presented as a book on self-help, or, to use Hilgard's well-chosen words, "a manual on the art of handling people." Study in this field does not replace trained clinical help. Although the text should help students to understand the "why's" of existence, personality theory is not directly concerned with psychiatric therapy.

## WHAT CONSTITUTES A THEORY— PERSONALITY OR OTHER?

There is a basic difference between personality theories and theories found in the general area of psychology. In the former case we are concerned with studying the individual in all the facets of his person and determining how these factors explain and predict his behavior. The emphasis is primarily upon normal, everyday behavior. The reasons for man's behavior become the rallying point for personality theory. In the latter case, there are many theories concerning smaller aspects of man's behavior but none concerning the unifying aspects of human behavior. There are theories explaining color combinations, motivation for food rewards, selection and placement of employees in industrial firms, and many others designed to explain behavior in terms of only one direct goal or objective. Many of the valuable theories in psychology try to answer a specific question in a specific field. The work of Roethlisberger, for example, at the Hawthorne Works of the Western Electric Company, revolved around theories of motivation, but these studies used theories designed to improve production and morale *in a specific situation.* Personality theory, on the other hand, concerns itself with motivation as a prime mover in life and throughout life, for both men and women, in all cultural climates: they are designed to grapple with over-all aspects of man's behavior in *all* kinds of situations.

Some confusion may arise from the differences between an hypothesis and a theory. From English and English we find that an hypothesis is an explanation of a complex set of data admittedly tentative and not yet proven, while a theory is a developed hypothesis supported by very substantial evidence.[1] Speculation may lead to an hypothesis, which in turn may lead to a theory, which, if the evidence appears irrefutable, may eventually be established as a law. It is interesting to note that at one time the study of psychology was organized around "laws" of behavior, a term now generally disreputable, although one notes signs of emerging laws of behavior creeping into the literature of behaviorists in psychology. (See especially Brown and Ghiselli, *Scientific Method in Psychology,* p. 161; and for the sophisticated student, see also Egon Brunswik's chapter, "The Conceptual Framework of Psychology," in Vol. I, Pt. 2, of the *International Encyclopedia of Unified Science,* University of Chicago Press, combined edition, 1955.)

As stated previously, we find that a theory is created out of an hypothesis; when the evidence seems overpowering, a theory eventually evolves out of this tested hypothesis. We must now turn our attention to the basic question of what a theory should include. First of all, a theory is a man-made scheme which proceeds from assumptions of hypotheses, having a logical inner consistency which leads to testable or empirically oriented reality. The more precisely a theory is constructed, the more fruitful it is in actual use. None of the theories in this book concerning personality fully meets the above definition. However, few theories in any field meet the fullest requirements of optimal definitions. It is not the intent of this work to test each personality theory as to its perfection when held up against the perfection of a definition, but to try to illuminate and educate the reader toward the content of each theory. We are merely interested in formulating a basis for theory construction, so that the reader may better acquaint himself with the rubric of the theoretical approach.

## WHAT SHOULD A THEORY DO?

A theory should be simple and forthright enough to make the idea it is trying to present understandable. It should use *clear language* and not be couched in neologisms.

A theory should be *useful* so that it leads to meaningful progress in the evolution of man toward better life goals.

A theory should *bring together* what is known in an orderly manner, incorporating this into a meaningful whole.

A theory should *clarify* man's thinking.

---

[1] H. B. English and A. C. English, *A Comprehensive Dictionary of Psychological and Psychoanalytical Terms* (Longmans, 1958), p. 246.

A theory should lead to *accurate prediction* before the fact, not after the fact.


## STRUCTURING THE TERM *PERSONALITY*

The reader will notice that there has been a deliberate attempt to avoid the task of defining personality yet. It is not that the word cannot be defined: it can and has been defined by many astute and intelligent writers. There are some objections to defining the term *personality* at this point, however, particularly for the beginning student in the field of personality study. Personality is better defined *after* one has expended considerable effort and energy in studying the concept: it is almost better considered as a concept than as a word. So many phenomena are involved in the term *personality* that clear-cut Websterian definitions are prone to truncate and confuse rather than to expand and clarify.

It is not unknown for man, in his intellectual pursuits, to study a phenomenon without the support of a unanimously accepted definition. Probably outstanding in the field of psychology of this kind is the study of *intelligence*. Many definitions exist for this word, and there is anything but agreement as to what it means, but vast amounts of research, testing, and academic placement are done in the name of intelligence as a behavioral phenomenon.

In essence, the theory of personality to which one subscribes also determines the way in which one will define personality for his own use. This is not to set semantic traps for the novitiate, but to state a truism. Just as one tends to define marriage or religion from the frame of reference of his own marriage or religious beliefs, so one is led to do similarly with personality and the theory he considers the most acceptable. The term *love* is defined in the dictionary, but from those definitions spring so many variations in theme as to make the original definitions an academic question. This does not, we must admit, keep us from trusting that love will operate as each of us conceives it should!

Thus, as we have stated before, one must study personality theories to saturation point before one is capable of defining personality to his own satisfaction. This state of affairs may promote some modicum of motivation: if you wish to be satisfied with a definition of personality, then the path is well marked—study the theories of personality.

All of the above is not intended to beg the question of defining the term *personality* in some measured order. If precise definition seems to be impossible for the moment, let us see what dimensions of personality lend themselves to preparing a definition of the term.

Basically we find that two major areas of consideration are found in personality theory, and though they appear dichotomized, there are common elements between them. Some definitions consider that man's personality is largely biophysical. These definitions concern themselves with what the human being actually is. In contrast to this are the definitions which concern themselves with the effect personalities have upon one another, the biosocial definitions. Under this umbrella of classification most definitions and theories of personality can be fitted without too much effort.

Further attempts to structure the term *personality* and the theories revolving around it may be summarized and outlined as follows:[2]

| *Nomothetic (largely American) (Methods designed to discover general laws.)* | *Idiographic (largely European) (Methods designed to understand single and particular individuals.)* |
| --- | --- |
| 1. Study parts or units of personality. | 1. Study personality as a unique whole which cannot be analyzed into smaller components. |
| 2. Research designed to find common bonds among all personalities. | 2. "Personality cannot be explained but can only be understood." |
| 3. Great emphasis on quantitative efforts. | 3. Emphasis on qualitative and unique aspects of personality. |

Still further attempts to define *personality* and the theories which surround it have recently led to advocating the term *personology* as the best approach. Reasons for this grew out of the confusion between character and temperament, both as synonymous terms for personality and as different kinds of personality. Character is now largely treated as the value and ethical norm of an individual. It connotes goodness and badness of content and inner dynamics of the self structure. Temperament is now generally accepted to be only a part of the general term personality and to describe an individual's characteristic emotional states.[3]

Another method which classifies definitions of personality first began with Allport in 1937 *(Personality: A Psychological Interpretation)*, and has been utilized by subsequent writers. (An excellent treatment of this approach is to be found in Hall and Lindzey, *Theories of Personality.)* In summary, the definitions seem to be clustered into

---

[2] See D. W. MacKinnon, The Structure of Personality, in J. McV. Hunt (ed.), *Personality and the Behavior Disorders* (Ronald, 1944), Vol. I, p. 7.

[3] *Ibid.*, Chap. 1.

seven different categories, which Allport drew out after finding some forty-seven distinctive definitions:

1. Biophysical:   probably the oldest; defines personality from organic dimensions as well as social characteristics; lends itself to quantification.

2. Biosocial:   the reactive stimulus value an individual has to others, who then define or describe in definitive terms the individual's personality for them; his effect upon others.

3. Unique:   no two personalities ever the same; each person is different.

4. Integrative:   one's personality organizes and integrates the myriad things of which life consists.

5. Adjustment:   the homeostatic agent for all of life's problems; the adjudicator of pressures and values.

6. Differential essential:   definitions which emphasize the most outstanding feature of the personality, not just uniqueness but the essential features which make each person different in some respect (somewhat allied to typologies).

7. Omnibus:   classification that defies categorization; all the other definitions of personality which do not fit into the first six classes.

Trait and type theories and definitions of personality add still another dimension to the field of personality study. Some definitions as they grow out of theoretical considerations cluster about the efforts to identify behavior in accordance with major traits. The term *trait* is greatly overused as a prefix for too many psychological terms, so that the word has lost much of the power of its meaning. Fundamentally, what is meant by "personality traits" is any enduring and persistent behavioral pattern by which one person can be readily distinguished from others. Thus, we may describe a person's personality as having the trait of honesty, or having the trait of courage. Traits are considered to lie within the individual, whether society gives him credit for the trait or not. They are inner driven ways of behaving. Types, on the other hand, are generally derived from labels which society gives to a personality. Confusion may arise in distinguishing the terms when, at times, the same word is used to describe a trait or a type, such as "One of his strongest traits is honesty," or "He certainly is an honest type of person." The difference then lies not in the behavioral characteristic so much as where the characteristic originates. Traits come from within the individual. Types come from outside of the individual and are designations placed upon the individual for convenience in labelling. At one time it was considered that there could be many traits but that types were restricted in number. However, through the loose use of the terms, especially by lay people, that distinction can scarcely now be made. The average individual is inclined to prefix any convenient adjective to the term *type* and thus describe another's personality.

As a final consideration toward the definition of *personality*, we turn to a pragmatic method, such as that found in Bell, *Projective Techniques* (p. 7). Bell is not trying to define personality nor even to create a personality theory. He attempts to give the underlying assumptions that seem to be involved in creating and using a projective test of personality. From these assumptions students of personality theory may gain a broader insight into the term *personality*.

First, personality is a dynamic and moving force. It is never fixed or rigid. Whatever the personality is, it changes from day to day; whether a person becomes more set in character, or develops in a forward-looking direction. One of the irrefutable facts of life is that daily man grows one day older. So we subscribe to the thesis that personality is not a "cast in the bronze" fact.

Second, personality is of a structured nature. Whatever the dimensions of it may be, it consists of *something*. Beyond the obvious fact of the flesh and blood body, personality may be considered to have inner dynamics, whether they be called drives or dynamisms or forces or id or life style; there is more to man's personality than his body.

Third, personality is a behaving and reacting thing: it does not remain dormant.

Fourth, except possibly for Allport, personality consists of more than what we see on the surface. Whether this is called the unconscious or the persona or the image, the evidence would indicate that not all of what man possesses as a personality is apparent on the surface of his physiognomy or actions.

## BIBLIOGRAPHY

BOOKS

Allport, G. W., *Personality: A Psychological Interpretation* (N.Y.: Holt, Rinehart and Winston, 1937).

Bell, J. E., *Projective Techniques* (N.Y.: Longmans, 1948). (Courtesy David McKay Co.)

Bettelheim, B., *Love Is Not Enough* (N.Y.: Free Press, 1950).

Brown, C. W., and E. E. Ghiselli, *Scientific Method in Psychology* (N.Y.: McGraw-Hill, 1955).

Brunswik, E., The conceptual framework of psychology, in *International Encyclopedia of Unified Science*, combined edition, *1*, Pt. II (Chicago: Univer. of Chicago Press, 1955), pp. 656–760.

Conant, J. B., *On Understanding Science* (New Haven: Yale Univer. Press, 1947).

English, H. B., and A. C. English, *A Comprehensive Dictionary of Psychological and Psychoanalytical Terms* (N.Y.: Longmans, 1958). (Courtesy David McKay Co.)

Hall, C. S., and G. Lindzey, *Theories of Personality* (N.Y.: Wiley, 1957).

Hempel, C. G., *Fundamentals of Concept Formation in Empirical Science* (Chicago: Univer. of Chicago Press, 1952).

MacKinnon, D. W., The structure of personality, in J. McV. Hunt (ed.), *Personality and the Behavior Disorders, 1,* Pt. 1 (N.Y.: Ronald, 1944), pp. 3–48.

PERIODICALS

Frank, J. D., The Great Antagonism: The U.S. versus the U.S.S.R., *Atlantic, 202,* No. 5, pp. 58–63.

# Successful Adjustment: A Frame of Reference

W. MASON MATHEWS

Today, Thursday, February 25, 1960, I formally open the thirty-seventh annual meeting of the American Orthopsychiatric Association. To our guest speakers, our members, fellows and friends, I wish to extend warmest greetings. Our program is a rich one and I believe one in which each of you will find material of great interest and considerable value. Your President, your Board, Chairmen and members of the Program, Arrangements and Public Relations Committees, and your Executive Secretary and the staff from the Central Office, will in every way in their power try to make these next three days pleasant and successful ones for you.

Before formally commencing the program with this morning's session, I should like to repeat from last year one paragraph of Dr. Stanislaus Szurek's opening comments: "May the spirit of this Association's historical eagerness to learn more and more of the whole truth about ourselves and about our fellow men, may the spirit of its tolerance and respect for anyone's relevant ideas—ideas which have been independently and freely derived by each and every one of us from our work and tested in that work—may this spirit preside over all our deliberations and thus enhance our individual and mutual sense of human dignity!"

Over recent decades there has been a gradual but clearly increasing trend to consider more intently what normal, healthy, *successful adjustment* is and its importance both to the well-being of the individual and to the well-being of society. To most efficiently use any of the various approaches to promoting better human adjustment, a practical and workable frame of reference is essential with which to compare, for any individual, internal patterns, both of satisfaction and dissatisfaction; and external behavior patterns, both acceptable and unacceptable. Movement of the individual toward successful adult adjustment is in large measure related to his internal organization. How one learns to perceive, to relate feeling to thinking, to channel, control and guide one's desires, is primarily the product of experience combined with the innate capacity of the individual to deal with these everyday factors. Values and value systems of people become clear or confused as a result of

From *American Journal of Orthopsychiatry*, Oct. 1960, pp. 667–675. Copyright 1960, the American Orthopsychiatric Association, Inc. Reproduced by permission.

the way they experience their world. Experience is the most manageable variable influencing growth. That Man and Society believe this, is evidenced by the efforts of parents, teachers, friends, acquaintances, employers and others to influence and manage every type of human behavior; and in the mores of such societal institutions as family, school and church; and in the very laws of the land. How to provide experience of the right kind and amount to encourage *successful adjustment* is less clear and at times causes tremendous doubt and confusion. Our volatile and changing beliefs about child rearing, causes of delinquency, mental illness, learning successes and failures, are some examples of such confusion and lack of clearness. It is essential that we learn what successful growth and adjustment is and, further, determine how to encourage optimal growth and truly successful individual and group adjustment. Any improvement over our present methods, techniques and approaches to helping make man's adjustment more successful would be indeed a real boon to the world.

A frame of reference firmly anchored to *successful adjustment* must be sufficiently flexible to provide a framework within which to understand the infant, the toddler, the child in nursery school and in primary school, the adolescent, and the adult, young, middle-aged, and old. It must constitute a reference standard for the person with things, with ideas and with other persons; for people with other people and with true groups of people. Is it possible to provide a definition which could encompass all this? I believe it is, at least at the operational point. In parent management of children, learning successes and difficulties in the public schools, establishing proper goals in psychotherapy—in fact, in all work with people a clear definition of *successful adjustment* is mandatory if we are to see where we are going in these areas. Where can we seek reliable resources with which to create at least an operational definition? One which presupposes that whatever definitiveness is achieved for any point in human development must to a large extent hold for every other point of development. In an effort to approach a workable definition of *successful adjustment,* ideas from a number of important sources have been considered.

A. H. Maslow describes "self-actualizing" as a process of fulfilling the potential inherent in the person (7, Ch. 12). Maslow further believes that a person actualizes himself best if his background is full of certain need gratifications. If there have been meaningful experiences, physical satisfaction, love, security, and respect, then the individual can be free to self-actualize or achieve *successful adjustment.* His perception of reality is clearer. He accepts himself and others better. He becomes creative, has better autonomy, improves interpersonal relations and in general has a deeper feeling for self and for mankind as a whole.

William Blatz presents his concept of "independent security" as the state of consciousness which accompanies a willingness of a person to accept the consequences of his own decisions and actions (2, Ch. 9). This independent security comes as learning. It involves a task to be done by the individual, who must either actively work at the task or give up. If he works at it, he will by overcoming his feelings of inadequacy, and achieving success with the task, thus attain independent security through learning how to solve problems with his work, in interpersonal and intrapersonal relations, and actually in all areas of his living.

Harry Stack Sullivan's "non-parataxic interpersonal relations" is defined by him as referring to a person with clear, realistic ideas of other people which are not unduly confused by past experiences (9, pp. 102–106). This implies that there must be a clear awareness of and a belief in oneself as well as others. When distortions of reality and ambivalence concerning other people commence in the child, it can confuse the meaning of experience so that in later life this confusion interferes with accurate perceptions of self, other people and situations. Contrariwise, where reality is not greatly distorted and where the attitudes and beliefs of the so-called "mothering person" or persons about self and others are realistic and positive, then there tends to be little or no confusion in the meaning of experience to the growing child and hence he becomes a successfully adjusted adult who is clear about self and others and fully aware of interpersonal relations.

Alfred Adler uses the term "social feeling" and sees this as involvement with all mankind (1, pp. 30–32). To achieve this, the person must have experience which will not make his power striving only a means to compensate for inferiority, and his competition with others so intense and deadly that there can be no way for him to love them (humanistically) or them to love him. Rather it is important for him to have experience during growth which permits warm identification with others and clear feeling of self-adequacy. For Adler this identification and self-adequacy seems to be the real focus of personality and hence allows for *successful adjustment.*

Erich Fromm's "productive orientation" approaches the understanding of human growth in a slightly different way (4). Here the principal idea hinges on the individual striving through his life to find real personal meaning within his own world. Man, according to Fromm, is filled with immense loneliness. *Successful adjustment,* then, comes only when man is free enough to join with his fellow men in a loving, productive way. Through such experiences real self-fulfillment can happen—hence better interpersonal relations which will lead to a better society.

Otto Rank speaks of "creativity" as relating to the individual who accepts and affirms his own will and his own individuality (8). The awareness of oneself as one really is, with assets and liabilities in clear relief, frees the person from false self-images and permits more *successful adjustment*. Basic to this is the assumption that the individual has positive, integrative, constructive elements at the core of his being and that through the use of the will, growth toward a satisfying self-concept can emerge; then this self-security will permit a more reality-oriented interaction with other humans and the world in general.

Of course, the writing of many other authors provides material of great value in attempting a clearer picture of *successful adjustment*. Those used of the many studied were selected because collectively their major assumptions typify most sources of material throwing light on the mature, healthy, normal, i.e., successfully adjusted, personality. How to combine these basic criteria into one definitive statement broad enough to allow for all levels of development and varying situational conditions is a problem. Reading in Marie Jahoda's book (6, p. 19) W. W. Boehm's statement—"Mental health is a condition and level of social functioning which is socially acceptable and personally satisfying"—and Mary L. Northway's statement from the introduction of Margaret Fletcher's book (3, p. xvi)—"We are concerned with helping children become people who face up to life situations, make decisions about what they want to do and how they want to live, and accept the outcome of these decisions with serenity and a further willingness to go ahead"—encouraged me to introduce a practical, operational definition worked out some 20 years ago to explain, through illustration, child-rearing practices and the relationship of experience to adult attitudes in releasing the growth, learning and adjustment potential of children. It stated: "A successful person is one who lives and grows in such a way that he is actively aware, relatively satisfied and feels largely successful with his internal adjustment and as a result of this exhibits behavior that is generally approved by him and relatively acceptable to the outside world."

Such a definition becomes a goal, perhaps never fully reached but attainable in large measure. Experience with people, ideas and things provides the crucible in which growth toward such a goal occurs. Experience which allows for physical satisfactions, emotional fulfillment and intellectual challenge is essential. When one's world provides food, love, trust, sex, freedom, limits, responsibility, and respect as a consistent part of one's life and when these experiences are provided in a way that produces feelings of satisfaction and success, then there is real encouragement to behave appropriately in the eyes of self and others. From birth, for many years it is the responsibility of significant adults to thoughtfully provide the kinds of experience which will challenge, satisfy and fulfill the growth potential of the child to the greatest extent possible. As the infant moves through childhood and beyond, the responsible efforts of the significant adults do not lessen; they only change toward a more cooperative peer position. To the extent that adulthood attains *successful adjustment,* man is free to join his fellow men in a loving, creative and productive way. This results in a truly creative and effective individual of great value to himself, to his group and to society. The experience of parents, teachers, child therapists, and to some extent researchers, is replete with situations which illustrate the validity of the above definition.

Two babies ten weeks old, in an agency home pending adoption, were equally alert, vigorous and generally above average developmentally. Four women cared for the babies in the nursery. The general pattern of care was consistent and fair. Two of these significant mothering persons smiled at, played with, and in other ways gave attention to the babies whenever near them. The other two adults gave physical care but were casual or indifferent when in contact with the babies. To the warm approach the two babies responded by becoming more alert, active and aware of things outside of themselves. With the more casual, detached approach of the other "mothering adults" the babies were restless, irritable, and many times showed signs of withdrawal; i.e., the babies would show pained stillness, their eyes would focus on nothing, and they would become passive. Adoptive parents were finally selected. It was agency policy to have frank discussions with new parents about their baby, his development, their attitudes and values, what relationships and methods he had been used to and which of these seemed most successful.

The parents of one infant were able to understand, and quickly became emotionally involved in a healthy way. They used the conferences to help them work at loving and helping their baby develop. Through the first year this baby was active and happy. As the parents continued spending time with him as he began to grow, allowing him freedom with his toys and at the same time maintaining a consistent living schedule for him, establishing limits only where necessary but holding consistently to them, this baby made extremely rapid progress. For him, locomotion was early. His attention to objects and general surroundings was high; soon he showed evidence of distinguishing between discrete objects. His awareness and delight with his parents and other adults gave evidence of the beginning of very positive feelings for people. Real confidence in self and trust in others was shown by the way the baby when almost a year old could interact with not too familiar adults, i.e., the agency social worker and psychologist. He seemed to have met his developmental tasks positively and for this period of his life made a successful adjustment. This pattern of positive and thoughtful management was continued, and when the child was five years old he entered kindergarten and was quite successful.

The parents who adopted the other baby had the same contacts and information that had been given to the other parents. They seemed unable to realize more than intellectually what was offered them. As soon as the baby became theirs they showed fairly constant anxiety and disturbance over how to manage the child. They had many conflicts between and within themselves. Sometimes they would let the baby "cry out" his distress; at other times they would pick him up and cuddle him. Feeding and other schedules were not consistent. The experience of this baby consisted of an excess of situations laden with anxiety, fear and periods of remoteness rather than warmth and very positive feelings. Through the first year the child made fair progress though he was more irritable, less willing to try things and at times responded poorly to adults, especially when his mother brought him to the agency. After three years his adjustment was of great concern to the parents and added help was given to them. Again they seemed unable to use this very positively, and at entrance to kindergarten the child was seen as emotionally immature and likely to have school difficulties.

Two boys of eight with similar personalities and background experiences were in a camp setting. The families of the boys corresponded to the adoptive parents already described. The parents of one boy were emotionally warm, only mildly demanding, with a consistent way of relating to each other, providing good climate, clear explanations of situations and, generally, showing real respect for the child. The boy was outgoing with people, showing real enthusiasm and warmth for his peers, respect and liking for his counselor, and clear ability to manage himself in a new situation. His first time in a camp and staying overnight with nonrelatives presented him, as it would any boy his age, with a difficult task. His ability to manage his anxiety around homesickness and other troublesome experiences was clear. He would ask for explanations, information and reassurance from his counselor. He managed soon to draw two cabinmates into a trip around camp to get acquainted. Over and over this boy met difficult situations and used his successes and personal skill in leadership and in artcrafts to make it clear that he could enjoy, learn and be successful.

The parents of the other boy were emotionally less secure, the mother having a great deal of anxiety and tension, the father somewhat hostile and inconsistent, and both wavering between a negative, indecisive family structure and a reasonable and clear set of expectations for their boy. They were intelligent but could not feel free or secure enough to really believe in themselves or their child. The son cried at parting with the parents, and for some distance they followed the bus taking the children to camp. In camp the boy rushed aimlessly to unpack, talked incessantly of what he liked and was going to do, asked questions of the counselor but seemed not to hear the answers, bragged to his cabinmates, and soon was in trouble with an old camper who was striving to be the cabin leader. This boy's tension, anxiety and fear of new situations prevented him from using rather clear answers that had been given to his questions. There was also some beginning dislike on the part of his fellows. These things seriously interfered with his adjusting to the new situation. As a result, he started the first night feeling lonely, homesick, picked upon and generally unsuccessful. It required careful work by the counselor and his supervisor to find the boy's strengths and use them to build in him feelings of trust, security and success with the adults, his peers and the various activities of the program. Because of this attention from trained adults the boy became in the following weeks fairly happy and independent, and developed good ability to think through problems, manage himself and relate to his peers. Had this supervision not been given, less and less successful adjustment probably would have occurred.

Two young women receiving premarital counseling came from usual middle class families. The parents of each had been married only once; the marriages had lasted for 25 and 28 years. There were several children in each family. One girl indicated that her parents were comfortable, warm, realistic people who had always talked freely and frankly about most family matters but had not given much information or help to the girl about her coming marriage. She had had college courses in child development and family life. As she posed problems around child rearing, living in a distant city, and her ideas which were at variance with her fiancé's, she showed some worry and concern. As she talked, her own strengths quickly appeared. She was, with only mild support of the counselor, able to see several possible solutions for each question and had little difficulty in seeing alternate courses of action, choosing a preferred one but admitting that alternate choices were acceptable. She was able later to talk honestly and frankly with her fiancé and reach compromises that were acceptable to both. Four years later the couple had two children, and from her description of their marriage she and her husband had been able in spite of many rough periods to continue frank communication, reaching mutually acceptable decisions, were still very much in love, and believed their children were developing successfully.

The second girl described her family as quite rigid in many of their beliefs, keeping the children out of as much important family discussion as possible, never explaining situations clearly, worrying about trusting or not trusting her. Her mother had conveyed the idea that marriage was very difficult, sex was to be endured, and that love did not last. She was tense and anxious throughout the counseling sessions. It was difficult for her to bring up her real concerns and when these did appear she would become tearful and confused or try to intellectualize and avoid the real issue. After a great many sessions she had made some progress but was still beset with anxiety and indecision. She could never talk frankly with her fiancé but kept indicating that if they loved each other all would work out. She was seen again three years after marriage. They had one child, and her description of the marriage was "so-so." Her husband was away from home a lot and seemed never to want to listen to her difficulties at home. She complained of loneliness, inability to help her child do well with his eating and sleeping, and in general felt that the family situation was not good. She knew that much of this was her fault, that her parents had left her no alternative but to remain distant from people, to doubt herself, and to be afraid to face situations honestly and talk them out. She and her husband were able to accept recommendations to get professional help and a year later had made some improvement.

Two men soon to reach retirement age had both had successful family and job experiences. The man who had done the better with his life had had less emotional difficulty with adjustment. He had always been able to find satisfaction and produce well even if he had to accept his second or third choices of courses of action. He had always believed a wide field of interest was useful and had developed many hobbies and other outlets for his needs and talents. He believed that life was good; people were pleasant and helpful whenever they knew you wanted their help. He had a firm belief that he could learn new ways even when he was older. He stated that his parents, teachers, employers, wife and friends had always reinforced this belief by their actions toward him. However, they had also made him feel that life for old people was very different. He had anticipated his retirement and was very concerned that society saw retirement as "going to pasture" and waiting for death. After talking this over with his counselor, it was not difficult for him to see that there were many people who did not have these values. After several supportive interviews he was able to plan realistically with his wife and children. He worked out an agreement with several employers to do part-time work and was able to find time for developing some of his hobbies into private money-making possibilities. Several years later he described his life as fuller than ever before. His private business was yielding a fair income and he felt well physically and had more freedom and enjoyment with his work, his family and friends than he had thought possible.

The other man had been very productive in his field, was widely read and apparently well liked. His parents had always taught him to be careful with people, that they were apt to take advantage of one and show friendliness only in order to get what they wanted. He said that his experience had taught him that in general they were right. He was immensely worried over retirement, knew of nothing to do that would satisfy him, was unhappy that his money-making days were over, resented the fact that his fairly well-off children planned to add to his income and felt that he and his wife were in for a somber life from then on. Even with a great deal of support and help from his counselor, this pattern persisted. He kept referring to what his mother and father taught him, to be independent because in the last analysis you can really only depend on yourself. It was always best to give all one's time to one's work and home; hobbies were pleasures one could ill afford. He finally said, "I know this isn't right but I can't change now. No matter what I do people will not respect me any more." In follow-ups on two occasions some years later, little change was revealed. He and his wife though financially secure lived alone, were very frugal, obviously believed they were old and not worth very much and seemed to have accepted the "just hanging on 'til I die" attitude.

If the foregoing illustrations are viewed within the concept of developmental tasks set forth by Havighurst, the material will be best understood in relation to the concept of *successful adjustment*. He states: "A developmental task is a task which arises at or about a certain period in the life of the individual, successful achievement of which leads to his happiness and to success with later tasks, while failure leads to unhappiness in the individual, disapproval by society and difficulty with later tasks" (5). To clarify the illustrations further, they should be viewed in terms of three notable task sources: characteristics of physical maturation, the constantly reinforcing cultural presence of society, and the vital life core of the individual to become and create.

The stream of *successful adjustment* is wide and any individual at any time may find himself at a different point between its shores as well as a certain distance downstream. Variable experiences bring out, hold back or divert each individual's innate potential. The case illustrations show both of these concepts clearly. From a practical, operational point of view (it must be remembered that this was all that was proposed) the definition of *successful adjustment* holds very well. Hence, it provides a very usable frame of reference in which to view human adjustment throughout life. It does constitute a reference standard for the individual and ideas, feelings, things and relationships, of many kinds. Such an operational standard does not permit discriminations of fine differentials within or between individuals whose adjustment is quite variable but still clearly successful. It should, however, accentuate such differentialness where *successful adjustment* merges into the unsuccessful, unhealthy, maladjusted or pathological. Actually though it serves well here, it could be improved a great deal. Herein, of course, lies the weakness of all attempts at any kind of differential diagnosis. Even with rigorous research approaches, this, as yet, has not been overcome. However, the more exact gathering and handling of data with application of specific numerical values to the results in order to deal with them, does make the individual variables stand out more clearly and hence may somewhat increase our ability to distinguish finer differentials. There should be an ever increasing emphasis on such research.

On the whole, and especially in cooperative professional work, *successful adjustment* as a frame of reference serves many practical purposes for social workers, psychiatrists, psychologists, teachers, parents and others in their efforts at broadly assessing, determining helping plans, and interpreting results. It applies equally well in vocational, educational and therapeutic planning and provides an especially useful starting point to help parents and teachers examine the strengths and weaknesses of themselves and children.

## REFERENCES

1. Adler, Alfred, *Understanding Human Nature* (New York: Permabooks, 1949).
2. Blatz, W., *Understanding the Young Child* (Toronto: Clarke, Irwin, 1944).
3. Fletcher, Margaret I., *The Adult and the Nursery School Child* (Univ. of Toronto Press, 1958).
4. Fromm, Erich, *Man for Himself* (New York: Rinehart, 1947).
5. Havighurst, Robert J., *Developmental Tasks and Education* (Chicago: Univ. of Chicago Press, 1948).
6. Jahoda, Marie, *Current Concepts of Positive Mental Health* (New York: Basic Books, 1958).
7. Maslow, A. H., *Motivation and Personality* (New York: Harper, 1954).
8. Rank, Otto, *Will Therapy, and Truth and Reality* (New York: Knopf, 1945).
9. Sullivan, H. S., *Conceptions of Modern Psychiatry* (Washington: William Alanson White Psychiatric Foundation, 1947).

# Interpersonal Behavior
# and Healthy Personality

SIDNEY M. JOURARD

*Many of our basic needs can be satisfied only through
relationships with other persons. Other people are frequently
the source of frustration or irritation, but we can hardly
remain fully human without some form of communicative
contact with our fellow man.[1] This is not to say that
moments of separation from others are dangerous to one's
well-being; indeed, there is some evidence that the healthiest
personalities need and actively seek periods of solitude in
order to contemplate and to discover their authentic feelings
and beliefs.[2]*

*Why do we need other people? What do we need them
for, and what do we need from them? What are some of the
more common bases for man's dependency upon his fellows?
And how must a person behave toward others so that they
will, in turn, provide him with whatever he needs from
them? First, we will examine some aspects of dependency,
and then we shall turn to a discussion of interpersonal behavior in its relation to the health of personality.*

## DEPENDENCY IN INFANTS

A newborn human infant is among the most helpless of living
organisms. The repertoire of instrumental action which the human
infant can perform is limited to a few automatic reflexes: swallow-
ing, eliminating, crying, and gross motor movements. For sheer
survival, the infant needs other people—parents or parent-
surrogates—to behave in ways which will bring all manner of
need-objects to him. The mother must provide food and arrange

---

Reprinted with permission of The Macmillan Company from *Personal Adjustment*
by Sidney M. Jourard. © by The Macmillan Company 1958, 1963.

[1] The reader perhaps has known people who live far away from other people or
who never interact with others, and he may have noticed that such individuals
seem "odd"—different in their values, emotional reactions, and so on, from the
average person. Fromm regards interaction with others as a *sine qua non* for being
*human. Cf.* Fromm, E., *The Sane Society* (New York: Rinehart, 1955), pp. 33–36. For
an account of *desocialization* and its bearing on "behavior pathology," see Cameron,
N. and Margaret, Ann, *Behavior Pathology* (New York: Houghton, 1951),ch. 16.

the environment so that the child will stay alive, relatively free from pain, and able to grow. As the child develops physically, so that he becomes more capable of learning, he needs other people as identification-models so he can become increasingly socialized. He needs to hear people talk, for example, so he can learn to talk. He needs, in his early days, a lot of mothering[3]—caressing, holding, and social stimulation; there is evidence that without such close mothering, his physical development will be impaired, and his social development will be deviant. The child needs other people to reward and punish him so he can learn to behave in socially acceptable ways. He needs to be in contact with peers, other children his age, so he can learn to compete, co-operate, play games, and so on. Contact with other people is thus seen as crucial for many aspects of a child's healthy development: physical survival and health; the learning of many skills important in the solution of problems and the gratification of assorted needs; and the learning of attitudes, values, morals, and social roles, essential in defining the child's membership in varied groups.

## DEPENDENCY IN ADULTS

The adult, by virtue of a vastly increased skill-repertoire, is much more self-reliant than the infant or young child, but he still needs other people for many reasons. Most of the satisfactions which make life worth while in fact can be gratified only in relation to, or with the co-operation of, other people.

*Technical dependency.* In a society so complex as ours, no man can ever hope in his lifetime to encompass all the skills necessary to solve all his problems and gratify all of his wants. Division of labor and specialization in knowledge and technique are enormously

---

For an account of the effects of sensory deprivation, as well as isolation from people, see Fiske, D. W., "Effects of Monotonous and Restricted Stimulation," in Fiske, D. W. and Maddi, S. R., *Functions of Varied Experience* (Homewood: Dorsey Press, 1961), especially pp. 122–143; also Heron, W., "The Pathology of Boredom," *Sci. Amer., 196*, 52–56 (1957); Byrd, R., *Alone* (New York: Putnam, 1938); and Solomon, P., Leiderman, H., Mendelson, J., and Wexler, D., "Sensory Deprivation. A Review," *Amer. J. Psychiat., 114* 357–363 (1957).

[2] Maslow notes that "self-actualizing people" have periodic strong needs for privacy and solitude. *Cf.* Maslow, A. H., *Motivation and Personality* (New York: Harper, 1954), pp. 212–213.

[3] See Ribble, M., *The Rights of Infants* (New York: Columbia U.P., 1943). This small volume is devoted to a discussion of what the infant needs a mother *for* and what he needs *from* a mother in order optimally to grow. Rene Spitz, a child psychiatrist, has undertaken some interesting research on mother-infant relationships and their consequences. See Spitz, R., "Hospitalism," in *Psychoanalyt. Stud. Child,* I (New York: International Universities Press, 1945).

developed in the Western world, so each man is dependent upon many other people for their specialized skill and knowledge.

The question may be asked, "How can an individual get the other person who has the needed skills to utilize them in his behalf?" In our society, this is generally accomplished on a *quid pro quo* basis; the needful individual "buys" the knowledge or skill from its possessor with money or anything else that is deemed of value equivalent to the skill. In some instances, if the skill or knowledge is very scarce, the possessor will set high or unusual prices for the purchase of his skill-commodity.

*Self-esteem dependency.* The adult may need other people to behave toward him in certain prescribed ways in order to maintain his self-esteem. Thus, if a person has acquired a "self-ideal" which specifies, essentially: "I am not a worth-while self-respecting individual unless other people (in general, or else certain classes of people) admire me, or listen to me seriously, or just plain like me," then it becomes apparent that he needs them to behave in the requisite ways. When they do not, he will be overwhelmed with feelings of inadequacy, worthlessness, or what is commonly called depression.[4] In our society, almost everyone's self-esteem is strongly determined by the presence of approval or accepting-responses from others; but there is also great variability to be found in just how a person needs others to act toward him in order to maintain self-esteem. These individual differences stem from individual differences in life experiences. To illustrate: The author knows several men who feel depressed and inadequate if an attractive woman does not seem to be favorably impressed by their appearance and behavior. A student undergoing personality therapy had a very curious set of conditions which had to be met in order that he might experience self-esteem. It was necessary that his father, *and only his father,* approve of his behavior. When the needed approval-response was obtained from his father, he would be elated, happy, and would hold himself in very high esteem. At the faintest indication of paternal disapproval, the student would be literally overwhelmed by self-hate, depression, and the conviction that he was a worthless individual. In his most severely depressed moments, he

---

[4] Horney has called attention to the various conditions which must be met in order that a neurotic person will not unleash upon himself a veritable onslaught of self-hate. See her *Neurosis and Human Growth* (New York: Norton, 1950), ch. 5. Fenichel also has indicated how neurotics come to depend, for the maintenance of self-esteem, on "external sources of supply." See Fenichel, O., *The Psychoanalytic Theory of Neurosis* (New York: Norton, 1945), pp. 387 ff.

would even consider self-destruction. However, no one but his father could affect him in this way.

The reader might well ask himself this question: "How do I need other people [be specific in referring to other people, e.g., mother, father, spouse, boss, friend, and so on] to behave toward me in order that I continue (or begin) to feel self-esteem?" The answers should provide considerable illumination to the motives for much behavior which occurs in the presence of those people. Very often, in order to obtain the needed behavior from the other, the individual has to "buy" it with behavior that conforms with the other's demands and expectations. This means that wherever there is a conflict between one's own wants and the other's demands, the wants must be sacrificed; when they are acceded to, the consequence is that the other withdraws the needed praise or approval, and the person loses self-esteem.

*Security dependency.* Security has been defined in many ways. In this context, security means the belief that everything one values and needs is safe from threat. People need and value many things for many reasons. So long as the need- and value-objects are available and assured, the person is secure. Anything which threatens to remove, or restrict, the availability of the need- and value-objects provokes insecurity, or more precisely, *anxiety*. Anxiety always implies the anticipation of pain or some form of unpleasantness; in this context, the pain or unpleasantness is produced by deprivation of the need-objects. It is, literally, "frustration-anxiety," the apprehension of frustration.

Since other people do provide us with many things we need and value, then to that extent we are dependent on these other people for our security.[5] As long as the other people are willing and able to act in ways that satisfy our wants (wants which we cannot satisfy by ourselves), then we feel secure. Anything which threatens the relationship with the "dependency-object" will provoke anxiety in the dependent person. He cannot satisfy all his wants by his own behavior; he needs the other person. If the other person is not available or is no longer willing to act in need-satisfying ways, then the dependent person faces the frightening prospect of deprivation.

As with self-esteem dependency, the individual whose security is dependent upon the intervention of other people must buy their skill, knowledge, or needed behavior in assorted ways. He must conform with their expectations and demands; he must get them to

---

[5] Blatz, W., *Understanding the Young Child* (Toronto: Clarke, Irwin, 1944), ch. 9.

like him; in more general terms, he must govern his behavior by their wishes so as not to jeopardize his friendly relationships with them.

In our society, there are many satisfactions which are possible to achieve *only if other people in general like you.* This objective state of affairs makes "likability" a trait of fundamental importance to the individual and the experience of being disliked a near catastrophe. (Later in this chapter, we will discuss this in greater detail.) When one is disliked, it may have the consequence of making many valued ends and many satisfactions completely inaccessible. Riesman's "other-directed" character is the logical outgrowth of the social conditions which make each of us dependent upon others for important need-satisfactions. Since other people will "come across" only if they like us, then we come to seek their approval and affection just as we seek money: not for its own sake, but for what it will enable us to acquire. And so in our society, many people dread being disliked just as they dread financial bankruptcy, and for the same reasons.

*Identity-dependency.* A person's sense of personal identity may be defined as a conviction or belief he *is* somebody, that he has characteristics which set him off from other people. In order that the sense of identity be strengthened, it is important that other people recognize, appreciate, value, encourage, and react to these individual idiosyncrasies. When other people react to an individual on a *formal* basis, when they see him as simply one member of a broad class or category of people, they actually deindividualize the person. Such behavior makes him feel much less an individual person and much more the embodiment of his social role. For example, a wife may be perceived and reacted to by her spouse as "the wife": "I'll have to ask the wife." For him, she is a wife, not a person. A recruit in the army soon learns that his personal idiosyncrasies, so lovingly recognized and catered to by his mother, are ignored by his sergeant; for the latter, he is just another GI. And the army chef cooks for "the men"—not for John, Bill, or Arthur.[6]

---

[6] The child psychoanalyst Erikson has recently been calling attention to the role of the sense of identity in personality growth. *Cf.* Erikson, E. H., *Childhood and Society* (New York: Norton, 1950). See also, by the same author, "The Problem of Ego Identity," *J. Amer. Psychoanalyt. Assoc., 4,* 56–121 (1956). Jeanne Watson, in an ongoing study, sees interpersonal behavior (sociability) as a means by which identity is defined: Watson, Jeanne, "Sociability as a Medium for Definition of the Self." (Mimeographed manuscript, 1956, Committee on Human Development, University of Chicago.) See also Maslow, A. H., *Toward a Psychology of Being* (Princeton, N.J.: Van Nostrand, 1962), chs. 7, 9.

The sense of identity is an important aspect of personality health; a person could not be called healthy if he lacked a sense of identity or if he suffered a weakened sense of identity. But it is clear the sense of identity is strongly dependent upon the reactions of other people to the self. If others will not recognize and respond to one's idiosyncrasies, the person loses palpably in the sense of identity and feels much less a person. We conclude that people are dependent upon others for the reinforcement of the identity-sense.

*Direction-dependency.* Personality hygienists place a positive valuation on autonomy, one aspect of which is self-direction (or, more literally, real-self-direction). By this is meant the person makes his own decisions; he follows his own will and not the will of others. But it happens that people become, in consequence of certain kinds of life-history experiences, "alienated from their real selves." When this has occurred, the individual loses the sense of being self-directing, and he will experience the need for some source of direction other than his own will. Earlier (Chapter 6) we noted certain patterns which emerge from self-alienation. From among these patterns of behavior-direction, let us discuss *authority-direction* and *peer-group direction.* The authority-directed character, or *authoritarian-character,* is an individual who feels lost unless he is in a position subordinate to some authority figure.[7] The directing agents for his behavior might be his parents, his superior officer in the armed services, or his boss. The peer-group-directed character has substituted the will of his peers for his own; he strives to ascertain what others do in a given situation and allows their example or their wishes to be his guide to conduct. He is the compulsive conformer which Fromm[8] and Riesman[9] have described; more recently, experimental psychologists have begun investigating his traits in more detailed fashion.[10]

*Love-dependency.* Love is a basic requirement for personality health and for happiness, and it is obvious we are dependent upon other people for their love. We need the love of (selected) other people.

---

[7] See Fromm, E., *Escape from Freedom* (New York: Rinehart, 1941), pp. 141–178, for a discussion of authoritarianism. For an empirical study of authoritarian characters, see Adorno, R. W., Frenkel-Brunswik, Else, Levinson, D. J., and Sanford, R. N., *The Authoritarian Personality* (New York: Harper, 1950).

[8] Fromm, E., *op. cit.,* pp. 185–206.

[9] Riesman, D., *The Lonely Crowd* (New Haven, Conn.: Yale, 1950)—the discussion of the other-directed character.

[10] *Cf.* Crutchfield, R. S., "Conformity and Character," *Amer. Psychologist, 10,* 191–198 (1955).

One of the reasons we pursue affection so assiduously is that affection in another person is a signal that loving-behavior will be forthcoming from him. Love-dependency is a form of dependency which is quite compatible with personality health. In our culture, we place such great emphasis on the positive value of independence and autonomy we are likely to overlook the fact that the need for love is a healthy need, and its satisfaction does not necessarily rob a person of his identity or independence. Indeed, a person deprived of love will find difficulty in relating to other people in socially acceptable and personally satisfying ways. Or, he may become quite indiscriminate in his quest for persons to love him.[11]

We have reviewed man's dependence upon his fellows for survival during infancy, for technical assistance, approval, security, reinforcement of his identity, direction, and love. Let us now turn to a discussion of interpersonal behavior—man's ways of behaving toward his fellow man—and explore its implications for his personality health.

## INTERPERSONAL BEHAVIOR

The behavior of a person in relation to or in the presence of his fellows has been subjected to intense study over the past decade, and will doubtless remain a subject of keen interest to psychologists for many years to come. The reason for this aroused interest in interpersonal behavior stems from the observation that man's personality characteristics are strongly determined and influenced by his relations with others. Martin Buber, a philosopher whose writings have stimulated many contemporary psychologists and psychiatrists, has made the statement, "The *I* in the primary word *I-Thou* is a different *I* from that of the primary word *I-It*."[12] In another context, Buber asserts that the essential nature of man will reveal itself for study only as man is involved in relations with other men as distinct individuals.[13] Buber's statement about the difference between the "I" of I-Thou and the "I" of I-It means that man, when he interacts with other men as persons, behaves and functions *differently* from man when he deals with things or with other people who are treated as things. An observer who studied man only in relation to an impersonal environment would get an entirely different view of man from one who observed men in their relationships with other people.

---

[11] See Horney, K., *op. cit.,* ch. 9.

[12] Buber, M., *I and Thou* (2nd ed.; New York: Scribners, 1958), p. 3.

[13] Buber, M., *Between Man and Man* (Boston: Beacon, 1955), pp. 199–205.

INTERPERSONAL COMPETENCE

Man, living in society as he does, is obliged to suppress and delimit his behavior to that range which is compatible with the smooth functioning of the over-all group or society. To the extent that his behavior conforms with rules, laws, customs, and the legitimate expectations of others, the man will remain free from criticism, punishment, and censure. In order that conformity with social expectation be facilitated, people are obliged to learn *roles*—patterns of approved and expected behavior—that are associated with one's sex, one's age level, one's position in the family: viz., father, mother, son; occupational roles; and so on. Healthy personality calls for facility at the learning and enactment of these roles in relationships with other people. But a potential threat to health is implicit to roles. Roles call for *suppression* of all behavior and emotion that is inappropriate to the role-definition. This suppression is necessary so that ordinary social relations will proceed along smooth, frictionless paths. People need to be able to predict the responses of others in their everyday transactions. We depend upon our parents behaving like parents, not like children. We expect a physician to behave like a physician when he is in his clinic, not like a playboy. But we have shown elsewhere (Chapter 4) that prolonged suppression of feelings and behavior tendencies can undermine health and that spontaneity and expressiveness are positive factors in wellness. This suggests that healthy personality calls for the ability to reconcile the often conflicting demands of role-behavior and "real-self" behavior. That is, healthy personalities should be able to confine their interpersonal behavior to the limits prescribed by their roles, when this is appropriate, and they should be able to abandon such formality and be themselves in the fullest spontaneity in their relations with others when the situation permits it. Such openness and spontaneity is appropriate in "personal relations" between people, and we shall devote the next chapter to discussion of factors in healthy personal relations. But if a person can assume a variety of roles in his transactions with others, and if he can abandon formal roles and be himself in his personal relations, he is manifesting a special type of skill which we shall call *interpersonal competence*.[14] Such interpersonal competence is an identifying characteristic of healthy personality. Two aspects of such competence are *role-versatility* and *role-adequacy*. These terms refer to the desirable ability to fulfill a variety of roles (versatility) in

[14] This term has been borrowed from Foote, N. N. and Cottrell, L. S., *Identity and Interpersonal Competence* (Chicago: U. of Chicago, 1955).

socially acceptable ways (adequacy). Let us discuss role-behavior and explore its relation to the health of personality.

### ROLE-BEHAVIOR AND HEALTHY PERSONALITY

An individual will enact many roles in his relationships with others. He may be obliged to play the role of husband, father, son, employee, boss, and so on. Each social role a person adopts carries with it certain prescriptions concerning how he must or should behave. Naturally, as a person plays any role, *he is obliged to suppress behavior which is not relevant to the role in question.* If, for example, the role of son requires that the person display only respect, obedience, and submission, then the son must suppress all rebellious, hostile, or self-assertive behavior. A person may avoid certain roles, or strongly resist having the role thrust on him, when the behavior required by that role threatens his self-structure or else interferes with the satisfaction of important needs. Thus, a person may reject the role of husband because such a role will require him to assume responsibility for others, and he may believe he is incapable of holding down a job. Marriage may require him to give up a close relationship with his mother, or with some friends, and since he needs those relationships in order to maintain a sense of identity, security, or self-esteem, he will avoid marriage.

Some roles dovetail nicely with the needs and values of the person, allowing him to find many important satisfactions. Thus a man may seek out the role of the leader, or the follower, because these roles require him to engage in interpersonal behavior which guarantees him safety, satisfactions, and self-esteem.[15]

Although an adult person has some freedom to choose various roles, e.g., occupational roles, some are ascribed to him by society because of sex, age, and the social group into which he has been born. As with all roles, the sex-role, the age-role, and the roles that are assigned because of group membership involve restriction and prescription of certain behavior patterns. The idiosyncratic needs of the person may be satisfied or thwarted by these roles, and so a discussion is warranted of *assigned* roles and personality health.

*Sex-roles.*  One's sex is determined at the instant of conception, but masculine and feminine behavior and personality are *culturally*

---

[15] There is an extensive literature on role-theory. The interested student will find an excellent introduction to this area in Lindzey, G. (ed.), *Handbook of Social Psychology*, I, (Cambridge, Mass.: Addison-Wesley, 1954), ch. 6.

defined and determined. Each person has to learn or be trained in his sex-role. Each society differs in its concept of masculine and feminine behavior, as Mead has convincingly demonstrated.[16] She showed that in three New Guinea tribes, there was considerable difference from tribe to tribe in the typical male and female roles. In one group, the Arapesh, men and women alike were passive, "maternal," co-operative, and nonaggressive. In the Mundugamor, a tribe geographically close to the Arapesh, men and women alike were fierce, cruel, aggressive, and self-assertive. A third tribe, the Tchambuli, showed a different pattern of sex-typing. The men were passive, dependent, individuals who spent their time cultivating the arts, while the women were assertive, and had to cultivate the gardens and make a living.

In America, rigid definition of sex-roles is gradually breaking down. Thus, many middle-class men take an active role in child care, in housekeeping, while their wives do many things which once were deemed to be a male prerogative: They keep the budget, spend the money, and work at occupations that formerly were strictly male. In some European countries, male and female behavior contrasts in certain ways with the American concept of masculinity and femininity. Thus, in Latin countries, a man can comfortably kiss another man, and he can cry openly without shame. But these men might look askance at the American woman who likes to wear trousers. For them, women belong in dresses.

In order to "wear" one's sex-role comfortably, a person has to be trained into it. Yet, some men have been reared in ways that promote the development of traits ordinarily regarded as effeminate; they may also have acquired, in process of growing up, the cultural concepts of the male role. Therefore, they find it a strain to "be a man." In acting in manly ways, they are going against their (acquired) "nature." But if they were to act in the ways which were most natural for them, they might experience a considerable threat to their sense of identity as a man and expose themselves to much ridicule. The same considerations apply to women. The individual who has acquired a rigid concept of male and female roles may experience a high degree of inner discomfort and conflict. If he acts just as he feels, he may undergo a threat to his self-concept. If he acts in accordance with his sex-role, he may suffer from considerable frustration of strong needs for self-expression. Some individuals are so insecure about their sexual

---

[16] See Mead, M., *Male and Female* (New York: Morrow, 1949). This is an excellent discussion of cultural variation in sex-typing by a leading anthropologist.

identity that they must "overprotest." Instead of being content to be manly, they must be "supermanly." They exaggerate their manly traits as if to convince themselves and others that they are indeed men. If anyone questions the masculinity of such a person, he may become dangerously aggressive. His life involves a continual quest for reassurances of his own masculinity. A woman who questions her own femininity may adopt the same adjustive procedures.

A common occurrence is that of role-conflict. Sociologists have pointed out that this is becoming increasingly common, especially among women, as our social system undergoes changes. The woman is obliged to be a housekeeper, a glamor girl, and a stimulating companion to her husband. It may be difficult for her to do justice to all of these roles, so that she comes to doubt her identity as a woman.[17]

Some women, as the psychoanalysts have pointed out, are very resentful of the woman's role in society and envious of the apparent freedom and more privileged position of the male in our society. This pattern has been metaphorically described among the analysts as "penis-envy." Mead has shown that just as women may envy the male, so some men may envy certain female prerogatives, such as their role in the bearing of children. In this connection she speaks of "womb-envy."[18]

Since sex-roles are relatively fixed by society, each person, man and woman, must find ways of fitting himself to his sex-role, of coming to terms with it. Some men and women find their sex-role too constraining, and they adopt many of the patterns of the opposite sex, both sexually and behaviorally.

The healthy personality is able to redefine his own personal sex-role in ways that dovetail better with his needs. Consequently, he has greater freedom to express and act out his real self and is much less easily threatened. Thus, a healthy man can do many things that might be deemed effeminate by other men, and yet he will not experience any threat to his masculinity. He may wash dishes, change babies, perform jobs such as hairdressing or ballet, yet still feel manly. A rigid concept of one's sex-role can promote the development of unhealthy personality.

---

[17] See Parsons, T., "Age and Sex in the Social Structure of the United States," in *Essays in Sociological Theory* (Glencoe, Ill.: Free Press, 1954). See also Jourard, S. M., "Some Lethal Aspects of the Male Role," *J. Existent. Psychiat.*, 2, 333–344 (1962). In this paper, I speculate on the possible relationship between the tendency of men to die sooner than women and the tendency of men to be less "self-disclosing" than women.

[18] Mead, M., *op. cit.*

*Age-roles.* Each society expects a progression of behavior in its members, a progression that will keep pace with the person's chronological age. If a person is keeping pace with his age-roles, he is said to be mature. If he is behind other people his age, he is said to be immature, or *fixated.* If he reverts to behavior characteristic of a younger age, he is said to display *regression,* and if he shows a premature development of traits expected from older persons, he is said to display *precocity.* As with sex-roles, age-roles may conflict sharply with the person's needs. He may not be ready to progress to the next age-role when the time for it comes. Or, he may enforce conformity with his age-role on himself, at considerable cost in satisfactions.

By the time an individual has become an adult, as this is defined in his culture, he acquires a vested interest in regarding himself as mature. Yet, need-gratifications may be possible only if he behaves in immature ways.

The healthy personality feels sufficiently secure about his identity as a mature adult that he can regress when he wants to or when he feels like it without any marked threats to self-esteem or to his sense of identity. A person who is insecure about his maturity may strive to convince himself and others that he is mature and avoid any regressive behavior like the plague. Thus, some men may not allow themselves to be taken care of even when they are gravely sick because it would imply that they had regressed. Some women may refuse tenderness and solicitude from a man because of the implication that they are not independent adults. Some adults cannot play because frolicsomeness feels childish to them and threatens their self-esteem.

# THE QUESTION OF

# NORMALITY

*. . . Sanity is a madness put to good uses.*

Santayana

No subject in psychology has created so much debate and discussion as the question of normality. Most attempts to define normality have given rise to lengthy explanation. The reasons are apparent to the psychologist: cultural expectations, which often differ from group to group, dictate the appropriateness of human responses; changing societies alter the patterns of established human behavior; and most important, as individuals we find ourselves judging the appropriateness of each other's behavior. This is because from early childhood we learn to evaluate our behavior in terms of the behavior of others. We make value judgments about the appropriateness of our actions. Many judgments are based on instruction received from parents, teachers, and other authority figures. As a result of this ego-involvement we consider ourselves "normal." In short, it is always the *other* person whose behavior might not be "normal."

The readings of this section are concerned with the various models of normality. These selections present views concerning adjustment and the effects of adjustment on racism.

Kisker's *The Theoretical Models of Normality* presents five major models by which normality can be assessed. *Behavior Characteristics of the Normal Personality* by Schneiders is concerned with the quality and characteristics of normal adjustment. Grier and Cobbs' excerpt, *The Black Norm*, presents what is necessary for the black American to cope with and to withstand the psychic stresses brought about by discrimination. The last selection, Haas' *Is Anybody Normal?*, presents contrary notions of adjustment and discusses conforming to group standards.

# The Theoretical Models of Normality

GEORGE W. KISKER

There are five major models by means of which normality ordinarily is determined. These models include (*a*) the subjective model, (*b*) the normative model, (*c*) the cultural model, (*d*) the statistical model, and (*e*) the clinical model.

## THE SUBJECTIVE MODEL

In the subjective model, normality is a personal judgment on the part of each individual. The judgment is made by establishing oneself as the standard of comparison. If other people are similar to ourselves, we are likely to consider them normal. If they are sufficiently different from ourselves by deviating in their patterns of action and thinking, it is probable that we would consider them abnormal.

*Everyone is queer*
*Save thee and me,*
*And sometimes I think*
*Thee a bit queer, too.*

> Quaker Proverb

The subjective model insists that people are either normal or not normal. There is no overlapping, and there is no transition from one to another. "Once a thief, always a thief" is a popular belief that applies equally well to mental illness. "You can't change human nature" is an idea rooted deep in the thinking patterns of the great majority of people. This view assumes a qualitative difference between those who are normal and those who are not. It implies that people who are not normal are of a completely different kind.

## THE NORMATIVE MODEL

In the normative model, an ideal of behavior is established, and those who most nearly approach the ideal are considered the most normal. Complete normality, according to this view, is perfection.
The great religious leaders of the world, including Buddha,

From *The Disorganized Personality* by George W. Kisker. Copyright © 1964 by McGraw-Hill, Inc. Used by permission of McGraw-Hill Book Company.

Confucius, Mohammed, Moses, and Christ, ordinarily are regarded as the most ideal of all personalities. Many men aspire to emulate the selfless behavior of these eminent historical figures. The monastic life, and the lives of the saints, are vivid examples of the efforts of some men and women to attain the ideals of human perfection. A rare few manage to reach degrees of perfection far beyond anything attained by the masses of people. These few become idealized, and serve as models of behavior to which other men aspire. The great philosophers, members of nobility, and creative geniuses also have been regarded from time to time as models of normality.

The weakness in the normative model is that seemingly ideal personalities, when examined closely, reveal a full share of human frailties and shortcomings. A more fundamental flaw in the normative model is that it is based ultimately on the idea of "what ought to be." Such a concept has no place in scientific investigation. Science is not concerned with what ought to be or what should be. It is concerned only with the world as it exists.

THE CULTURAL MODEL

The cultural model is based on the assumption that normality is the standard approved by the greatest number of people. If enough people adopt a hairstyle, article of clothing, type of dance, manner of speech, or way of behaving, it is assumed to be normal. The cultural view was expressed by Ruth Benedict, an American anthropologist, who said (1), "Normality, within a very wide range, is culturally defined. It is primarily a term for the socially elaborated segment of human behavior in any culture; and abnormality is a term for the segment that that particular civilization does not use." The cultural view also is expressed in the following comment by a psychiatrist (2): "Whenever we try to give a definition of what mental health is, we simply state our preference for a certain type of cultural, social, and ethical order."

There are many examples of the cultural determination of normality and abnormality. Homosexuality, or sexual relationships between members of the same sex, is frowned upon and considered abnormal in our society. But at other times and in other places, such behavior has been considered quite acceptable and normal. The severe view of this type of behavior in the Old Testament is indicated by the admonition (3): "If a man also lieth down with a man as he lieth with a woman, both of them have committed an abomination. They shall verily be put to death. Their blood shall be upon them." However, in ancient Greece, sexual love among members of the same sex was looked upon favorably, and even encouraged. Plato said (4): "They (speaking of homosexuals) act in this way because they have a strong soul, manly courage, and a virile character." Today, in our culture, homosexual behavior is neither an abomination nor a sign of strong character. It is looked upon as an expression of a disturbed personality. Here, then, are three sets of attitudes toward the same behavior. Each attitude is a function of the culture in which the behavior occurs.

Similarly, in our culture, it is a crime for an adult to engage in sex relations with a child. But in certain sections of India, it is normal for adult men to engage in sex activities with girls as young as eight years (5). Also, we vigorously oppose sex play among children. Yet in other societies, such play is not only tolerated, but actively encouraged. Among the Trobriand Islanders, sex relations begin with six-year-old girls and ten-year-old boys (6).

What is normal and what is abnormal varies from one culture to another, and the situations which precipitate mental disturbance may differ because of variations in social patterning. Otto Klineberg, a social psychologist, said that abnormality is social "not only because it occurs in social situations, but also because it is embedded in the very structure of a society, and can only be understood against the background of the culture in which it occurs"(7).

There are three types of evidence for the cultural model of abnormality. This evidence includes (*a*) behavior considered abnormal in our culture but normal in other cultures, (*b*) behavior considered normal in our society but abnormal in others, and (*c*) types of abnormalities not found in Western civilization.

Behavior that would be abnormal in our culture but which is normal in other cultures includes the "insult complex" of the Northwest Coast Indians who consider almost anything an insult, the exaggerated fear and suspicion of the natives of Dobu, the taboo on touching found among the Polynesians, the common practice of using drugs to induce visual and auditory perceptual disturbances among the Plains Indians, the trance states of the Yogis, and the general acceptance of homosexuality in a number of cultures.

An example of behavior which is normal in our culture, but which would be considered abnormal in other cultures, is our emphasis on personal initiative and competitiveness. Such behavior would be regarded as abnormal among the Zuñi Indians of New Mexico. Similarly, the emphasis on acquisitiveness found in our culture is discouraged in certain other societies.

The cultural model of abnormal behavior also is supported by the occurrence among different societies of behavior disorders which are peculiar to them. Such conditions as *arctic hysteria, amok, latah, witigo,* and similar reactions . . . do not appear to have counterparts in our culture. While it is possible that the basic susceptibility to personality disorganization is due to inborn factors, the form taken by the disturbance is influenced to a considerable degree by social forces.

The legal concept of abnormality is a special case of the cultural model. This view assumes that normal behavior is that which is consistent with the codified regulations of society, while abnormal behavior is inconsistent with the rules of society. The difficulty with the legal criterion of abnormality is that it measures behavior in terms of rules, regulations, ordinances, and laws, which have been established arbitrarily, and with little consideration for the complexities of human behavior. The legal world is still burdened to some extent by the archaic concept of determining "insanity" by the test of whether an individual knows right from wrong. The assumption is that if this distinction can be made, the individual is "sane"; if the distinction cannot be made, the individual is "insane." Nothing could be more incorrect.

While the legal concept has been modified in some states, using the ability to distinguish between right and wrong as a measure of mental competency is completely without justification. Serious forms of personality disorganization are found in some men and women who would have little trouble in making such a distinction, while the distinction cannot be made by other people who have never shown any symptoms of mental illness.

## THE STATISTICAL MODEL

The statistical conception of normality says that the "average" is normal. There is an average weight, height, hat size, shoe size, and clothing size. The closer the average is approached, the more normal the person is considered to be. A man would not be normal if he wore a size ten hat, or a size fourteen shoe.

The statistical model is best illustrated by the normal distribution curve. This curve is derived by plotting cases along a base line, with the number of cases indicated on the vertical axis. The bell-shaped appearance of the curve is due to the fact that most cases fall in the middle of the distribution, with fewer and fewer cases trailing off at the lower and upper ends. According to the statistical

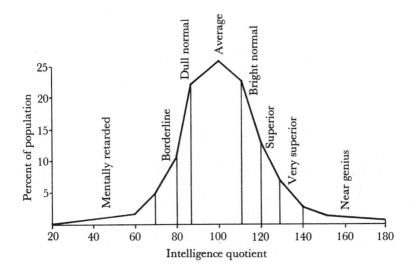

*The normal distribution curve. (Adapted from
L. M. Terman,* Measuring Intelligence, *1937.)*

model, cases falling at the middle of the distribution are the most normal cases. As cases fall farther and farther toward the ends of the distribution, the degree of abnormality increases.

The statistical criterion of abnormality is illustrated clearly in the case of intelligence. Most people have average intelligence. When intelligence test scores are plotted along a base line, the majority of the scores fall into the middle section of the distribution. Relatively few people have high intelligence, fewer have very high intelligence, and a rare few are geniuses having an extraordinary capacity for imaginative creation, original thought, invention or discovery. Similarly, some people have low intelligence, fewer have very low intelligence, and a relatively small number are mentally retarded. For this reason, fewer and fewer cases are plotted as the ends of the distribution are approached. When large numbers of cases are involved, the typical bell-shaped curve appears.

Individuals with abnormally high intelligence and abnormally low intelligence are at either end.

Unfortunately, this approach does not lend itself conveniently to the analysis of the personality. While the statistical model is an adequate means of portraying relatively uncomplicated traits and of representing simple biological measurements, it cannot reflect the subtle complexities of a total personality. The difficulty is not in the nature of the model, but in the present inability of science to formulate personality variables in a way in which they can be handled meaningfully by statistical techniques. The inability to isolate and quantify the variables of personality makes the statistical model largely ineffective in the field of personality disturbance at the present time.

Another difficulty with the statistical model is that the frequent occurrence of a given type of behavior is not necessarily healthy, desirable, or normal. Many physical conditions, such as tooth cavities, hardening of the arteries, high blood pressure, and defective vision, are so frequently encountered that they are average in the statistical sense. Similarly, millions of people are anxious, worried, fearful, guilt-laden, depressed, and emotionally unstable. Yet the mere frequency of these conditions does not make them normal.

THE CLINICAL MODEL

The clinical view of normality emphasizes the effectiveness of the organization and functioning of the individual personality. The approach is frankly a relative one, and appreciates fully the multidimensional nature of personality. While the model draws freely upon social criteria, the major emphasis is placed upon freedom from disabling symptoms. In a broad sense, the clinical model is concerned with mental health.

One of the advantages of the clinical model is that nondisabling symptoms may be present and may in fact add to the effectiveness of the personality organization. One psychologist put it this way(8):

*When I'm in an airplane, I don't want my pilot to be some slap-happy, easy-going bundle of joy who is too busy laughing and relating to the stewardesses to worry about the instruments. I prefer a tense, rigid man who is so loaded down with obsessions and compulsions that he can not take his eyes off the dial. If I am lying on the operating table, I am not interested in knowing that my surgeon is a nice fellow with a lot of empathy for his nurses. For all I care his nurses can hate him—as long as he knows what he is doing and has them on their toes.*

While the clinical model of normality is probably the most useful approach to the problems of mental health and illness, it is not completely independent of the other models. In fact, it is impossible to draw a sharp line between the various models of normality. A particular model is valid only to the degree that it serves a particular purpose. The important thing is to recognize the subjective nature of the concepts of normality and abnormality and to exercise the necessary caution in making interpretations in this field.

## REFERENCES

1. Benedict, Ruth, "Anthropology and the abnormal," *J. gen. Psychol.*, 1934, X, p. 59.
2. Szasz, T. S., "Some observations on the relationship between psychiatry and the law," *Amer. med. Ass. Arch. Neurol. Psychiat.*, 1956, LXXV, p. 297.
3. Leviticus. 20:13.
4. Jowett, B. (trans.), *The dialogues of Plato* (New York: Random House, Inc., 1953).
5. Ellis, H., *Studies in the psychology of sex* (New York: Random House, Inc., 1942), 2 vols.
6. Malinowski, B., *The sexual life of savages in North-western Melanesia* (New York: Liveright Publishing Corporation, 1929).
7. Klineberg, O., *Social psychology*, 2d ed. (New York: Holt, Rinehart & Winston, Inc., 1954).
8. Havemann, E., "Who's normal? Nobody, but we all keep trying," *Life*, Aug. 8, 1960, XLIX, p. 78.

# Behavior Characteristics
# of the Normal Personality

ALEXANDER A. SCHNEIDERS

## THE QUALITY OF NORMAL ADJUSTMENT

For any single problem arising in the course of human experience there may be several possibilities for solution. The outcome depends on experience in the handling of problems, availability of substitute responses, adaptability, level of maturity, and similar factors. Some of these responses are normal and healthy and thus fulfill the criteria of adequate adjustment; others are abnormal or maladjustive and may contribute to the breakdown of personality and mental health or to the disruption of the relations between the individual and reality.

Suppose, for example, that a boy's father is offered a position in another city, which means a change of residence for the entire family. This would involve breaking up old friendships, changing schools, learning to live in a new and strange environment, relinquishing family ties, and so on. A situation like this can be deeply frustrating and may lead to a number of adjustment problems. Whether or not it does depends on the boy's reactions, and it is these reactions that will determine the quality of adjustment. The boy could, for example,

Accept the change in a spirit of adventure
Plead with his father not to accept the position
Become resigned to a situation over which he has no control
Accept the situation in a mature and realistic fashion
Elect to remain in his home town and live with relatives
Refuse to make the change
Fail in school subjects as a protest against the change
Develop resentment, hostility, and aggression
Become moody and depressed
Exploit his mother's reluctance to make the change

Rejoice over his father's good fortune in getting a better
position
Develop hysterical symptoms in an effort to prevent the
change
Threaten self-destruction if forced to change residence
Accuse his father of ruining his life
Develop symptomatic disorders that would preclude the
change of residence

The possibilities are numerous, and no one could tell for sure
what the outcome is going to be. Some of these possible reactions
would promote good adjustment, and others would just as surely
lead to adjustment difficulties. The question then arises whether
the quality of adjustment varies in a straight line, or whether it is
discontinuous. Is all adjustment (good and bad) essentially the
same, varying only in degree or in accidental characteristics? Or
are adjustment processes discrete, so that we can draw a sharp line
between those that are normal and adequate and those that are
abnormal or maladjustive in character (Shoben, 1957).

CONTINUUM OF ADJUSTMENT PROCESSES

The precise quality of any adjustment process has a lot to do with
the essential nature of adjustment. The more fully we understand
the difference between good and bad adjustment, the more certainly will we grasp the basic nature of the adjustment process. In
the sense that all adjustment processes, regardless of individual
characteristics, represent attempts by the person to secure the gratification of basic needs and desires, and to reduce conflicts, frustrations, and tensions associated with these motivations, we may say
that *they are all essentially alike.* From this viewpoint the difference
between adjustment and maladjustment is a matter of degree,
which could be determined in any single instance by applying
some reliable criterion such as maturity. As one writer says, "The
pathological individual does not differ from the normal in some
quality or essence which he possesses but the normal person does
not. Nor does the normal possess certain qualities that the poorly
adjusted person does not. The difference is merely one of degree.
. . . The only difference between the normal person and the abnormal is a quantitative one" (Symonds, 1949, p. 384).

In other words, therefore, the more that any response fulfills the
selected criterion, the greater the degree of adjustment. Pathologi-
cally immature responses, then, would represent the extreme of
maladjustment. Using the example described earlier, we could say

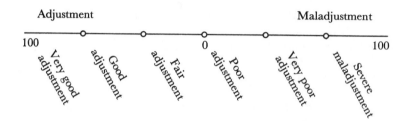

*Continuum of adjustment processes.*

that acceptance of the father's change in position in a realistic and mature fashion is an instance of very good adjustment, whereas the development of symptomatic disorders, or of resentment, hostility, and depression exemplifies gross maladjustment. The figure above is a simple diagrammatic representation of this *continuum of human adjustment,* which extends from the extreme of unusually good adjustment to that of severe maladjustment. Human nature being what it is, the majority of responses would tend to cluster in the middle range.

From another point of view, maladjustive responses may be said to differ fundamentally from those that are adjustive. Between the normal person's rational, healthy acceptance of reality and the complete rejection or distortion of reality by the psychotic patient, there is a gap that cannot be readily bridged by the concept of quantitative variation. There seems to be, in other words, *a qualitative difference* between responses that are essentially normal and those that are essentially abnormal. This distinction was anticipated in our earlier discussion of psychological normality. This argument is based on the character or quality of the response itself. There is a *real qualitative difference* between the acceptance of reality and its distortion or rejection. Thus complete maladjustment, from the *quantitative* point of view, would mean maximum failure in attempting to meet the demands of self or of reality, whereas *qualitatively,* it would signify pathological distortion of one's relation to self and to reality. Expressed concretely, the paranoid patient is severely maladjusted because of the pathological quality of his delusions which distort his relation to reality, whereas the person who consistently fails to meet the requirements of daily living, in academic, social, or marital situations, is also poorly adjusted even though no pathology is involved. In the latter case, however, it is the *degree of failure* rather than the nature of the response that determines the quality of adjustment.

Some writers recognize qualitative as well as quantitative differences between normality and abnormality. Pointing to the fundamental difference between physical health and disease, Page says:

> This viewpoint, which is known as the *pathological criterion* of abnormality, is also applicable to certain forms of mental disorder. For example, normal individuals do not appear to have the same kind of emotional and thought disturbances that are observed in some mental patients. . . . The pathological criterion does not differentiate the normal from the superior group, but it is not improbable that qualitative differences also exist between these two groups.[1]

Between the extremes of good and poor adjustment, there is the *nonadjustive* type of response which also varies qualitatively from the other two. The majority of responses, whether psychologically good or bad, are adjustive in the sense that they reduce tension, frustration, and conflict; however, there are some responses that seem to have no adjustive significance. To this class belong many mannerisms, eccentricities, and peculiarities of conduct or expression, such as continuous humming, wearing odd-looking clothes, speaking with an affected accent, habitually squinting, or pursing one's lips. These responses have little to do with adjustment and thus merit no further consideration (Shaffer, 1936, p. 257).

### CLASSIFICATION OF ADJUSTIVE RESPONSES

The wide range in complexity of adjustive responses makes it somewhat difficult to set up a satisfactory classification that would serve all purposes. But several possibilities can be studied to advantage.

First of all, adjustive responses can be classified by *symptoms and causes.* Here the categories of neurotic, psychotic, psychopathic, and epileptic are used. This classification is more suited to the aims of abnormal psychology and psychiatry than to those of adjustment psychology, since our primary purpose is to study the process of

---

[1] Page, J. D., *Abnormal psychology* (New York: McGraw-Hill, 1947), pp. 14–15. Used by permission of McGraw-Hill Book Company.

adjustment, whether normal or abnormal. Adjustments can also be grouped in terms of the *kinds of response* involved. This classification is particularly useful to the study of adjustment because it centers attention on the mental and behavioral processes involved in adjustive behavior. Within this classification we can distinguish (1) normal adjustment, (2) adjustment by means of defense reactions, (3) adjustments by escape and withdrawal, (4) adjustments by illness, and (5) adjustments by aggression. For these different forms we have adopted the general term "patterns of adjustments," which are described in Part Three.

Finally, adjustments can be classified in terms of the *problems or situations* involved. In this category would be included personal, social, family, academic, vocational, and marital adjustments. This grouping is also consonant with the aims of adjustment psychology, which describes the adjustment process in all of its different phases. These we will study in the section on mental hygiene (Part Four). There are, of course, many interrelations between these two groupings, and we shall find that the different patterns of adjustment condition the varieties of adjustive behavior in a complex and intricate manner. By studying such relations we can bridge the gap between the more abstract study of adjustment processes and their occurrence in everyday, concrete situations.

## NORMAL ADJUSTMENTS

### CHARACTERISTICS OF NORMAL ADJUSTMENTS

The term "normal adjustment" is used here to denote those ways of behaving or reacting that do not involve the difficulties or negative characteristics associated with maladjustive and abnormal responses. Everyone recognizes the difference between a calm, deliberate attack on a problem and one that is disorganized, over-emotional, and lacking in direction. For example, the worker who calmly accepts criticism and sets about correcting whatever deficiencies exist is responding normally, and the student who redoubles his efforts in order to overcome low grades, instead of rationalizing his poor performance or blaming his teachers, is making a normal adjustment. Examples like these could be multiplied endlessly; it is probable that the majority of human responses belong in this category.

These responses are characterized in certain ways that enable us to identify them without too much difficulty. First of all, they can be identified by a relative *absence of excessive or damaging emotionality.*

In persons who respond normally to problems or reality demands, there is always a certain degree of emotional tranquility and control, which enables them to size up the situation intelligently and to go about resolving the difficulty.

Normal adjustments are characterized also by a relative *absence of psychological mechanisms*. A straightforward approach to a problem, conflict, or frustration is more clearly indicative of normal response than the devious route of such mechanisms as rationalization, projection, sour grapes, or compensation. Falling back on the specious reasoning of rationalization is less a normal adjustment than the frank admission of personal weaknesses or lack of adequate effort.

Normal adjustments are also largely *free of the sense of personal frustration*. A feeling of frustration, as we will see later, makes it difficult or even impossible to react normally to problem situations. If, for example, a student feels hopelessly frustrated in his academic efforts or social aspirations, it becomes increasingly difficult for him to organize his thinking, feelings, or behavior effectively in those situations in which he feels frustrated. Therefore, instead of reacting normally, he is likely to use outmoded responses, psychological mechanisms, or other nonadjustive responses.

From a more positive point of view, normal adjustments are characterized by *rational deliberation and self-direction*. The basic human ability to think through problems, conflicts, or frustrations, and to organize thinking and behavior so that difficulties can be resolved is the surest guarantee of normal adjustment. This characteristic is illustrated daily in the efficient handling of economic problems, marital difficulties, responsibilities in school, social relations, sex conflicts, vocational frustrations, disappointments, and tragedies. Conversely, the absence of rational deliberation and self-direction is a sure sign of inadequate adjustment.

Normal adjustment is further characterized by the *ability to learn*. This point is clearly exemplified in marital adjustment which demands continuous growth. Personal, selfish aims must be relinquished, at the same time that necessary habits, skills, attitudes, and interests are developed, without which adjustment is impossible. In situations like this, therefore, normal adjustment is characterized by *continuous learning*.

The ability to learn reminds us of another characteristic of normal adjustment, which is the *utilization of past experience*. This of course is one of the ways in which we learn. It is often noted that the psychopathic personality, with a high degree of maladjustment, is characterized by the inability to profit from past experience. This inability lies at the basis of many other adjustment difficulties as well. Normal adjustment, then, requires effective use of past experience. For example, the worker who finds that he cannot meet the responsibilities of his job with less than seven hours' sleep is adjusting normally when he arranges a schedule that will insure adequate rest. Inadequate personalities are notoriously lacking in this ability.

Finally, we may note that normal adjustments are consistently associated with a *realistic, objective attitude,* one that, based on learning, past experience, and rational deliberation, *enables us to evaluate a situation, problem, or personal limitation as it actually is.* Suppose, for example, that the loss of a job, a serious injury, or the death of one's parents is regarded as an irreversible catastrophe, from which recovery is impossible. In such a case, the chances of adjusting normally to the situation are pretty slim. Similarly, to appraise one's own personal qualities unrealistically is likely to impede good adjustment. To view one's self realistically and objectively is one of the clearest signs of the normal personality. It acts as a protection against distortions of the self concept and the damaging influences such distortions can have on adjustment and mental health.

Here, then, are some of the characteristics of normal, healthy adjustments. Understanding them thoroughly will pave the way to a clearer understanding of the behavior characteristics of the normal personality.

# The Black Norm

WILLIAM H. GRIER AND PRICE M. COBBS

We submit that it is necessary for a black man in America to develop a profound distrust of his white fellow citizens and of the nation. He must be on guard to protect himself against physical hurt. He must cushion himself against cheating, slander, humiliation, and outright mistreatment by the official representatives of society. If he does not so protect himself, he will live a life of such pain and shock as to find life itself unbearable. For his own survival, then, he must develop a *cultural paranoia* in which every white man is a potential enemy unless proved otherwise and every social system is set against him unless he personally finds out differently.

Every black man in America has suffered such injury as to be realistically sad about the hurt done him. He must, however, live in spite of the hurt and so he learns to know his tormentor exceedingly well. He develops a sadness and intimacy with misery which has become a characteristic of black Americans. It is a *cultural depression* and a *cultural masochism*.

He can never quite respect laws which have no respect for him, and laws designed to protect white men are viewed as white men's laws. To break another man's law may be inconvenient if one is caught and punished, but it can never have the moral consequences involved in breaking one's own law. The result may be described as a *cultural antisocialism*, but it is simply an accurate reading of one's environment—a gift black people have developed to a high degree, to keep alive.

These and related traits are simply adaptive devices developed in response to a peculiar environment. They are no more pathological than the compulsive manner in which a diver checks his equipment before a dive or a pilot his parachute. They represent normal devices for "making it" in America, and clinicians who are interested in the psychological functioning of black people must get acquainted with this body of character traits which we call the *Black Norm*. It is a normal complement of psychological devices, and to find the amount of sickness a black man has, one must first

From Chapter VIII of *Black Rage* by William H. Grier and Price M. Cobbs, © 1968 by William H. Grier and Price M. Cobbs, Basic Books, Inc., Publishers, New York.

total all that appears to represent illness and then subtract the Black Norm. What remains is illness and a proper subject for therapeutic endeavor. To regard the Black Norm as pathological and attempt to remove such traits by treatment would be akin to analyzing away a hunter's cunning or a banker's prudence. This is a body of characteristics essential to life for black men in America and woe be unto that therapist who does not recognize it.

# Is Anybody Normal?

KURT HAAS

## ADJUSTMENT AND CONFORMITY

Partially to avoid the difficult scientific and philosophical problems inherent in any attempt to state what normality is, the notion of "adjustment" has been proposed. *Adjustment* is defined as the ability to get along with others. Psychological health is seen as consisting of the skills necessary to fit ourselves in with others and respond as desired by those with whom we associate. Psychologists have dubbed this an environment-centered approach to normality. Normality is viewed as the ability to adjust to our surroundings even when, at times, the environment is itself abnormal.

Many psychologists, such as Dr. Abraham Maslow of Brandeis University, are dissatisfied with definitions of normality that imply that man may retain his psychological well-being simply by fitting himself into a particular culture. The sadistic fanatic, it is pointed out, who slips comfortably into the role of party stalwart in an autocratic society is thus "well adjusted," but hardly normal in any ethical-psychological sense. An environment-centered definition of normality means that a particular culture or group, whether it be a settlement of religious idealists or a delinquent street gang, is the final arbiter of normality. The society that is itself sick therefore demands that all its members manifest a similar disorder. A person who is actually dangerously disturbed—a juvenile delinquent, for example—may be considered well adjusted by the disordered standards of his own social group.

Another critic of the emphasis on adjustment is Erich Fromm. In his quest for normalcy, i.e., adjustment, the individual in our culture is led to take on what Fromm has called a "marketing orientation." Personality is shaped to a considerable degree by the demands and expectations of our social equals—the so-called "market." The market-oriented personality develops those qualities that can best be sold. In his book *Man for Himself,* Fromm suggests that the basic characteristic of the "marketing orientation is emptiness ... the lack of any specific quality which is not subject to change."

Since any particular trait might someday conflict with the requirements of the market, the essence of this personality is that "no specific and permanent kind of relatedness is developed." The market-oriented personality confuses normality with the ability to blend in with the personal requirements of the society in which he lives and moves. He loses all sense of individuality and creativity.

To what extent, however, is adjusting to and conforming with the wishes of the groups in which we live a necessity? There is no answer equally applicable to all. Individuals continually find that they need to shape their own behavior to coincide with the inclinations of the majority. A businessman or professional may dislike suit and tie but wear them because they are a requisite indicator of his position. A PTA mother may not care for the superficial niceties that typify her contact with other members, but she conforms in order to enable herself to carry out her more valued functions. All of us must decide the degree to which we are willing to curb ourselves so that we may work in the ways most effective for us. The student or employee who consistently arrives late to class or job because, as he states, he cannot be bothered to conform to arbitrary deadlines is not expressing his individual creativity. He is permitting what may be relatively petty or immature motives to interfere with what should be more cherished goals. The ordinary and everyday discipline we exercise over ourselves, conforming to what is reasonable, is called by social scientists "respect for legitimate order." By subordinating some of our own wishes so that we may live and work together with other human beings, we recognize that society is legitimately entitled to some ordering of events and circumstances. Slavish conformity is not required. Illinois University Professor O. H. Mowrer has pointed out, "It seems empirically well established that, by and large, the good men in a society are the conforming and happy men. Only by making one's peace with one's society and 'playing the game' does one seem to achieve the kind of freedom and fulfilment that attend the good life."

That a measure of conformity is necessary does not mean society requires people to become empty, market-oriented shells and lose all feelings of personal worth. Probably too much emphasis is placed on adjustment in our own culture. It is only one ingredient of psychological health. The normal personality retains his identity and initiative even though he adjusts to the demands that his role imposes upon him. At the same time that he makes limited concessions so that he is enabled to live on a reasonably harmonious basis with those about him, he maintains the essential qualities that make him a unique human being. Furthermore, when conflict takes place, as it frequently does when one attempts to reconcile *ethically appropriate* individual needs with group demands, the normal person is likely to work through and incorporate social needs and follow through his own original satisfactions. As Professor Mowrer puts it,

> In my judgment the most effective kind of "radical" is a man (or woman) who has made all the renunciations that his society asks him to make, has accepted his full share of personal and social responsibility, and then steps forward to make his criticisms. The trouble with most self-styled radicals is that they are immature, irresponsible individuals who don't want to grow up and who cavil against society instead. Lenin obviously had this in mind when he said that the curse of a revolutionary movement is that it always attracts as followers a lot of people who are still adolescent in their mentality and social outlook. And I suspect that something of a similar nature might be said about neurotics.[1]

## CULTURE AND ETHICS

Normality cannot be considered apart from ethical requirements. Every society defines normal behavior not only in psychological and emotional terms but also with respect to the degree to which the behavior is "good" or "bad." But the definitions of acceptable and unacceptable vary widely. American parents encourage a considerable amount of aggressiveness and achievement orientation in their children. What we consider ethically desirable and healthy competitiveness, the cooperation-centered Balinese might view as an unfortunate personality quirk. The degree to which normality is dependent upon cultural values and definitions is explained by Dr. Mowrer in the following terms:

> We find that, regardless of the way in which the details of approved action and attitude differ from one society to another, there is one thing common to life in all societies. Every human society is organized and conducted on the basis of certain principles—which are best described as social ethics. These principles have been worked out over a long period of time, with many mistakes and much suffering. Each individual born into a human society is under pressure to adopt the approved ways of that society, and each individual

---

[1] Mowrer, O. H., "What is Normal Behavior?" in Arthur Weider, ed., *Contributions Toward Medical Psychology* (New York: The Ronald Press Company, 1953), p. 147.

experiences in the course of his own development some of the struggles, difficulties, and dilemmas which were involved in the evolution of his society. To the extent that an individual is able in his lifetime to assimilate the historically hard-won wisdom of society and to experience the fruits thereof, he may be said to be normal; to the extent that he fails, he is abnormal.

Since this is a struggle in which individuals in every society must engage, we arrive in this way at a conception of normality which is not culture-bound and yet which takes due account of the enormous importance of the culture-assimilation process.[2]

All societies are confronted with the problems of preserving life and property, protecting their young, and ensuring a certain degree of loyalty to their own codes. As a consequence, most cultures evolve ways to prohibit behavior they consider inimical to their well-being. Sociologists designate the degree to which behavior is regulated as mores, norms, and folkways. The facing figure describes the regulatory structure in our own culture and the types of sanctions applied. At the top, where absolute conformity is required, there are injunctions such as those against theft, murder, and treason. These morally sanctioned norms are called mores. Failure to conform is rare, and one who does not conform is severely punished. At the bottom of the list the nonmoral norms— social techniques and manners—appear. Deviation from these is considered poor taste, bad manners, or eccentricity.

## RELATIVE, ABSOLUTE, AND DULL NORMALITY— A NOTE OF CAUTION

The definition of particular behavior as normal or otherwise is to a large extent dependent upon the culture and setting in which it occurs. Whether a visual hallucination is regarded as evidence of mystical powers or psychosis depends upon whether the experience occurs among certain groups of Plains Indians or on Main Street U.S.A. It has become apparent that many human experiences and activities cannot be described as normal or abnormal on an absolute basis. Their status is *relative* to the society and setting in which they occur. But the recognition of relative definitions of normality has led to the erroneous conclusion that *all* conduct is relative to circumstances and that there are no absolute criteria for abnormality.

---

[2] Ibid., p. 167.

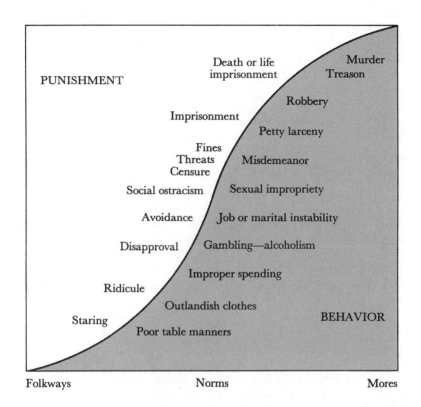

*Society defines acceptable behavior
and appropriate punishment.*

Overemphasis on the relative basis for assessing normality frequently results in the attitude that nobody knows what's normal
anyway. Some social scientists have even supported this contention
by writing that "We all need to define 'right' for ourselves" or "As
long as two people agree, it's all right." What is considered normal,
acceptable ethical conduct is thus left to the judgment of one or
two individuals, and the ancient history and experience of the
entire human race is disregarded. It is made to appear that all
standards are relative, that whatever is not openly permitted or
sanctioned in the United States is "all right anyway," since

somewhere else it is bound to meet with approval. The view that all human activities are relative to their social context is not true. Just as an infected appendix or a broken leg is universally considered abnormal, so is a hostile mother who severely rejects her children. All parts of this earth believe sexual contact between close relatives and between mature members of the same sex abnormal. Every culture sets ethical standards governing property, propriety, and the relationship between individuals and groups. All societies regard unwarranted severance and disruption of family ties as an abnormality. In fact, the list of absolutes is endless. In his article "Society, Culture and the Human Organism," C. S. Ford lists over fifty specific acts that more than eight out of ten cultures throughout the world carefully regulate. There are absolute criteria of normality as well as merely relative ones.

Normal and ethical behavior join at the point where relative and absolute standards of behavior coincide. The universal patterns of behavior that men have lived by in every social setting have enabled them to distinguish themselves from unreasoning, unfeeling animals. These are the absolutes of conduct, the worldwide ethics, which are closely interwoven with all standards for normal behavior.

Equally as common as not understanding that there are absolute criteria for normality is the false belief that normality is synonymous with dullness and insipidity. To be identified as normal is, according to some, to be labeled an uninteresting bore. A typical instance of such confusion occurred in the pages of *The New York Times Magazine* in an article, "Close-up of the Normal Wife," by Rena Corman (September 8, 1963). Corman reported a long-range and valuable study of affectively healthy individuals conducted by a group of behavior scientists. Despite the fact that the normal families investigated were physically healthy, emotionally sound, and led deeply satisfying lives, the investigators, interjecting their own viewpoint, concluded that their subjects' normality made them mundane and dull.

> What would you do if given $5,000,000? A 22-year-old (normal) woman, pregnant for the first time and living in a new home, gave a typical reply: "Well, we'd pay off this house and get all the furniture we need for it right away, instead of a piece at a time. Joe (her husband) would get a new car, too. . . . I guess we'd invest the rest. Maybe we'd need it for the future. . . . Of course, we'd give to charities, too, and our church. . . . And maybe Joe would retire and we'd travel some."

The investigators felt that much more imaginative responses came from some former juvenile delinquents, one of whom said, "Gosh, I'd never thought of more than one million. But I have plenty of things I'd like to do with it. First of all, I'd hire a French chef and get me a Rolls-Royce. And I'd hire a special attorney just to 'fix' my traffic tickets. I'd set up a public golf course, and endow a museum, and build a hospital for crippled children and—say, Doc, do you think you could up the ante to 10 million?"

Not only were the normals alleged to have less fertile imaginations but their values and pastimes were made to seem ludicrous.

21 DEAD IN LOS ANGELES RIOTS
600 HURT; 20,000 TROOPS CALLED
PRESIDENT CONDEMNS VIOLENCE

KENNEDY IS KILLED BY SNIPER
AS HE RIDES IN CAR IN DALLAS;
JOHNSON SWORN IN ON PLANE

Radio Listeners in Panic,
Taking War Drama as Fact

Many Flee Homes to Escape 'Gas Raid From
Mars'—Phone Calls Swamp Police at
Broadcast of Wells Fantasy

ASSASSINATION OF TRUMAN FOILED
IN GUN FIGHT OUTSIDE BLAIR HOUSE;
PUERTO RICAN PLOTTER, GUARD DIE

MANIAC IN MILWAUKEE SHOOTS COL. ROOSEVELT;
HE IGNORES WOUND, SPEAKS AN HOUR, GOES TO HOSPITAL

# DISPLACED REACTIONS:

# SOME CASE STUDIES

*... Oh the nerves, the nerves; the mysteries of this machine*
*called Man! Oh the little that unhinges it: poor creatures*
*that we are!*

Dickens

This section is divided into two parts. The first deals with the pathology of displacement based on group reactions such as group hysteria. The second deals with displacement of individuals and presents popular cases of neuroses and psychoses.

Part One begins with Weisz and Taylor's analysis of the psychiatric characteristics of presidential assassins. In their article, *The Assassination Matrix,* the authors also make constructive suggestions for preventing or minimizing presidential assassinations. The following reading, *They Saw A Game,* is an analysis of a Princeton-Dartmouth football game which opposing spectators viewed with varying reactions. The authors Hastorf and Cantril make a critical analysis of the conditions following this famous event. The final article in this section, Cantril's *Invasion from Mars,* analyzes why Howard Koch's "War of the Worlds" radio broadcast of 1937 invoked hysterical reactions in some individuals and groups. An excerpt from Koch's "War of the Worlds" radio script follows the evaluation.

Part Two begins with Thigpen and Cleckley's *A Case of Multiple Personality.* This case is a classic illustration of the rare disorder regarded by most psychologists as a condition stemming from a conflicting set of motives responsible for creating two or more personalities. Schizophrenia, a psychotic reaction which generally characterizes itself as a retreat from reality, is illustrated in the next reading, *The Three Christs of Ypsilanti.* This excerpt by Rokeach is a study into three paranoid schizophrenics, each of whom believes he is Christ. The last excerpt, from Rubin's *Lisa and David,* is a graphic presentation of autism and schizophrenia. Autism, or a state of "emotional refrigeration," is characterized by extreme withdrawal and obsessiveness. Lisa's symptoms are classed as schizophrenic; David's are autistic.

# PART ONE

# The Assassination Matrix

ALFRED E. WEISZ AND ROBERT L. TAYLOR

*The eight armed attacks on American Presidents are
wrapped in a web of the assassins' mental derangement, the
victims' fatalism, and the social environment. Preventive
systems could be improved.*

In the 180 years since George Washington took office, the American republic has been served by 37 Presidents. Known attempts have been made to assassinate eight of them, and four times the assassins were successful.

Within days of the last national election, men accused of plotting to take the life of Richard M. Nixon were arrested in New York and Chicago. Last June Robert F. Kennedy, a candidate for the presidency, was fatally shot in the kitchen of a Los Angeles hotel as he walked away, virtually without protection, from his California primary celebration. A scant two months before, Martin Luther King was killed by a sniper's bullet as he stood on the balcony of a motel in Memphis, an ironic fate for one who had preached so fervently against violence.

These events, considered with the murder only five years ago of President Kennedy and the violent deaths of Malcolm X and George Lincoln Rockwell, underscore that the threat of assassination is increasing in this country. They also, even in brief outline, point up the way in which the mental state of the killer, the attitude of the victim, and the social environment interact to result in assassination. Our purpose is to explore these relationships as they have occurred in presidential assassination, reviewing the pertinent psychiatric and historical literature and suggesting some approaches to preventive intervention.

Nine men—seven loners and the pair who endangered Harry S. Truman—have been involved in the recorded attempts to kill

Reprinted from *Stanford Today*, Winter 1969, Series II, No. 1, with permission of the publisher, Stanford University. Copyright by the Board of Trustees of the Leland Stanford Junior University.

American presidents. All were Caucasian males ranging in age from 24 to 40. All were smaller than average in stature. With the exception of John Wilkes Booth they came out of obscurity to attempt political murder. Five of the nine were born outside the United States, but all were citizens of this country at the time of the event. Marriage was attempted by four of these men but was disrupted within a short period in two instances. Striking socioeconomic deterioration occurred over the year prior to assassination in seven of the nine. All of the attacks were made with handguns except for the Italian rifle allegedly used by Lee Harvey Oswald.[1]

In every case but one there is considerable evidence that the assassins were severely deranged. Their commonest ailment was delusions of grandeur and persecution, a type of disordered thinking most often, but not exclusively, associated with the diagnosis of paranoid schizophrenia.

At age 32, two years before he became the first man to make an armed attack on an American President, Richard Lawrence came to believe that he was Richard III of England and that Andrew Jackson was trying to cheat him out of large sums of money. His mental derangement was so apparent after his abortive assassination attempt that even the prosecuting attorney for the District of Columbia (who was Francis Scott Key, author of the lyrics of the "Star-Spangled Banner") encouraged the defense to plead insanity.

John Wilkes Booth was obsessed with the idea that Lincoln had been elected by a fraudulent vote count and that the President wanted to become a king. The grandiosity of his thinking can be seen in this excerpt from Booth's diary, made after the death of Lincoln: "Our country owed all her troubles to him, and God simply made me the instrument of his punishment . . . I bless the entire world."

As an adolescent, the future murderer of James A. Garfield posted a notice stating, "Charles J. Guiteau, Premier of England, will deliver a lecture in St. James Hall, London." At age 39 this divorced, unemployed lawyer with several arrests and at least one conviction for fraud in his record attempted to frame the platform for the Republican Party and wrote the President that he would be willing to accept the ambassadorship to Austria. At his trial he vehemently denied that he was insane and testified that God had directed him to kill the President.

---

[1] Statements concerning Lee Harvey Oswald are based on the Warren Commission Report with recognition that questions concerning this assassination still exist.

Leon F. Czolgosz was so delusional about being poisoned that six months before he killed William McKinley he bought and cooked his own food, refusing to let his stepmother prepare his meals or even to eat food which he prepared if she was in the house.

When McKinley was shot, John Schrank dreamed that he saw the murdered President rise from his coffin and accuse Theodore Roosevelt (who succeeded to the presidency) of arranging his death. When Roosevelt flouted the two-term tradition by running for president on the Bull Moose ticket, Schrank decided that his dream of years before was a divine mandate to avenge McKinley's death. Police found among his personal papers a note which read, "Theodore Roosevelt is in conspiracy with European monarchs to overthrow our Republic. . . . We want no king."

Giuseppe Zangara, born to poverty in Italy, was put to work at age six by his father. His resentment of authority spread until it became a murderous rage directed toward all heads of state. He often complained of stomach problems and moved to Miami because the warmer temperature seemed to ease the discomfort. But seven years later the autopsy following his execution failed to reveal any abnormality of the gastrointestinal tract.

The exceptions to delusional tendencies were Oscar Collazo and Griselio Torresola. At first glance, their belief that killing the President of the United States would provide a spark to the faltering Puerto Rican nationalist movement would seem to be poor judgment near delusional in proportion. But by definition a belief is not a delusion if it is shared by a significant number of people in the person's environment. These men were active members of an ultra-nationalist party, and many of their associates shared the same beliefs. In addition the two men demonstrated a capability for cooperative planning and action not usually associated with severe emotional disturbance.

At age 13 Lee Harvey Oswald was evaluated by the chief psychiatrist of the New York Youth House for Boys as potentially dangerous on the basis of his strongly suspicious nature and inability to verbalize hostility. Eleven years later, after the assassination of John F. Kennedy, the same doctor said in a *Life* interview, "Psychologically he had all the qualifications of being a potential assassin. Such a criminal is usually a person with paranoid ideas of grandiosity who can get satisfactory self-vindication only by shocking the entire world and not just a few people. He had to show the world he was not unknown, that he was someone with whom the world had to reckon . . . ."

Distractibility and excessive ambivalence were characteristic of several of the assassins. Although they had brooded about their plans for weeks, months, or even years, some were temporarily dissuaded by surprisingly minor considerations.

Guiteau was prepared and in position to shoot Garfield several times, only to change his mind at the last moment, once because Mrs. Garfield was with the President. Schrank passed up an opportunity in Chicago two days before he finally made his attempt on Theodore Roosevelt. Not wanting to damage Chicago's civic reputation, he waited until his intended victim moved on to Milwaukee. Zangara really meant to shoot President Hoover but was reluctant to leave the warm climate of Florida for the chill of winter in Washington. He kept postponing his trip, and when he heard that President-elect Franklin Roosevelt would soon be in Miami, he changed his intended victim.

Five of the assassins were lifelong bachelors. Collazo and Torresola were married; Guiteau was divorced; Oswald was separated from his wife at the time of Kennedy's death. In this and other ways their lives seem marked by interpersonal alienation and loneliness.

Lawrence was described as a well-behaved "loner" as a child. Booth loudly espoused the Southern cause, but when war came he abandoned his supposed comrades for the North. Czolgosz was described as a quiet, shy child without friends. He claimed to be an anarchist and a socialist, but he acted so strangely at one anarchist meeting he was thought to be a government spy. A note found in Schrank's suitcase after his arrest read, "I never had a friend in my life. My uncle was more than a friend, and God has been my guardian." Zangara prized solitude so much that on one occasion he rented two adjoining houses in order to avoid neighbors. Poignantly, Lee Harvey Oswald was the founder and sole member of the New Orleans Fair Play for Cuba Committee.

Socioeconomic deterioration has been a frequent prelude to the act of assassination. Lawrence gave up his job as a housepainter two years before his attempt. Booth was forced to space his stage appearances at longer and longer intervals because of laryngitis, Guiteau had suffered a downhill financial course for seven years before his violent act, and Czolgosz was described as a "vagabond" by his own family. Schrank inherited a $25,000 tenement but gave up work and lived in cheap Bowery rooms during the year before his assassination attempt, and Zangara left a lucrative contractor's business to move to Florida. Oswald had never been a steady worker and, although he was not really sinking into lower socioeconomic levels, his wife frequently berated him for not being able to earn a living.

Displacement of hostility to the head of state is a phenomenon which researchers have associated with presidential assassination. David A. Rothstein studied men in a medical center for federal prisoners whose offense included threatening the President. He published a study in *Archives of General Psychiatry* drawing remarkable parallels between the lives of his patients and the life of Oswald. Rothstein noted that his patients had turned in adolescence from their unhappy family life to find a family substitute such as military service, political organizations, or even mental hospitals and prisons. In this new "family" the wished for dependency gratifications were again denied, resulting in a displacement of rage from parents onto the recently rejecting organization. If this organization was governmental, the natural focus for the anger became the chief of state.

We turn now to the role of the head of state himself in eliciting his own assassination. The fatalistic stance of victims such as Lincoln, Garfield, and both Kennedys is striking. John Kennedy stated a view common to these four men: "I will not live in fear. What will be, must be." Fatalistic speculation may be a personally comforting defense against the real danger involved in being a controversial, political leader. But the man who repeatedly and publicly proclaims his vulnerability to assassination may be encouraging the delusional and grandiose isolate who dreams of accomplishing at least one important and publicly recognized act in his lifetime.

Fatalism may also contribute to negligent, counterphobic behavior by the chief of state that results in even greater danger. John Cottrel in his *Anatomy of an Assassination* documents many instances in which Lincoln exposed himself to unnecessary risks. He would ride on horseback through Washington unescorted at night, and several times returned to the White House with bullet holes in his hat. His intention to attend the play at Ford's Theater the fatal night was preannounced. Cottrel writes, "Lincoln was not merely casual about his own safety; he was downright reckless." Robert Kennedy declared, "If I'm elected President, you won't find me riding around in any of those awful [bulletproof] cars." Unnecessary exposure creates situations in which potential assassins with limited cognitive abilities have less difficulty in carrying out their deeds.

The social environment is another factor which works its effect on the would-be assassin. There is in our society a sanction, a lingering throwback to an earlier age, for violence as a way to overcome threatening circumstances. Loren Eiseley tells us in *The Immense Journey:*

> The need is not really for more brains.
> The need is now for a gentler, a more tolerant people,
> than those who won for us
> against the ice, the tiger, and the bear.

Killing is not legally or socially defined as an unequivocal criminal act. Capital punishment and war give qualified sanction to the taking of human life, implying that killing is sometimes a legitimate means of conflict resolution. The message appears to be that in dealing with social issues of sufficient importance, killing is justified. When a would-be assassin is convinced of the overwhelming importance of his cause and begins to search for ways to achieve it, killing provides a "legitimate" answer. The role of the assassin's environment in this decision is far from clear, but it seems reasonable to assume that certain social inconsistencies may mesh with the assassin's poor concept of reality, making assassination seem a justifiable act.

In at least one other culture the role of homicide in politics has reached phenomenal proportions. In 1962 Paul Friedrich wrote in *Psychiatry* that in the Tarascan village of Acan, in Mexico, which at no time numbered more than 1,500 persons, there had been 77 political homicides in the previous 35 years. A study of Tarascan political life would help clarify the role of social environment in the genesis of assassination.

A large segment of the population develops hostile feelings after the assassination of a President. Paul B. Sheatsley reported in *Public Opinion Quarterly* on the reactions of more than 1,000 persons surveyed immediately after the death of John F. Kennedy. Not surprisingly, three out of four "felt angry that anyone should do such a terrible deed." More remarkable was the intensity of feeling in 11 percent of those interviewed who "hoped the man who killed him would be shot down or lynched." The increased number of assassinations and threats around the world following John Kennedy's murder, the killing of Lee Harvey Oswald by Jack Ruby, and the shooting of a Jordanian grocer subsequent to Robert Kennedy's assassination lend further support to the idea that violence can be contagious.

A study published in *The Psychoanalytic Review* provides evidence that people with negative feelings toward the victim of assassination suffer the most serious and prolonged reactions. Richard M. Suinn administered questionnaires to 50 college students after John Kennedy's assassination. Those who had the strongest emotional reactions to the President's death were not, as might be expected, the Kennedy Democrats but those who differed from the President politically.

Thus far we have dealt with the psychiatric characteristics of presidential assassins, the vulnerability of their victims, and society's inconsistent attitude toward killing as a means of conflict resolution. We turn now to what we hope are constructive suggestions for preventing or minimizing presidential assassination.

The first three assassins gave clear warnings of their intent but were not apprehended beforehand. Lawrence personally accosted Vice-President Van Buren and threatened that President Jackson would suffer if Congress did not pay the large sums he fancied were owed him. Booth, after hearing that Lincoln deplored Louisiana's failure to give the franchise to Negroes, was heard to say, "Now, by God, I'll put him through!" Guiteau, whose request for an ambassadorship went unheeded, wrote to President Garfield demanding the resignation of the Secretary of State, "otherwise you and the Republican Party will come to grief."

Today laws of this country make it an offense to threaten the life of the head of state, and certainly some potential assassins have been identified and held before they could commit their violent acts. But Philip Solomon has noted in the *Journal of the American Medical Association* the reluctance of physicians to carefully evaluate the violence potential of emotionally disturbed patients. Patients with the diagnosis of paranoid schizophrenia should be seen as a high risk group. When they express thoughts of injuring the President or other political leaders, their statements, no matter how wild they may seem, should be taken seriously and thoroughly assessed.

The ambivalence and distractibility that have characterized the assassins suggests that establishing certain administrative blocks would be one reasonable approach to prevention. A good example would be a waiting period between the announced intention to own and the actual possession of lethal weapons. In some instances the potential assassin might be unable to navigate these blocks, or the impulse might pass during the time consumed in moving through the procedures. These obstacles would not deter the thoughtful planner but could be of considerable hindrance to vacillating men like Zangara, who wouldn't leave the warm climate of

Florida to carry out his intention of shooting President Hoover, or Schrank, who chose not to attempt assassination in Chicago in order to protect the city's name.

Fatalistic statements and negligent self-exposure to danger by assassination victims have been documented. To what degree these findings are the result of retrospective scrutiny remains unknown. A study of the attitudes of assassinated and non-assassinated heads of state toward protection might clarify the role of the victim. French President Charles de Gaulle, for example, has survived three assassination attempts over the past few years. What protection systems were used? How does de Gaulle feel about assassination?

"Mixing with the people" is strongly embedded in the political tradition of the United States, but it has also proved to be an accomplice to assassination. But protection is virtually impossible without the cooperation of the man to be protected. We are not arguing for a reverse paranoia that would result in the fear of an assassin at every street corner, nor for the desirability of restricting public figures only to electronic communication and other mass media. We do suggest that Presidents and candidates be prohibited by enforceable laws from close contact with large crowds in places where their presence has been publicly announced in advance.

In a bureaucratic system the citizen with a complaint against a governmental agency usually faces a number of hurdles. There is suggestive evidence that when the potential assassin faces this frustration he turns his wrath against the person who is the symbol of government, the President. Thus, Lawrence fired on Jackson only after unsuccessfully trying to have his claims for money heard in Congress. Months before President Kennedy was assassinated Lee Harvey Oswald protested to the Navy Department that he had been wrongfully given an undesirable discharge from the Marines.

The ombudsman system of mediating between expanding bureaucratic government and the individual originated in 19th century Sweden and is still largely confined to the Scandinavian countries and New Zealand. Ideally, the ombudsman functions as an independent and impartial arbiter between government and individual. He is readily identifiable as a grievance receiver and may be instrumental in aiding a discontented citizen to state his complaint in an intelligible and effective fashion.

An ombudsman system would serve to intercept the delusional discontent of the disorganized complainer before it becomes directed toward the President. In those instances where the ombudsman is confronted by a person with persistent irrational complaints, unaffected by appropriate explanations, referral for possible psychotherapy and counseling could be made.

We are not suggesting that an ombudsman system be instituted solely as a preventive measure for assassination. The ombudsman would hear all manner of complaints and could be of great value in an era of dissident minorities who feel alienated from a powerful establishment.

A preventive effort designed to reduce the contagion of violence and aimed primarily at ambivalent, mentally disordered potential assassins would be the creation of violence prevention centers, functioning in much the same way as the widening network of suicide prevention centers. There is ample dynamic overlap between suicide and homicide. As early as 1910 Wilhelm Stekel stated "No one kills himself who has never wanted to kill another, or at least, wished the death of another," and Rothstein observed that potential political assassins often have strong self-destructive tendencies. Certainly the life expectancy of an assassin is short.

Volunteers who are now being trained to counsel suicidal individuals could readily expand their expertise to homicide prevention. A fundamental therapeutic approach with both is the strengthening of boundaries that separate destructive thoughts from actions. Suicide prevention workers are already skilled at making sophisticated estimates of the seriousness of an individual's violent or self-destructive plans. They could facilitate appropriate dispositions, ranging from further supportive psychotherapy to recommendation for confinement.

The *Uniform Crime Reports* published annually by the FBI note that most homicides and aggravated assaults are committed within the family unit or among neighbors or acquaintances, not as a result of planned felonies. The conclusion is made that "criminal homicide is, to a major extent, a social problem beyond police prevention." In light of this information the establishment of combined suicide-homicide-violence prevention centers, like the suggestion for an ombudsman system, would have significance far beyond the problem of presidential assassination.

BIBLIOGRAPHY

Briggs, L. V., *The Manner of Man That Kills: Spencer, Czolgosz, Richeson* (Gorham Press, 1921).

Cottrel, John, *Anatomy of an Assassination* (Frederick Muller, Ltd., 1966).

Donovan, Robert J., *The Assassins* (Harper and Brothers, 1952).

Hastings, Donald W., "The Psychiatry of Presidential Assassination," *Journal Lancet*, March, April, May, and July, 1965.

Jackson, Don, "The Evolution of an Assassin," *Life*, February 21, 1964.

Kimmel, Stanley P., *The Mad Booths of Maryland* (Bobbs-Merrill Co., 1940).

# They Saw A Game: A Case Study

ALBERT H. HASTORF AND HADLEY CANTRIL

On a brisk Saturday afternoon, November 23 [sic], 1951, the Dartmouth football team played Princeton in Princeton's Palmer Stadium. It was the last game of the season for both teams and of rather special significance because the Princeton team had won all its games so far and one of its players, Kazmaier, was receiving All-American mention and had just appeared as the cover man on *Time* magazine, and was playing his last game.

A few minutes after the opening kick-off, it became apparent that the game was going to be a rough one. The referees were kept busy blowing their whistles and penalizing both sides. In the second quarter, Princeton's star left the game with a broken nose. In the third quarter, a Dartmouth player was taken off the field with a broken leg. Tempers flared both during and after the game. The official statistics of the game, which Princeton won, showed that Dartmouth was penalized 70 yards, Princeton 25, not counting more than a few plays in which both sides were penalized.

Needless to say, accusations soon began to fly. The game immediately became a matter of concern to players, students, coaches, and the administrative officials of the two institutions, as well as to alumni and the general public who had not seen the game but had become sensitive to the problem of big-time football through the recent exposures of subsidized players, commercialism, etc. Discussion of the game continued for several weeks.

One of the contributing factors to the extended discussion of the game was the extensive space given to it by both campus and metropolitan newspapers. An indication of the fervor with which the discussions were carried on is shown by a few excerpts from the campus dailies.

For example, on November 27 (four [sic] days after the game), the *Daily Princetonian* (Princeton's student newspaper) said:

> This observer has never seen quite such a disgusting exhibition of so-called "sport." Both teams were guilty but the blame must be laid primarily on Dartmouth's doorstep.

Princeton, obviously the better team, had no reason to rough up Dartmouth. Looking at the situation rationally, we don't see why the Indians should make a deliberate attempt to cripple Dick Kazmaier or any other Princeton player. The Dartmouth psychology, however, is not rational itself.

The November 30th edition of the *Princeton Alumni Weekly* said:

But certain memories of what occurred will not be easily erased. Into the record books will go in indelible fashion the fact that the last game of Dick Kazmaier's career was cut short by more than half when he was forced out with a broken nose and a mild concussion, sustained from a tackle that came well after he had thrown a pass.

This second-period development was followed by a third quarter outbreak of roughness that was climaxed when a Dartmouth player deliberately kicked Brad Glass in the ribs while the latter was on his back. Throughout the often unpleasant afternoon, there was undeniable evidence that the losers' tactics were the result of an actual style of play, and reports on other games they have played this season substantiate this.

Dartmouth students were "seeing" an entirely different version of the game through the editorial eyes of the *Dartmouth* (Dartmouth's undergraduate newspaper). For example on November 27 the *Dartmouth* said:

However, the Dartmouth-Princeton game set the stage for the other type of dirty football. A type which may be termed as an unjustifiable accusation.

Dick Kazmaier was injured early in the game. Kazmaier was the star, an All-American. Other stars have been injured before, but Kazmaier had been built to represent a Princeton idol. When an idol is hurt there is only one recourse—the tag of dirty football. So what did the Tiger Coach Charley Caldwell do? He announced to the world that the Big Green had been out to extinguish the Princeton star. His purpose was achieved.

After this incident, Caldwell instilled the old see-what-they-did-go-get-them attitude into his players. His talk got results. Gene Howard and Jim Miller were both injured. Both had dropped back to pass, had passed, and were standing unprotected in the backfield. Result: one bad leg and one leg broken.

The game was rough and did get a bit out of hand in the third quarter. Yet most of the roughing penalties were called against Princeton while Dartmouth received more of the illegal-use-of-the-hands variety.

On November 28 the *Dartmouth* said:

Dick Kazmaier of Princeton admittedly is an unusually able football player. Many Dartmouth men traveled to Princeton, not expecting to win—only hoping to see an All-American in action. Dick Kazmaier was hurt in the second period, and played only a token part in the remainder of the game. For this, spectators were sorry.

But there were no such feelings for Dick Kazmaier's health. Medical authorities have confirmed that as a relatively unprotected passing and running star in a contact sport, he is quite liable to injury. Also, his particular injuries—a broken nose and slight concussion—were no more serious than is experienced almost any day in any football practice, where there is no more serious stake than playing the following Saturday. Up to the Princeton game, Dartmouth players suffered about 10 known nose fractures and face injuries, not to mention several slight concussions.

Did Princeton players feel so badly about losing their star? They shouldn't have. During the past undefeated campaign they stopped several individual stars by a concentrated effort, including such mainstays as Frank Hauff of Navy, Glenn Adams of Pennsylvania and Rocco Calvo of Cornell.

In other words, the same brand of football condemned by the *Prince*—that of stopping the big man—is practiced quite successfully by the Tigers.

Basically, then, there was disagreement as to what had happened during the "game." Hence we took the opportunity presented by the occasion to make a "real life" study of a perceptual problem.[1]

PROCEDURE

Two steps were involved in gathering data. The first consisted of answers to a questionnaire designed to get reactions to the game and to learn something of the climate of opinion in each institution. This questionnaire was administered a week after

---

[1] We are not concerned here with the problem of guilt or responsibility for infractions, and nothing here implies any judgment as to who was to blame.

the game to both Dartmouth and Princeton undergraduates who were taking introductory and intermediate psychology courses.

The second step consisted of showing the same motion picture of the game to a sample of undergraduates in each school and having them check on another questionnaire, as they watched the film, any infraction of the rules they saw and whether these infractions were "mild" or "flagrant." [2] At Dartmouth, members of two fraternities were asked to view the film on December 7; at Princeton, members of two undergraduate clubs saw the film early in January.

The answers to both questionnaires were carefully coded and transferred to punch cards. [3]

## RESULTS

Table 1 shows the questions which received different replies from the two student populations on the first questionnaire.

Questions asking if the students had friends on the team, if they had ever played football themselves, if they felt they knew the rules of the game well, etc. showed no differences in either school and no relation to answers given to other questions. This is not surprising since the students in both schools come from essentially the same type of educational, economic, and ethnic background.

Summarizing the data of Tables 1 and 2, we find a marked contrast between the two student groups.

Nearly all *Princeton* students judged the game as "rough and dirty"—not one of them thought it "clean and fair." And almost nine-tenths of them thought the other side started the rough play. By and large they felt that the charges they understood were being made were true; most of them felt the charges were made in order to avoid similar situations in the future.

When Princeton students looked at the movie of the game, they saw the Dartmouth team make over twice as many infractions as their own team made. And they saw the Dartmouth team make over twice as many infractions as were seen by Dartmouth

---

[2] The film shown was kindly loaned for the purpose of the experiment by the Dartmouth College Athletic Council. It should be pointed out that a movie of a football game follows the ball, is thus selective, and omits a good deal of the total action on the field. Also, of course, in viewing only a film of the game, the possibilities of participation as spectator are greatly limited.

[3] We gratefully acknowledge the assistance of Virginia Zerega, Office of Public Opinion Research, and J. L. McCandless, Princeton University, and E. S. Horton, Dartmouth College, in the gathering and collation of the data.

*Table 1.* Data from first questionnaire

| Question | Dartmouth Students (N = 163)% | Princeton Students (N = 161)% |
|---|---|---|
| 1. Did you happen to see the actual game between Dartmouth and Princeton in Palmer Stadium this year? | | |
| Yes | 33 | 71 |
| No | 67 | 29 |
| 2. Have you seen a movie of the game or seen it on television? | | |
| Yes, movie | 33 | 2 |
| Yes, television | 0 | 1 |
| No, neither | 67 | 97 |
| 3. (Asked of those who answered "yes" to either or both of above questions.) From your observations of what went on at the game, do you believe the game was clean and fairly played, or that it was unnecessarily rough and dirty? | | |
| Clean and fair | 6 | 0 |
| Rough and dirty | 24 | 69 |
| Rough and fair* | 25 | 2 |
| No answer | 45 | 29 |
| 4. (Asked of those who answered "no" on both of the first questions.) From what you have heard and read about the game, do you feel it was clean and fairly played, or that it was unnecessarily rough and dirty? | | |
| Clean and fair | 7 | 0 |
| Rough and dirty | 18 | 24 |
| Rough and fair* | 14 | 1 |
| Don't know | 6 | 4 |
| No answer | 55 | 71 |
| (Combined answers to questions 3 and 4 above) | | |
| Clean and fair | 13 | 0 |
| Rough and dirty | 42 | 93 |
| Rough and fair* | 39 | 3 |
| Don't know | 6 | 4 |
| 5. From what you saw in the game or the movies, or from what you have read, which team to you feel started the rough play? | | |
| Dartmouth started it | 36 | 86 |
| Princeton started it | 2 | 0 |
| Both started it | 53 | 11 |
| Neither | 6 | 1 |
| No answer | 3 | 2 |

* This answer was not included on the checklist but was written in by the percentage of students indicated.

| Question | Dartmouth Students (N = 163)% | Princeton Students (N = 161)% |
|---|---|---|
| **6. What is your understanding of the charges being made?**\*\* | | |
| Dartmouth tried to get Kazmaier | 71 | 47 |
| Dartmouth intentionally dirty | 52 | 44 |
| Dartmouth unnecessarily rough | 8 | 35 |
| **7. Do you feel there is any truth to these charges?** | | |
| Yes | 10 | 55 |
| No | 57 | 4 |
| Partly | 29 | 35 |
| Don't know | 4 | 6 |
| **8. Why do you think the charges were made?** | | |
| Injury to Princeton star | 70 | 23 |
| To prevent repetition | 2 | 46 |
| No answer | 28 | 31 |

\*\* Replies do not add to 100% since more than one charge could be given.

students. When Princeton students judged these infractions as "flagrant" or "mild," the ratio was about two "flagrant" to one "mild" on the Dartmouth team, and about one "flagrant" to three "mild" on the Princeton team.

As for the *Dartmouth* students, while the plurality of answers fell in the "rough and dirty" category, over one-tenth thought the game was "clean and fair" and over a third introduced their own category of "rough and fair" to describe the action. Although a third of the Dartmouth students felt that Dartmouth was to blame for starting the rough play, the majority of Dartmouth students thought both sides were to blame. By and large, Dartmouth men felt that the charges they understood were being made were not true, and most of them thought the reason for the charges was Princeton's concern for its football star.

When Dartmouth students looked at the movie of the game they saw both teams make about the same number of infractions. And they saw their own team make only half the number of infractions the Princeton students saw them make. The ratio of "flagrant" to "mild" infractions was about one to one when Dartmouth students judged the Dartmouth team, and about one "flagrant" to two "mild" when Dartmouth students judged infractions made by the Princeton team.

It should be noted that Dartmouth and Princeton students were thinking of different charges in judging their validity and in assigning reasons as to why the charges were made. It should also be noted that whether or not students were spectators of the game in the stadium made little difference in their responses.

## INTERPRETATION: THE NATURE OF A SOCIAL EVENT[4]

It seems clear that the "game" actually was many different games and that each version of the events that transpired was just as "real" to a particular person as other versions were to other people. A consideration of the experiential phenomena that constitute a "football game" for the spectator may help us both to account for the results obtained and illustrate something of the nature of any social event.

Like any other complex social occurrence, a "football game," consists of a whole host of happenings. Many different events are occurring simultaneously. Furthermore, each happening is a link in a chain of happenings, so that one follows another in sequence. The "football game," as well as other complex social situations, consists of a whole matrix of events. In the game situation, this matrix of events consists of the actions of all the players, together with the behavior of the referees and linesmen, the action on the sidelines, in the grandstands, over the loud-speaker, etc.

Of crucial importance is the fact that an "occurrence" on the football field or in any other social situation does not become an experiential "event" unless and until some significance is given to it: an "occurrence" becomes an *"event"* only when the happening has significance. And a happening generally has significance only if

*Table 2.* Data from second questionnaire checked while seeing film

| Group | N | Total number of infractions checked against | | | |
| | | Dartmouth Team | | Princeton Team | |
| | | Mean | SD | Mean | SD |
| Dartmouth students | 48 | 4.3* | 2.7 | 4.4 | 2.8 |
| Princeton students | 49 | 9.8* | 5.7 | 4.2 | 3.5 |

*Significant at the .01 level.

[4] The interpretation of the nature of a social event sketched here is in part based on discussions with Adelbert Ames, Jr., and is being elaborated in more detail elsewhere.

it reactivates learned significances already registered in what we have called a person's assumptive form-world.[5]

Hence the particular occurrences that different people experienced in the football game were a limited series of events from the total matrix of events *potentially* available to them. People experienced those occurrences that reactivated significances they brought to the occasion; they failed to experience those occurrences which did not reactivate past significances. We do not need to introduce "attention" as an "intervening third" (to paraphrase James on memory) to account for the selectivity of the experiential process.

In this particular study, one of the most interesting examples of this phenomenon was a telegram sent to an officer of Dartmouth College by a member of a Dartmouth alumni group in the Midwest. He had viewed the film which had been shipped to his alumni group from Princeton after its use with Princeton students, who saw, as we noted, an average of over nine infractions by Dartmouth players during the game. The alumnus, who couldn't see the infractions he had heard publicized, wired:

> Preview of Princeton movies indicates considerable cutting of important part please wire explanation and possibly air mail missing part before showing scheduled for January 25 we have splicing equipment.

The "same" sensory impingements emanating from the football field, transmitted through the visual mechanism to the brain also obviously gave rise to different experiences in different people. The significances assumed by different happenings for different people depend in large part on the purposes people bring to the occasion and the assumptions they have of the purposes and probable behavior of other people involved. This was amusingly pointed out by the New York *Herald Tribune's* sports columnist, Red Smith.

> You see, Steve Ellis is the proprietor of Chico Vejar, who is a highly desirable tract of Stamford, Conn., welterweight. Steve is also a radio announcer. Ordinarily there is no conflict between Ellis the Brain and Ellis the Voice because Steve is an uncommonly substantial lump of meat who can support both halves of a split personality and give away weight on each end without missing it.
>
> This time, though, the two Ellises met head-on, with a sickening, rending crash. Steve the Manager sat at ringside in the guise of Steve the Announcer broadcasting a dispassionate,

[5] Cantril, H., *The "why" of man's experience* (New York: Macmillan, 1950).

unbiased, objective report of Chico's adventures in the ring. . . .

Clear as mountain water, his words came through, winning big for Chico. Winning? Hell, Steve was slaughtering poor Fiore.

Watching and listening, you could see what a valiant effort the reporter was making to remain cool and detached. At the same time you had an illustration of the old, established truth that when anybody with a preference watches a fight, he sees only what he prefers to see.

That is always so. That is why, after any fight that doesn't end in a clean knockout, there always are at least a few hoots when the decision is announced. A guy from, say, Billy Graham's neighborhood goes to see Billy fight and he watches Graham all the time. He sees all the punches Billy throws, and hardly any of the punches Billy catches. So it was with Steve.

"Fiore feints with a left," he would say, honestly believing that Fiore hadn't caught Chico full on the chops. "Fiore's knees buckle," he said, "and Chico backs away." Steve didn't see the hook that had driven Chico back. . . .

In brief, the data here indicate that there is no such "thing" as a "game" existing "out there" in its own right which people merely "observe." The "game" "exists" for a person and is experienced by him only in so far as certain happenings have significances in terms of his purpose. Out of all the occurrences going on in the environment, a person selects those that have some significance for him from his own egocentric position in the total matrix.

Obviously in the case of a football game, the value of the experience of watching the game is enhanced if the purpose of "your" team is accomplished, that is, if the happening of the desired consequence is experienced—i.e., if your team wins. But the value attribute of the experience can, of course, be spoiled if the desire to win crowds out behavior we value and have come to call sportsmanlike.

The sharing of significances provides the links except for which a "social" event would not be experienced and would not exist for anyone.

A "football game" would be impossible except for the rules of the game which we bring to the situation and which enable us to share with others the significances of various happenings. These rules make possible a certain repeatability of events such as first downs, touchdowns, etc. If a person is unfamiliar with the rules of the game, the behavior he sees lacks repeatability and consistent significance and hence "doesn't make sense."

And only because there is the possibility of repetition is there the possibility that a happening has a significance. For example, the balls used in games are designed to give a high degree of repeatability. While a football is about the only ball used in games which is not a sphere, the shape of the modern football has apparently evolved in order to achieve a higher degree of accuracy and speed in forward passing than would be obtained with a spherical ball, thus increasing the repeatability of an important phase of the game.

The rules of a football game, like laws, rituals, customs, and mores, are registered and preserved forms of sequential significances enabling people to share the significances of occurrences. The sharing of sequential significances which have value for us provides the links that operationally make social events possible. They are analogous to the forces of attraction that hold parts of an atom together, keeping each part from following its individual, independent course.

From this point of view it is inaccurate and misleading to say that different people have different "attitudes" concerning the same "thing." For the "thing" simply is *not* the same for different people whether the "thing" is a football game, a presidential candidate, Communism, or spinach. We do not simply "react to" a happening or to some impingement from the environment in a determined way (except in behavior that has become reflexive or habitual). We behave according to what we bring to the occasion, and what each of us brings to the occasion is more or less unique. And except for these significances which we bring to the occasion, the happenings around us would be meaningless occurrences, would be "inconsequential."

From the transactional view, an attitude is not a predisposition to react in a certain way to an occurrence or stimulus "out there" that exists in its own right with certain fixed characteristics which we "color" according to our predisposition.[6] That is, a subject does not simply "react to" an "object." An attitude would rather seem to be a complex of registered significances reactivated by some stimulus which assumes its own particular significance for us in terms of our purposes. That is, the object as experienced would not exist for us except for the reactivated aspects of the form-world which provide particular significance to the hieroglyphics of sensory impingements.

---

[6] Kilpatrick, F.P. (ed.), *Human behavior from the transactional point of view* (Hanover, N.H.: Institute for Associated Research, 1952).

# Invasion from Mars

HADLEY CANTRIL

On the evening of October 30, 1938, thousands of Americans became panic-stricken by a broadcast purported to describe an invasion of Martians which threatened our whole civilization. Probably never before have so many people in all walks of life and in all parts of the country become so suddenly and so intensely disturbed as they did on this night. Yet what justification is there for conducting an elaborate investigation of a panic which was, after all, ephemeral and not sufficiently important to be recorded by historians?

There are essentially two ways to rationalize this study: one is hopefully scientific, the other frankly didactic.

Such rare occurrences are opportunities for the social scientist to study mass behavior. They must be exploited when they come. Although the social scientist unfortunately cannot usually predict such situations and have his tools of investigation ready to analyze the phenomenon while it is still on the wing, he can begin his work before the effects of the crisis are over and memories are blurred. As far as the writer is aware, this is the first panic that has been carefully studied with the research tools now available. A complete description of this panic should, in itself, be of value to anyone interested in social problems.

Furthermore, the attempts to determine the underlying psychological causes for a widespread panic in 1938 should give us insight into the psychology of the common man and, more especially, the psychology of the man of our times. From this point of view the investigation may be regarded as more than a study of panic. For the situation created by the broadcast was one which shows us how the common man reacts in a time of stress and strain. It gives us insights into his intelligence, his anxieties and his needs, which we could never get by tests or strictly experimental studies. The panic situation we have investigated had all the flavor of everyday life and, at the same time, provided a semi-experimental condition for research. Students of social psychology should find here some useful

*Invasion from Mars* by Hadley Cantril (Princeton University Press, 1940, 1952). Reprinted by permission of Princeton University Press. Radio drama by Howard Koch. Copyright 1940 by Princeton University Press. Permission of Monica McCall, Inc.

research tools. They will see shortcomings in the methods employed and should be able to profit from mistakes which have been pointed out wherever the writer has detected them.

A more practical justification for such a study concerns the educational implications which an understanding of this panic may have. Although citizens are not confronted every day with potentially panic-producing situations, they do face social or personal crises where their good judgment is taxed to the limit. If they can see why some people reacted unintelligently in this instance, they may be able to build up their resistance to similar occurrences. And if they are ever caught in a really critical situation, the information recorded here may help them make a more satisfactory adjustment. At least it will be discovered how superficial and misleading is the account of one prominent social scientist who said that "as good an explanation as any for the panic is that all the intelligent people were listening to Charlie McCarthy." In spite of the unique conditions giving rise to this particular panic, the writer has attempted to indicate throughout the study the pattern of circumstances which, from a psychological point of view, might make this the prototype of any panic.

Localized panics are frequently reported on shipboard, in congested buildings that have caught fire, or in specific areas suffering some natural catastrophe. More widespread panics are comparatively rare. Nevertheless, panics such as that occurring in the United States on the evening of October 30, 1938, are by no means confined to our own country or our own times.

Panics resulting from financial crises and commercial miscalculations are probably as old as commerce itself. Prior to the eighteenth century such panics were generally due to an undersupply of goods, caused by crop failures, political disturbance, or the like. In the later stages of our expanding economy, an overabundance of goods has led to successive crises and business cycles generally accompanied by widespread fears among the increasing number of publics involved.

The most similar predecessor to the panic resulting from the *War of the Worlds'* broadcast occurred on January 16, 1926, in England during a period of unusual labor strife and shortly before the general strike. On that day the traditionally complacent English listener was startled by a description given by Father Ronald Knox (in the customary news broadcast) of an unruly unemployed mob. The mob was said to have attempted demolition of the Houses of Parliament, its trench mortars had brought Big Ben to the ground, it had hanged the Minister of Traffic to a tramway post. The London broadcast ended with the "destruction" of the British Broadcasting Corporation's station. After the broadcast, the newspapers, police and radio stations were besieged with calls from frantic citizens. However, the panic created by Father Knox's broadcast did not cause either as widespread or as intense a fear as the Orson Welles program.

The fact that this panic was created as a result of a radio broadcast is today no mere circumstance. The importance of radio's rôle in current national and international affairs is too well known to be recounted here. By its very nature radio is the medium par excellence for informing all segments of a population of current happenings, for arousing in them a common sense of fear or joy and for enciting them to similar reactions directed toward a single objective. It is estimated that of the 32,000,000 families in the United States 27,500,000 have radios—a greater proportion than have telephones, automobiles, plumbing, electricity, newspapers or magazines. Radio has inherently the characteristics of contemporaneousness, availability, personal appeal and ubiquity. Hence, when we analyze this panic, we are able to deal with the most modern type of social group—the radio audience—which differs from the congregate group of the moving picture theatre and the consociate group reading the daily paper. The radio audience consists essentially of thousands of small, congregate groups united in time and experiencing a common stimulus—altogether making possible the largest grouping of people ever known.

Because the social phenomenon in question was so complex, several methods were employed to seek out different answers and to compare results obtained by one method with those obtained by another. Such an approach seems advisable in analyzing any problem in social psychology. Otherwise, the investigator has difficulty in demonstrating that his assumption has not been "proved" merely because his method would give him no contradictory evidence. Furthermore, should the investigator reach no positive conclusions, he is unable to tell whether his presuppositions and theories are wrong or whether the fault lies in his method. The use of a pluralistic approach in a study such as this is particularly urgent since the phenomenon under consideration was of so transient a nature. Also, so far as was known, no other extensive investigation was being independently conducted on the problem, thus making it impossible to check one set of data and interpretations against another.

Much of our information was derived from detailed interviews of 135 persons. Over 100 of these persons were selected because they were known to have been upset by the broadcast. The names of the persons who were frightened were obtained almost entirely by the personal inquiry and initiative of the interviewers. The names of persons who were listed in the newspapers as having been frightened failed to produce more than a half-dozen interviews. Many more names were finally obtained than could possibly be interviewed with the limited funds available. Every attempt was made to keep the group fairly representative of the population at large. However, no pretense is made that the group *is* a proper sample of the total population, and the results and interpretations of the complete study do not depend on such a sample since these cases can be studied against the background of two extensive statistical surveys made prior to the intensive personal interviews. Twenty-eight persons who were not frightened but who tuned in late to the broadcast were included in the group interviewed.

The interviews were limited to the New Jersey area for reasons of finance and supervision. All names of respondents used in the text are fictitious and identifying characteristics are disguised, but the true flavor of the case studies is preserved. The interviewing began one week after the broadcast and was completed in about three weeks. The regrettable delay in getting to the respondents was unavoidable for two reasons: funds were not immediately available to begin the study; highly trained interviewers are difficult to obtain, and the danger of delaying the interval between such an experience and an interview is probably less than the danger of obtaining an inadequate or unreliable report from an unskilled interviewer.

Quotations have been freely used to illustrate psychological processes which are implied in the statistical figures. They have also been included at times wherever language failed and meaning could be better conveyed by the impression gained from a quotation.

Since the budget of the Princeton Radio Project was obviously unable to anticipate this particular study, the investigation was made possible by a special grant from the General Education Board. The interviews upon which most of the study is based were made by Mrs. Paul Trilling, Frances Ginevsky, Mrs. Richard Robinson, and Mrs. David Green. The writer is indebted to all of these women for their faithful reporting. Mrs. Green was especially inexhaustible and resourceful in gathering names of frightened persons.

Orson Welles and the Mercury Theatre have cooperated in every way by allowing the writer to examine material related to the broadcast. Howard Koch has kindly permitted us to publish for the first time his brilliant adaptation of the *War of the Worlds*. And Mr. H. G. Wells generously gave his permission for the use of the adaptation.

Dr. Frank Stanton, Director of Research for the Columbia Broadcasting System and Associate Director of the Princeton Radio Project, is to be thanked for his methodological advice and his careful reading and checking of the manuscript. The Columbia Broadcasting System has been kind enough to release the original script of the broadcast and the results of two special surveys commissioned by it and supervised by Dr. Stanton.

Hazel Gaudet, Research Assistant on the Princeton Radio Project, was in charge of the actual administration of the investigation. She not only made most of the tabulations based on the interviews, but many of the ideas reflected in the tabulations and the text were contained in her detailed memoranda to the writer. From first to last she was indispensable in the progress of the research.

Herta Herzog made an independent survey of the panic before this study was undertaken. On the basis of her experience and insight, we were able to prepare the interview schedule used here. She made the initial study of the checks attempted by the listeners and analyzed the case studies reported in Chapter VIII.

The author's greatest indebtedness is to Dr. Paul Lazarsfeld, Director of the Princeton Radio Project. He has not only given the writer innumerable suggestions for analysis and interpretation, but he has, with his rigorous and ingenious methodological help, provided the writer an invaluable intellectual experience. Because of his insistence, the study has been revised many times.

THE BROADCAST

At eight P.M. eastern standard time on the evening of October 30, 1938, Orson Welles with an innocent little group of actors took his place before the microphone in a New York studio of the Columbia Broadcasting System. He carried with him Howard Koch's freely adapted version of H. G. Wells's imaginative novel, *War of the Worlds*. He also brought to the scene his unusual dramatic talent. With script and talent the actors hoped to entertain their listeners for an hour with an incredible, old-fashioned story appropriate for Hallowe'en.

Much to their surprise the actors learned that the series of news bulletins they had issued describing an invasion from Mars had been believed by thousands of people throughout the country. For a few horrible hours people from Maine to California thought that hideous monsters armed with death rays were destroying all armed resistance sent against them; that there was simply no escape from disaster; that the end of the world was near. Newspapers the following morning spoke of the "tidal wave of terror that swept the nation." It was clear that a panic of national proportions had occurred. The chairman of the Federal Communications Commission called the program "regrettable."

What had these actors said in the brief hour at their disposal? What wild story had they let loose? With the permission of the Mercury Theatre on the Air, the Columbia Broadcasting System, and Mr. H. G. Wells, we are able to print the whole of the radio drama for the first time.

*(Excerpt)*
## COLUMBIA BROADCASTING SYSTEM
## ORSON WELLES AND MERCURY THEATRE
## ON THE AIR

### SUNDAY, OCTOBER 30, 1938
### 8:00 to 9:00 P.M.

CUE: *(Columbia Broadcasting System)*
*( . . . 30 seconds . . . )*

ANNOUNCER: The Columbia Broadcasting System and its affiliated stations present Orson Welles and the Mercury Theatre on the Air in *War of the Worlds* by H. G. Wells.

THEME

ANNOUNCER: Ladies and gentlemen: the director of the Mercury Theatre and star of these broadcasts, Orson Welles. . . .

ORSON WELLES

We know now that in the early years of the twentieth century this world was being watched closely by intelligences greater than man's and yet as mortal as his own. We know now that as human beings busied themselves about their various concerns they were scrutinized and studied, perhaps almost as narrowly as a man with a microscope might scrutinize the transient creatures that swarm and multiply in a drop of water. With infinite complacence people went to and fro over the earth about their little affairs, serene in the assurance of their dominion over this small spinning fragment of solar driftwood which by chance or design man has inherited out of the dark mystery of Time and Space. Yet across an immense ethereal gulf, minds that are to our minds as ours are to the beasts in the jungle, intellects vast, cool and unsympathetic regarded this earth with envious eyes and slowly and surely drew their plans against us. In the thirty-ninth year of the twentieth century came the great disillusionment.

It was near the end of October. Business was better. The war scare was over. More men were back at work. Sales were picking up. On this particular evening, October 30, the Crossley service estimated that thirty-two million people were listening in on radios.

## ANNOUNCER CUE

. . . for the next twenty-four hours not much change in temperature. A slight atmospheric disturbance of undetermined origin is reported over Nova Scotia, causing a low pressure area to move down rather rapidly over the northeastern states, bringing a forecast of rain, accompanied by winds of light gale force. Maximum temperature 66; minimum 48. This weather report comes to you from the Government Weather Bureau.

. . . We now take you to the Meridian Room in the Hotel Park Plaza in downtown New York, where you will be entertained by the music of Ramon Raquello and his orchestra.
*(Spanish theme song . . . fades)*

## ANNOUNCER THREE

Good evening, ladies and gentlemen. From the Meridian Room in the Park Plaza in New York City, we bring you the music of Ramon Raquello and his orchestra. With a touch of the Spanish, Ramon Raquello leads off with "La Cumparsita."
*(Piece starts playing)*

## ANNOUNCER TWO

Ladies and gentlemen, we interrupt our program of dance music to bring you a special bulletin from the Intercontinental Radio News. At twenty minutes before eight, central time, Professor Farrell of the Mount Jennings Observatory, Chicago, Illinois, reports observing several explosions of incandescent gas, occurring at regular intervals on the planet Mars.

The spectroscope indicates the gas to be hydrogen and moving towards the earth with enormous velocity. Professor Pierson of the observatory at Princeton confirms Farrell's observations, and describes the phenomenon as *(quote)* like a jet of blue flame shot from a gun. *(unquote.)* We now return you to the music of Ramon Raquello, playing for you in the Meridian Room of the Park Plaza Hotel, situated in downtown New York. *(Music plays for a few moments until piece ends. . . . sound of applause)*

Now a tune that never loses favor, the ever-popular "Star Dust." Ramon Raquello and his orchestra. . . .
*(Music)*

## ANNOUNCER TWO

Ladies and gentlemen, following on the news given in our bulletin a moment ago, the Government Meteorological Bureau has requested the large observatories of the country to keep an astronomical watch on any further disturbances occurring on the planet Mars. Due to the unusual nature of this occurrence, we have arranged an interview with the noted astronomer, Professor Pierson, who will give us his views on this event. In a few moments we will take you to the Princeton Observatory at Princeton, New Jersey. We return you until then to the music of Ramon Raquello and his orchestra.
*(Music . . .)*

## ANNOUNCER TWO

We are ready now to take you to the Princeton Observatory at Princeton where Carl Phillips, our commentator, will interview Professor Richard Pierson, famous astronomer. We take you now to Princeton, New Jersey.
*(Echo Chamber)*

## PHILLIPS

Good evening, ladies and gentlemen. This is Carl Phillips, speaking to you from the observatory at Princeton. I am standing in a large semicircular room, pitch black except for an oblong split in the ceiling. Through this opening I can see a sprinkling of stars that cast a kind of frosty glow over the intricate mechanism of the huge telescope. The ticking sound you hear is the vibration of the clockwork. Professor Pierson stands directly above me on a small platform, peering through the giant lens. I ask you to be patient, ladies and gentlemen, during any delay that may arise during our interview. Beside his ceaseless watch of the heavens, Professor Pierson may be interrupted by telephone or other communications. During this period he is in constant touch with the astronomical centers of the world. . . . Professor, may I begin our questions?

### PIERSON

At any time, Mr. Phillips.

### PHILLIPS

Professor, would you please tell our radio audience exactly what you see as you observe the planet Mars through your telescope?

### PIERSON

Nothing unusual at the moment, Mr. Phillips. A red disk swimming in a blue sea. Transverse stripes across the disk. Quite distinct now because Mars happens to be at the point nearest the earth . . . in opposition, as we call it.

### PHILLIPS

In your opinion, what do these transverse stripes signify, Professor Pierson?

### PIERSON

Not canals, I can assure you, Mr. Phillips, although that's the popular conjecture of those who imagine Mars to be inhabited. From a scientific viewpoint the stripes are merely the result of atmospheric conditions peculiar to the planet.

### PHILLIPS

Then you're quite convinced as a scientist that living intelligence as we know it does not exist on Mars?

### PIERSON

I should say the chances against it are a thousand to one.

### PHILLIPS

And yet how do you account for these gas eruptions occurring on the surface of the planet at regular intervals?

### PIERSON

Mr. Phillips, I cannot account for it.

### PHILLIPS

By the way, Professor, for the benefit of our listeners, how far is Mars from the earth?

### PIERSON

Approximately forty million miles.

### PHILLIPS

Well, that seems a safe enough distance.

### PHILLIPS

Just a moment, ladies and gentlemen, someone has just handed Professor Pierson a message. While he reads it, let me remind you that we are speaking to you from the observatory in Princeton, New Jersey, where we are interviewing the world-famous astronomer, Professor Pierson. ... One moment, please. Professor Pierson has passed me a message which he has just received. ... Professor, may I read the message to the listening audience?

### PIERSON

Certainly, Mr. Phillips.

### PHILLIPS

Ladies and gentlemen, I shall read you a wire addressed to Professor Pierson from Dr. Gray of the National History Museum, New York. "9:15 P.M. eastern standard time. Seismograph registered shock of almost earthquake intensity occurring within a radius of twenty miles of Princeton. Please investigate. Signed, Lloyd Gray, Chief of Astronomical Division." ... Professor Pierson, could this occurrence possibly have something to do with the disturbances observed on the planet Mars?

## PIERSON

Hardly, Mr. Phillips. This is probably a meteorite of unusual size and its arrival at this particular time is merely a coincidence. However, we shall conduct a search, as soon as daylight permits.

## PHILLIPS

Thank you, Professor. Ladies and gentlemen, for the past ten minutes we've been speaking to you from the observatory at Princeton, bringing you a special interview with Professor Pierson, noted astronomer. This is Carl Phillips speaking. We now return you to our New York studio.
*(Fade in piano playing)*

## ANNOUNCER TWO

Ladies and gentlemen, here is the latest bulletin from the Intercontinental Radio News. Toronto, Canada: Professor Morse of Macmillan University reports observing a total of three explosions on the planet Mars, between the hours of 7:45 P.M. and 9:20 P.M., eastern standard time. This confirms earlier reports received from American observatories. Now, nearer home, comes a special announcement from Trenton, New Jersey. It is reported that at 8:50 P.M. a huge, flaming object, believed to be a meteorite, fell on a farm in the neighborhood of Grovers Mill, New Jersey, twenty-two miles from Trenton. The flash in the sky was visible within a radius of several hundred miles and the noise of the impact was heard as far north as Elizabeth.

We have dispatched a special mobile unit to the scene, and will have our commentator, Mr. Phillips, give you a word description as soon as he can reach there from Princeton. In the meantime, we take you to the Hotel Martinet in Brooklyn, where Bobby Millette and his orchestra are offering a program of dance music.
*(Swing band for 20 seconds . . . then cut)*

## ANNOUNCER TWO

We take you now to Grovers Mill, New Jersey.
*(Crowd noises . . . police sirens)*

## PHILLIPS

Ladies and gentlemen, this is Carl Phillips again, at the Wilmuth farm, Grovers Mill, New Jersey. Professor Pierson and myself made the eleven miles from Princeton in ten minutes. Well, I . . . I hardly know where to begin, to paint for you a word picture of the strange scene before my eyes, like something out of a modern Arabian Nights. Well, I just got here. I haven't had a chance to look around yet. I guess that's *it*. Yes, I guess that's the ... *thing*, directly in front of me, half buried in a vast pit. Must have struck with terrific force. The ground is covered with splinters of a tree it must have struck on its way down. What I can see of the ... object itself doesn't look very much like a meteor, at least not the meteors I've seen. It looks more like a huge cylinder. It has a diameter of ... what would you say, Professor Pierson?

### PIERSON *(off)*

About thirty yards.

### PHILLIPS

About thirty yards. ... The metal on the sheath is ... well, I've never seen anything like it. The color is sort of yellowish-white. Curious spectators now are pressing close to the object in spite of the efforts of the police to keep them back. They're getting in front of my line of vision. Would you mind standing on one side, please?

### POLICEMAN

One side, there, one side.

### PHILLIPS

While the policemen are pushing the crowd back, here's Mr. Wilmuth, owner of the farm here. He may have some interesting facts to add. ... Mr. Wilmuth, would you please tell the radio audience as much as you remember of this rather unusual visitor that dropped in your backyard? Step closer, please. Ladies and gentlemen, this is Mr. Wilmuth.

### WILMUTH

I was listenin' to the radio.

### PHILLIPS

Closer and louder, please.

### WILMUTH

Pardon me!

### PHILLIPS

Louder, please, and closer.

### WILMUTH

Yes, sir—while I was listening to the radio and kinda drowsin', that Professor fellow was talkin' about Mars, so I was half dozin' and half . . .

### PHILLIPS

Yes, Mr. Wilmuth. Then what happened?

### WILMUTH

As I was sayin', I was listenin' to the radio kinda halfways . . .

### PHILLIPS

Yes, Mr. Wilmuth, and then you saw something?

### WILMUTH

Not first off. I heard something.

### PHILLIPS

And what did you hear?

### WILMUTH

A hissing sound. Like this: sssssssss . . . kinda like a fourt' of July rocket.

### PHILLIPS

Then what?

### WILMUTH

Turned my head out the window and would have swore I was to sleep and dreamin'.

## PHILLIPS

Yes?

## WILMUTH

I seen a kinda greenish streak and then zingo! Somethin' smacked the ground. Knocked me clear out of my chair!

## PHILLIPS

Well, were you frightened, Mr. Wilmuth?

## WILMUTH

Well, I—I ain't quite sure. I reckon I—I was kinda riled.

## PHILLIPS

Thank you, Mr. Wilmuth. Thank you.

## WILMUTH

Want me to tell you some more?

## PHILLIPS

No. . . . That's quite all right, that's plenty.

## PHILLIPS

Ladies and gentlemen, you've just heard Mr. Wilmuth, owner of the farm where this thing has fallen. I wish I could convey the atmosphere . . . the background of this . . . fantastic scene. Hundreds of cars are parked in a field in back of us. Police are trying to rope off the roadway leading into the farm. But it's no use. They're breaking right through. Their headlights throw an enormous spot on the pit where the object's half-buried. Some of the more daring souls are venturing near the edge. Their silhouettes stand out against the metal sheen.
*(Faint humming sound)*
One man wants to touch the thing . . . he's having an argument with a policeman. The policeman wins. . . . Now, ladies and gentlemen, there's something I haven't mentioned in all this excitement, but it's becoming more distinct. Perhaps you've caught it already on your radio. Listen: *(long pause)* . . . Do you hear it? It's a curious humming sound that seems to come from inside the

object. I'll move the microphone nearer. Here. *(pause)* Now we're not more than twenty-five feet away. Can you hear it now? Oh, Professor Pierson!

### PIERSON

Yes, Mr. Phillips?

### PHILLIPS

Can you tell us the meaning of that scraping noise inside the thing?

### PIERSON

Possibly the unequal cooling of its surface.

### PHILLIPS

Do you still think it's a meteor, Professor?

### PIERSON

I don't know what to think. The metal casing is definitely extra-terrestrial ... not found on this earth. Friction with the earth's atmosphere usually tears holes in a meteorite. This thing is smooth and, as you can see, of cylindrical shape.

### PHILLIPS

Just a minute! Something's happening! Ladies and gentlemen, this is terrific! This end of the thing is beginning to flake off! The top is beginning to rotate like a screw! The thing must be hollow!

### VOICES

She's a movin'!
Look, the darn thing's unscrewing!
Keep back, there! Keep back, I tell you.
Maybe there's men in it trying to escape!
It's red hot, they'll burn to a cinder!
Keep back there! Keep those idiots back!
*(Suddenly the clanking sound of a huge piece of falling metal)*

## VOICES

She's off! The top's loose!

Look out there! Stand back!

Ladies and gentlemen, this is the most terrifying thing I have ever witnessed. ... Wait a minute! Someone's *crawling out of the hollow top.* Some one or ... something. I can see peering out of that black hole two luminous disks ... are they eyes? It might be a face. It might be. ...

*(Shout of awe from the crowd)*

Good heavens, something's wriggling out of the shadow like a grey snake. Now it's another one, and another. They look like tentacles to me. There, I can see the thing's body. It's large as a bear and it glistens like wet leather. But that face. It ... it's indescribable. I can hardly force myself to keep looking at it. The eyes are black and gleam like a serpent. The mouth is V-shaped with saliva dripping from its rimless lips that seem to quiver and pulsate. The monster or whatever it is can hardly move. It seems weighed down by ... possibly gravity or something. The thing's raising up. The crowd falls back. They've seen enough. This is the most extraordinary experience. I can't find words. ... I'm pulling this microphone with me as I talk. I'll have to stop the description until I've taken a new position. Hold on, will you please, I'll be back in a minute.

*(Fade into piano)*

## ANNOUNCER TWO

We are bringing you an eyewitness account of what's happening on the Wilmuth farm, Grovers Mill, New Jersey.

*(More piano)*

We now return you to Carl Phillips at Grovers Mill.

## PHILLIPS

Ladies and gentlemen (Am I on?). Ladies and gentlemen, here I am, back of a stone wall that adjoins Mr. Wilmuth's garden. From here I get a sweep of the whole scene. I'll give you every detail as long as I can talk. As long as I can see. More state police have arrived. They're drawing up a cordon in front of the pit, about thirty of them. No need to push the crowd back now. They're willing to keep their distance. The captain is conferring with some-one. We can't quite see who. Oh yes, I believe it's Professor Pierson. Yes, it is. Now they've parted. The professor moves around one side, studying the object, while the captain and two policemen advance with something in their hands. I can see it now. It's a white handkerchief tied to a pole . . . a flag of truce. If those creatures know what that means . . . what anything means! . . . *Wait!* Something's happening!

\*　　\*　　\*　　\*　　\*　　\*　　\*

## THE HISTORICAL SETTING

The characteristic thoughts and judgments of any group of people are deeply rooted in the culture that surrounds them. The prevailing social conditions provide the context within which the individual must develop and make his adjustment. We naturally wonder if the social setting in the United States on October 30, 1938 was particularly conducive to the panicky behavior of people who happened to hear the broadcast. Are the times more out of joint now than they were in the golden nineties or in 1925? Were there fewer people able to orient themselves properly in 1938 than there might have been in other historical periods had a comparable situation arisen? And if conditions were particularly disturbed, did they affect all people equally? These are essentially questions for the historian and sociologist of the future. But with out present perspective and our present evidence we can discern certain characteristics of the social background which contributed to the arousal of the panic.

### INSTABILITY OF IMPORTANT SOCIAL NORMS

When a culture is highly stable and in a state of complete equilibrium, it means that the frames of reference of the individuals constituting the culture are in complete conformity with the norms of that culture. It means, furthermore, that the frames of reference of individuals are, for them, completely adequate pathways in an environment that is satisfying their needs. Such an ideal state of affairs has certainly never existed for long in any large cultural group. Unrest, change, frustration, dissatisfaction are the rule. For at least a segment of the population current norms are inadequate to meet personal physical and psychological needs. Individual frames of reference either do not conform to accepted norms, as is the case with the radical thinker, or do not adequately explain to the individual the dissatisfaction he is experiencing, as is the case with those who frankly confess they don't know what the remedy is, those who try one remedy after another, or those who land in the camp of a leader, such as Dr. Townsend, who has an oversimplified but understandable solution.

At the time of the Martian invasion many social norms, with their corresponding personal habits, were in a state of flux and change, many of the previously accepted social standards were either proving themselves inadequate to accommodate human needs or were in danger of being overthrown by outside ideologies. In either case many of the individuals who composed the culture were perplexed and confused.

*Unsettled Conditions.* Particularly since the depression of 1929, a number of people have begun to wonder whether or not they will ever regain any sense of economic security. The complexity of modern finance and government, the discrepancies shown in the economic and political proposals of the various "experts," the felt threats of Fascism, Communism, prolonged unemployment among millions of Americans—these together with a thousand and one other characteristics of modern living—create an environment which the average individual is completely unable to interpret. Not only do events occur that he is unable to understand, but almost all of these events seem to be completely beyond his own immediate control, even though his personal life may be drastically affected by them. He feels that he is living in a period of rapid social change, but just what direction the change should take and how it may be peacefully accomplished he does not know. For the most part, the potential consequences of forthcoming events are unpredictable.

This situation is not something known only to the public official, the big businessman, or the social scientist. The masses of people themselves know all this most poignantly. The material consequences of a disturbed economic order are not difficult for anyone to recognize. And most important for our purposes are the psychological consequences in terms of personal anxieties, ambitions, and insecurities of this awareness that all is not right with the world. A few random observations will illustrate what these unsettled conditions actually mean to people.

A recent poll of the American Institute of Public Opinion contained the question, "If you lost your present job (or business) and

| Persons on relief already | 17% |
| Could hold out one month or less | 19 |
| One to six months | 16 |
| Six months up to three years | 13 |
| Three years and over | 35 |

could not find other work, how long do you think you could hold out before you would have to apply for relief?"[1] The answers to this question reflect the basic insecurity of over half the population.[2]

The same ballot asked persons what social class they felt they belonged to and of what income class they considered themselves to be members. The answers to these two questions show that whereas only 6 per cent of the population regards itself as belonging to the lower *social* class and 88 per cent believe they are in the middle class, 31 per cent regard themselves as members of the lower *economic* class. Hence for a quarter of the population there is a discrepancy between their income and the social status to which they belong.

Popular education, advertising, and mass media of communication have deluged people with a knowledge of the potential abundancies of life. They derive real needs for automobiles, central heating, indoor plumbing, and dozens of other things which are now within their range of vision. Even in our small sample of case studies, we found that when people were asked to indicate from a list of eighteen possibilities, "Which of the following would you most like to have?" (such as a pretty home, travel, professional advancement), those persons with more than high school education checked twice as many things as less educated people. If education should be further extended while economic conditions remained static, one could safely predict that the discrepancy between the aspiration levels and the achievement levels of the masses would become even greater.

In the case of certain listeners to this broadcast, the general confusion in economic, political and social conditions does seem to have been a major cause of fantastic interpretation. And it was the people who were closest to the borderline of economic disaster who were most apt to take the program as news. We have already shown the high relationship between education and economic status and have seen that people of low education oriented themselves least adequately. But even when we equate people by their educa-

---

[1] Release of April 2, 1939.

[2] See *Consumer Incomes in the United States,* a report of the National Resources Committee for a graphic account of income distribution in the United States during 1936. Also the National Resources Committee report, *The Structure of the American Economy,* Part I: *Basic Characteristics,* 1939. Although the report has been widely quoted, the real significance of the low standards of living prevailing in the country are difficult to appreciate in any personal context unless one can actually observe the consequences or feel their implications in such books as *Grapes of Wrath, These Are Our Lives, Middletown in Transition.*

tional level and then compare their adjustment to the broadcast according to their economic circumstances, we find that poorer people tended to assume a false standard of judgment more frequently than others, irrespective of education (See table below.)

A few comments from the case studies will show how people felt, and why they were suggestible to news which perhaps seemed little less confused than the confused world they already knew.

"Everything is so upset in the world that *anything might happen.*"

"Things have happened so thick and fast since my grandfather's day that *we can't hope to know what might happen now.* I am all balled up."

"Ever since my husband lost his job a few years ago, *things seem to have gone from bad to worse.* I don't know when everything will be all right again."

"*Being we are in a troublesome world, anything is liable to happen.* We hear so much news every day—so many things we hear are unbelievable. Like all of a sudden 600 children burned to death in a school house, or a lot of people being thrown out of work. Everything seems to be a shock to me."

For many persons another bewildering characteristic of our present civilization is the mystery of science. For certain people without scientific training or without sufficient personal ability, initiative or opportunity to investigate the mechanisms surrounding them, the telephone, the airplane, poison gas, the radio, the camera are but specific manifestations of a baffling power. The principles by which such things operate are completely unknown. Such devices come from a world outside and lie within a universe of discourse completely foreign to the perplexed layman. Scientists in general are frequently referred to as "they." Many variations of this theme are found in the case studies. If science can create the things we have, why can't it create rocket ships and death rays?

Proportion of people in different educational and economic groups who interpreted the program as news (CBS survey)

| Economic Status | Education | | |
| | College (per cent) | High school (per cent) | Grammar school (per cent) |
| --- | --- | --- | --- |
| High | 28 | 31 | 43 |
| Average | 25 | 34 | 45 |
| Low | 0 | 44 | 53 |

*"I hear they are experimenting* with rocket ships and it seems possible that we will have them."

"So many odd things are happening in the world. *Science has progressed so far* that we don't know how far it might have gone on Mars. The way the world runs ahead anything is possible."

*War Scare.* This broadcast followed closely on the heels of a European war crisis. Not only did the crisis seem to be a very real one, but it was perhaps at the time a more widely known one than any in history—thanks to the medium of radio and the ingenuity and resourcefulness of the large broadcasting companies who had special reporters on the spot. During August, September and part of October 1938 millions of Americans were listening regularly to their radios, to the latest stories of a developing international crisis. Probably never before in the history of broadcasting had so many people in this country been glued to their sets. Stations at all hours were willing to interrupt prearranged programs for the latest news broadcast. Hence both the technique and the content of this broadcast tended to fit into the existing mental context which had resulted from world events of the previous weeks.

When our interviewers asked, "What major catastrophe could happen to the American people?" three-fourths of those in the frightened group as contrasted to half of those in the non-frightened group answered war or revolution. Evidence of the same feeling is seen in answer to the question, "What sort of a catastrophe did you think it was?" Here the largest single category of response, except that of a Martian invasion, was the belief that the catastrophe actually was an act of war or some foreign attack. Over a fourth of the people who were disturbed or frightened by the broadcast gave such answers. Further expression of the fear of war is revealed in the images that listeners had of the actual invaders. Although about half of the people who were frightened or disturbed had fantastic pictures of the invaders as Martians, giants, or creatures of semihuman form, almost one-fifth of them reported that they had visions of soldiers attacking with advanced military weapons. Persons in the frightened group were, then, apparently more concerned about war.

The European war scare left some persons bewildered and confused, with a very real, if vague dread of a new war. Others had definite ideas of the potential source of trouble, localizing it chiefly in Germany or Japan. The instability of the former peace-time norms and the fear that these would be upset in favor of new norms that were personally dangerous and unwanted was clearly reflected in the case studies.

*"The war talk has us so upset.* Conditions are so unsettled since Chamberlain went to see Hitler."

*"I feel insecure* because although we are not in the war, we are so near it. I feel that with new devices on airplanes, it is possible for foreign powers to invade us. I listened to every broadcast during the European crisis."

*"I'm afraid* of all those people in Europe, they could do anything."

"I felt the castastrophe was *an attack by the Germans,* because Hitler didn't appreciate Roosevelt's telegram."

"The announcer said a meteor had fallen from Mars and I was sure he thought that, but *in back of my head I had the idea that the meteor was just a camouflage.* It was really an airplane like a Zeppelin that looked like a meteor and *the Germans were attacking* us with gas bombs. The airplane was built to look like a meteor just to fool people."

"I felt *it might be the Japanese*—they are so crafty."

A few people interpreted the invasion as an extension of the war against the Jews.

"The Jews are being treated so terribly in some parts of the world, *I was sure something had come to destroy them* in this country."

"I worry terribly about the future of the Jews. Nothing else bothers me so much. I thought *this might be another attempt to harm them.*"

*The thrill of disaster.* It is a well known fact that people who suffer deeply or whose lot in life is generally miserable frequently compensate for their situations by seeking some temporary change or escape from their troubles. Dull lives may be cheered with bright clothing or gaudy furniture, harassed breadwinners may become fixtures at the local beer hall, worried housewives may zealously participate in religious orgies, repressed youths may identify themselves for a few hours with the great lovers or gangsters of the silver screen. There are many socially accepted ways of escape from the responsibilities, worries, and frustrations of life—the movies, the pulp magazines, fraternal organizations, and a host of other devices thrive partially because their devotees want surcease from their woes.

In addition to these more obvious escapes, there are two other conditions that may resolve the problems such persons face. In the first place, some social upheaval may dissipate the circumstances that create the frustration. The early days after a revolution generally bring with them freedom and license. Sometimes the upheaval may be of such a nature that the individual will in the end be in a worse situation than he was before. But because of the intense worries or anxieties he has, he may consciously or unconsciously welcome the cataclysm. Take, for example, a bank clerk who has embezzled certain funds to help a needy family. His conscience may bother him and he may always have the dread that some day he will be caught. But one day the bank is blown up, all the records are destroyed and he himself is badly injured. It is not hard to imagine that such a man would greet such a catastrophe. A few persons represented in the case studies showed signs of welcoming the invasion and their consequent extermination because of the relief it would give them.

*"I was looking forward with some pleasure to the destruction of the entire human race* and the end of the world. *If we have Fascist domination* of the world, *there is no purpose in living anyway."*

"My only thought involving myself as a person in connection with it was a delight that if it spread to Stelton *I would not have to pay the butcher's bill."*

"I looked in the icebox and saw some chicken left from Sunday dinner that I was saving for Monday night dinner. I said to my nephew, *'We may as well eat this chicken*—we won't be here in the morning.' "

"The broadcast had us all worried but I knew *it would at least scare ten years' life out of my mother-in-law."*

Another way in which people may get relief from their troubles is by submerging their own responsibilities and worries into a battle their whole society is having with some threatening force. We know, for example, that the suicide rate decreases in war time, presumably because potential suicides gain new securities and feel new responsibilities that are socially valued. Some of the frightened persons to the broadcast had a feeling of self-importance while they were listening or relaying vital information regarding the invasion to uninformed friends whom they thought they were helping. They were temporarily a member of the "in" group.

"I urged my husband to listen and said *it was an historical moment* possibly and he would be sorry afterwards to have missed it."

*"It was the thrill of a lifetime*—to hear something like that and think it's real."

"I had never heard anything like it before and I was excited even after I knew what it was about. *I felt like telling somebody all about it."*

Others seemed to enjoy the broadcast despite their fear because the event was aligning them with other people in a conflict for rights, privileges, or ideals they had been carrying on alone or with a minority group. A Jewish woman reported, for example:

"I realized right away that *it was something that was affecting everybody, not only the Jews,* and I felt relieved. *As long as everybody was going to die,* it was better."

Although comparatively rare, these instances of an ambivalent attitude to the ensuing destruction do serve as a mirror of the times. Such persons would probably not have experienced any pleasure or relief from their worries had they lived in a more ideal social order where democracy was secure, where every person played a rôle, or where money, food, or houses were plentiful.

So far we have indicated that the broadcast would not have aroused an extensive panic if people had enjoyed greater educational advantages which they might have followed through with satisfying jobs, sufficiently rewarding to accommodate more of their needs. The times also seemed out of joint because of the threat of an impending war in which this country might become involved. These dislocations in the culture probably account in large measure for the emotional insecurity we have found so important and for the lack of critical ability discovered especially in the lower education and income brackets of the population.

Throughout the whole discussion so far we have stressed the personal and unique nature of the subjective context which the listener called upon to interpret the broadcast. In our analyses we have been forced to conceptualize these various contexts by using classificatory rubrics. But as the author of the *War of the Worlds* has pointed out, "the forceps of our minds are clumsy forceps and crush the truth a little in taking hold of it."[3] Before seeking any final generalizations with which to explain the nature of a panic, we shall turn therefore to case studies of a few individuals who were panic-stricken to see how the factors we have mentioned so far are in individual lives interwoven with individual listening experiences.

---

[3] H. G. Wells, *Experiment in Autobiography* (New York: Macmillan, 1934), p. 180.

# PART TWO

# A Case of Multiple Personality

CORBETT H. THIGPEN AND HERVEY CLECKLEY

The psychiatric manifestation called multiple personality has been extensively discussed. So too have the unicorn and the centaur. Who has not read of these legendary quadrupeds? Their pictures are, perhaps tiresomely, familiar to any schoolboy. Can one doubt that during medieval times many twilight encounters with the unicorn were convincingly reported? Surely in the days of Homer there were men of Thessaly or Beotia who had seen, or even ridden, centaurs almost as wise as Chiron.

The layman who at college took a course in psychology may feel that for him *dual personality*, or *multiple personality*, is a familiar subject. Some psychiatrists' reactions suggest they are inclined to dismiss this subject as old hat. Nevertheless, like the unicorn and the centaur in some respects, multiple personality, despite vivid appearances in popularized books on psychology (2), is not commonly encountered in the full reality of life (1, 16, 17). Nearly all those perplexing reports of two or more people in one body, so to speak, that arouse a unique interest in the classroom, are reports of observations made in a relatively distant past. The most significant manifestations of this sort discussed in the current literature occurred in patients studied half a century or more ago (13, 23). It is scarcely surprising that practical psychiatrists today, never having directly observed such things as Morton Prince found in Miss Beauchamp or as Azam reported of Felida, might hold a tacitly skeptical attitude toward such archaic marvels and miracles. In the fields of internal medicine and chemistry the last, or even the middle, decades of the nineteenth century are close to us. In the relatively new field of psychopathology they are almost primeval, a dim dawn era in which we find it easy to suspect that a glimpse of a rhinoceros might have led to descriptions of the unicorn, or the sound of thunder been misinterpreted as God's literal voice.

A reserved judgment toward what cannot be regularly demonstrated is not necessarily deplorable. Some current tendencies suggest that our youthful branch of medicine may not yet have emerged

Thigpen and Cleckley, "A Case of Multiple Personality," *Journal of Abnormal and Social Psychology*, XLIX, No. 1, 1954, pages 135–144. Copyright 1954 by the American Psychological Association and reproduced by permission.

from its primordial and prerational phase. The discovery of *orgone* by one of our erstwhile leaders in the development of "psychodynamics" should not be ignored (4, 25). Enthusiastically adduced "proof" from an adult's dream that he was as an embryo significantly traumatized by fear of his father's penis, which during intercourse threatened him from his mother's vagina, is, we believe, the sort of evidence toward which our "resistance" is not without value (21). Despite Morton Prince's exquisitely thorough study of the celebrated Miss Beauchamp (23, 24) it is not surprising that decades ago McDougall should have warned us:

> It has been suggested by many critics that, in the course of Prince's long and intimate dealings with the case, involving as it did the frequent use of hypnosis, both for exploratory and therapeutic purposes, he may have moulded the course of its development to a degree that cannot be determined. This possibility cannot be denied (16, p. 497).

It is perhaps significant to note that, despite the light (or at least the half-light) they throw on most of the puzzling manifestations of psychiatric disorder, the studies of Prince and others on multiple personality are not even mentioned in some of the best and most popular textbooks of psychiatry used in our medical schools today (19, 26). When mentioned at all in such works, the subject is usually dismissed with a few words (11, 20). It is particularly noteworthy that Freud, during his years of assiduous investigation, apparently displayed no appreciable interest in the development of this disorder. Erickson and Kubie cite one brief allusion (9) which they term his "only reference to the problem" (6).

Psychiatrists who would not deny outright the truly remarkable things reported long ago about multiple personality, even when accepting them passively in good faith seem often to do so perfunctorily. In the midst of clinical work, with its interesting immediate experiences and pressing demands, few are likely to focus a major interest on what is known to them only through dust-covered records, on what they have never encountered, and don't expect to deal with. During the complications and excitements of a stormy sea voyage even the most sincere believer in the miracle of Jonah will probably not look to whales for his chief solution of problems that may arise from shipwreck.

Our direct experience with a patient has forced us to review the subject of multiple personality. It has also provoked in us the reaction of wonder, sometimes of awe.

One of us (C. H. T.) had for several months been treating a twenty-five-year-old married woman who was referred because of "severe and blinding headaches." At the first interview she also mentioned "blackouts" following headache. These were vaguely described by the patient. Her family was not aware of any thing that would suggest a real loss of consciousness or serious mental confusion. During a series of interviews which were irregular, since the patient had to come from some distance away, several important emotional difficulties were revealed and discussed. Encouraging symptomatic improvement occurred, but it was plain that this girl's major problems had not been settled. To the therapist, Eve White—as we shall call her—was an ordinary case with commonplace symptoms and a relatively complex but familiar constellation of marital conflicts and personal frustrations. We were puzzled during therapy about a recent trip for which she had no memory. Hypnosis was induced and the amnesia cleared up promptly. Several days after a visit to the office a letter was received.

What was the meaning of such a letter? Though unsigned, the postmark, the content, and the familiar penmanship in most of the message revealed to the therapist that this had been written by Eve White. The effect of this letter on the therapist was considerable. It raised puzzling questions for which there were no answers and set in motion thoughts that pursued various and vague directions. Had some child found the uncompleted page, scribbled those words, and, perhaps as a whim, mailed it in an already addressed envelope? Perhaps. The handwriting of the last paragraph to be sure suggested the work of a child. Could Eve White herself, as a puerile prank, have decided to disguise her characteristic writing and added this inconsequential note? And if so, why? Mrs. White had appeared to be a circumspect, matter of fact person, meticulously truthful and consistently sober and serious about her grave᾿ troubles. It was rather difficult to imagine her becoming playful or being moved by an impulse to tease, even on a more appropriate occasion. The "blackouts" which she had rather casually mentioned, but which did not seem to disturb her very much, suggested of course that a somnabulism or brief fugue might have occurred.

On her next visit she denied sending the letter, though she recalled having begun one which she never finished. She believed she had destroyed it. During this interview Eve White, ordinarily an excessively self-controlled woman, began to show signs of distress and agitation. Apprehensively and reluctantly she at last formulated a question: Did the occasional impression of hearing an imaginary voice indicate that she was "insane"?

*July.*

Dear Doctor,

Remembering my visit to _____ brought me a great deal of relief, to begin with.

Just being able to recall the trip seemed enough, but now that I've had time to think about it and all that occurred, it's more painful than I ever thought possible.

How can I be sure that I remember all that happened, even now? How can I know that it won't happen again? I wonder if I'll ever be sure of anything again.

While I was there with you it seemed different. Somehow it didn't matter so much, to have forgotten; but now it does matter. I know it's something that doesn't happen to _____

I can't even recall color schemes and I know that would probably be the first thing I'd notice.

My head hurts right on top. It has ever since the day I was down there to see you. I think it must be my eyes — I see little red & green specks — and I'm covered with some kind of rash.

baby please be quite down here don't let me done patience with her she too sweet and innocent and my self-control

*This letter in retrospect was the first intimation that our patient was unusual. The dramatic and unexpected revelation of the second personality shortly followed.*

To the therapist this information was startling. Nothing about Eve White suggested even an early schizoid change. Her own attitude toward what she now reported was in no respect like any of the various attitudes of patients who are in the ordinary sense experiencing auditory hallucinations. Yet, she insisted with painful embarrassment, she had on several occasions over the last few months heard briefly but distinctly a voice addressing her. Something about her reaction to this may be conveyed if we compare it to what we can imagine an experienced psychiatrist in robust mental health might feel if, with full retention of insight, he heard himself similarly addressed. While the therapist, hesitating a moment in wonder, sought for an adequate reply, an abstruse and inexplicable expression came, apparently unprompted by volition, over Eve White's familiar countenance. As if seized by a sudden pain she put both hands to her head. After a tense moment of silence, her hands dropped. There was a quick, reckless smile and, in a bright voice that sparkled, she said, "Hi there, Doc!"

The demure and constrained posture of Eve White had melted into buoyant repose. With a soft and surprisingly intimate syllable of laughter, she crossed her legs. Disconcerted as he was by unassimilated surprise, the therapist noted from the corner of his awareness something distinctly attractive about them, and also that this was the first time he had received such an impression. There is little point in attempting here to give in detail the differences between this novel feminine apparition and the vanished Eve White. Instead of that retiring and gently conventional figure, there was in the newcomer a childishly daredevil air, an erotically mischievous glance, a face marvellously free from the habitual signs of care, seriousness, and underlying distress, so long familiar in her predecessor. This new and apparently carefree girl spoke casually of Eve White and her problems, always using *she* or *her* in every reference, always respecting the strict bounds of a separate identity. When asked her own name she immediately replied, "Oh, I'm Eve Black."

It is easy to say that this new voice was different, that the basic idiom of her language was plainly not that of Eve White. A thousand minute alterations of manner, gesture, expression, posture, of nuances in reflex or instinctive reaction, of glance, of eyebrow tilting and eye movement, all argued that this could only be another woman. It is not possible to say just what all these differences were.

It would not be difficult for a man to distinquish his wife, or perhaps even his secretary, if she were placed among a hundred other women carefully chosen because of their resemblance to her, and all dressed identically. But few would wager that, however articulate he might be, he could tell a stranger, or even someone very slightly acquainted with her, how to accomplish this task. If he tries to tell us how he himself recognizes her, he may accurately convey something to us. But what he can convey, no matter how hard he tries, is only an inconsequential fragment. It is not enough to help us when we set out to find her. So, too, we are not able to tell adequately what so profoundly distinguishes from Eve White the carefree girl who took her place in this vivid mutation.

Even before anything substantial of her history could be obtained, the therapist reacted to the new presence with feelings that momentarily recalled from distant memory these words:

The devil has entered the prompter's box
And the play is ready to start.

Over a period of 14 months during a series of interviews totaling approximately 100 hours, extensive material was obtained about the behavior and inner life of Eve White—and of Eve Black. It is our plan to report on this more adequately in a book-length study. Here space limits our presentation to a few details.

Eve Black, so far as we can tell, has enjoyed an independent life since Mrs. White's early childhood.[1] She is not a product of disruptive emotional stresses which the patient has suffered during recent years. Eve White apparently had no knowledge or suspicion of the other's existence until some time after she appeared unbidden before the surprised therapist. Though Mrs. White has learned that there is a Miss Black during the course of therapy, she does not have access to the latter's awareness. When Eve Black is "out," Eve White remains functionally in abeyance, quite oblivious of what the coinhabitant of her body does, and apparently unconscious.

---

[1] The question: "How can the various personalities be called out?" has been asked. After the original spontaneous appearance of Eve Black it was at first necessary for Eve White to be hypnotized in order for us to talk with Eve Black. How Eve Black could "pop out" of her own accord at unpredictable times and yet could not come out on request, we do not know. Under hypnosis of Eve White, Eve Black could very easily be called forth. After a few hypnotic sessions, we merely had to request Eve White to let us speak to Eve Black. Then we called Eve Black's name, and Eve Black would come forth. The reverse was true when Eve Black was out and we wished to speak with Eve White. Hypnosis was no longer necessary for the purpose of obtaining the changes. This made things simpler for us but complicated Eve White's life considerably because Eve Black found herself able to "take over" more easily than before. A third personality, Jane, to be described below, emerged spontaneously and we have never had to employ hypnosis to reach her.

On the contrary, Eve Black preserves awareness while absent. Invisibly alert at some unmapped post of observation, she is able to follow the actions and the thoughts of her spiritually antithetical twin. The hoydenish and devil-may-care Eve Black "knows" and can report what the other does and thinks, and describes her feelings. Those feelings, however, are not Eve Black's own. She does not participate in them. Eve White's genuine and natural distress about her failing marriage is regarded by the other as silly. Eve White's love and deep concern for her only child, a little girl of four, is to us and to all who know her, warm, real, consistent, and impressive. Eve Black, who shares her memory and verbally knows her thoughts, discerns her emotional reactions and values only as an outsider. They are for the outsider something trite, bothersome, and insignificant. The devotion of this mother for her child, as an empty definition, is entirely familiar to the lively and unworried Eve Black. Its substance and nature are, however, so clearly outside her personal experience that she can evaluate it only as "something pretty corny."

During the temporary separation of her parents, which may become permanent, this little girl is living with her grandparents in a village. Because her earnings are necessary for her child's basic welfare, the mother has no choice but to work and live in a city approximately a hundred miles from the child. Having apparently known little but unhappiness with her husband, she was finally forced to the conclusion that her young and vulnerable child had little chance of happy or normal development in the home situation, which, despite her best efforts, continually grew worse. She now endures the loneliness, frustration, and grief of separation from her warmly loved daughter, who is the primary object of her life and feeling, and who, she has good reason to fear, is likely to grow up apart from her. Perhaps, it seems to her sometimes, she will become to her as years pass little more than a coolly accepted stranger.

Vulnerable, uningenious, and delicately feminine, Eve White characteristically perserves a quiet dignity about personal sorrow, a dignity unpretentiously stoic. Under hypnosis one can come closer to the sadness and the lonely despair she feels it her task not to display. Even then no frantic weeping occurs, no outcries of self-pity. Her quiet voice remains level as she discussed matters that leave her cheeks at last wet from silent tears.

Despite access to this woman's "thoughts" Eve Black has little or no real compassion for her. Nor does she seem in any important sense actively, or purposefully, cruel. Neutral or immune to major affective events in human relations, an unparticipating onlooker, she is apparently almost as free of hatefulness, or of mercy, or of comprehension, as a bright-feathered parakeet who chirps undisturbed while watching a child strangle to death.

It has been mentioned that Eve Black's career has been traced back to early childhood. She herself freely tells us of episodes when she emerged, usually to engage in acts of mischief or disobedience. She lies glibly and without compunction, so her account alone can never be taken as reliable evidence. Since Eve White, whose word on any matter has always proved good, still has no access to the other's current awareness or her memory and, indeed, did not until recently even faintly suspect her existence, it has been impossible through her to check fully and immediately on Eve Black's stories. Her memory has, however, afforded considerable indirect evidence since she has been able to confirm reports of punishments she received, of accusations made against her, for deeds unknown to her but described to us by Eve Black.

Some stories have been substantiated through others. Both of this patient's parents, as well as her husband, have been available for interviews. They recall several incidents that Eve Black had previously reported to us. For instance, the parents had had to punish their ordinarily good and conforming six-year-old girl for having disobeyed their specific rule against wandering through the woods to play with the children of a tenant farmer. They considered this expedition dangerous for so young a child, and their daughter's unaccountable absence had caused them worry and distress. On her return Eve received a hearty whipping despite her desperate denials of wrongdoing or disobedience. In fact these very denials added to her punishment, since the evidence of her little trip was well established and her denial taken as a deliberate lie. Eve Black had previously described this episode to us in some detail, expressing amusement about "coming out" to commit and enjoy the forbidden adventure and withdrawing to leave the other Eve, sincerely protesting her innocence, to appreciate all sensations of the whipping.

The adult Eve White recalled this and several other punishments which she had no way of understanding and which sometimes bewildered her in her relations with her parents.

Irresponsibility and a shallowly hedonistic grasping for ephemeral excitements or pleasures characterize Eve Black's adult behavior. She succeeded in concealing her identity not only from the other Eve but also from her parents and the husband. She herself denies marriage to this man, whom she despises, and any relation to Eve White's little girl except that of an unconcerned bystander. Though she had often "come out" in the presence of all these people, she went unrecognized until she agreed to reveal herself to them in the therapist's office.

Her wayward behavior, ill will, harshness, and occasional acts of violence, observed by Mr. White and the parents, were attributed to unaccountable fits of temper in a woman habitually gentle and considerate.

During her longer periods "out," when she expresses herself more freely in behavior so unlike that of Eve White, she avoids her family and close friends, and seeks the company of strangers or of those insufficiently acquainted with her alternate to evaluate accurately the stupendous transformation.

Once we had seen and spoken with Eve Black, it seemed to us at first scarcely possible that, even in the same body as her alternate, she could for so long have concealed her separate identity from others. Yet, who among those acquainted with her would be likely to suspect, however unlike herself Eve appeared at times to be, such a situation as that voluntarily revealed to us by the patient? No matter how many clues one is given, no matter how obvious the clues, one will not be led to a conclusion that is inconceivable. One will seek explanations for the problem only among available hypotheses.

Not knowing the only concept into which successive details of perception will fit, even a very astute man may observe a thousand separate features of something his imagination has never shaped without grasping the gestalt, without being able to put into a recognizable whole the details he has so clearly detected. Only our previous familiarity with three-dimensional space enables us to see the representation of depth in a picture. What is for us still unconceived can give us a thousand hints, boldly flaunt before us its grossest features, and remain for us undelineated, formless, uncomprehended as an entity.

The astonishingly incompatible gestures, expressions, attitudes, mannerisms, and behavior which Eve occasionally displayed before intimates provoked thought and wonder, demanded explanation. But who in the position of these people would be likely to find or create in his mind the hypothesis that forms a recognizable image? Let us remember too that Eve Black, until she voluntarily named herself to the therapist, meant to remain unrecognized. When it suits her, she deliberately and skillfully acts so as to pass herself off as Eve White, imitating her habitual tone of voice, her gestures, and attitudes. Let us not forget that she is shrewd. Would it not, after all, require a sledge-hammer blow from the obvious to drive into an unsuspecting acquaintance the only hypothesis that would lead to her recognition?[2]

Psychometric and projective tests conducted on the two Eves by a well-qualified expert were reported thus:

### Psychological Consultation Report

This twenty-five-year-old married female patient was referred for psychological examination with a provisional diagnosis of dual personality. Two complete psychological examinations were requested, one of the predominant personality, Mrs. White, the other, . . . of the secondary personality, Miss Black.

The patient is the oldest of three siblings, having twin sisters. She quit school two months before graduation from high school. She was employed as a telephone operator. She has been married six years and has a girl four years old. Patient states that she did things recently she cannot remember having done, and expresses serious concern about this condition. The following psychological tests were administered in both examinations:

Wechsler-Bellevue Intelligence Scale

Wechsler Memory Scale

Drawings of Human Figures

Rorschach

*Test behavior:* Patient was neat, friendly, and cooperative. However, while Mrs. White was more serious, more conscientious, and displayed more anxiety, Miss Black appeared somewhat less anxious and was satisfied with giving more superficial responses. Still the basic behavior pattern was very similar in both personalities, indicating that inhibitory forces were not markedly abolished even in the role of the desired personality. Speech was coherent, and there were no distortions in ideation or behavior according to the assumed personality. No psychotic deviations could be observed at the present time.

*Tests results:* While Mrs. White is able to achieve an IQ of 110 on the Wechsler-Bellevue Intelligence Scale, Miss Black attains an IQ of 104 only. There is evidence that the native intellectual endowment is well within the bright normal group; however, in Mrs. White's case anxiety and tenseness

---

[2] Eve White's husband and parents were troubled by the inexplicable changes in her. They assumed them to be "fits of temper" about which she lied. Her mother called the fugues of her daughter these "strange little habits." Apparently these people observed the same changes that we have observed, but unlike ourselves, they have not had the conception of multiple personality in mind. Lacking it, they could not use it as an explanatory construct.

interfere, in Miss Black's superficiality and slight indifference
as to achievement are responsible for the lower score. While
Mrs. White shows more obsessional traits, Miss Black shows
more hysterical tendencies in the records. It is interesting to
note that the memory function in Miss Black is on the same
level as her Intelligence Quotient, while Mrs. White's memory
function is far above her IQ, although she complained of a
disturbance of memory. The only difficulty encountered by
both personalities is on recall of digits, a performance in which
telephone operators usually excel! On the other hand, the
Rorschach record of Miss Black is by far healthier than the
one of Mrs. White. In Miss Black's record a hysterical tendency is predominant, while Mrs. White's record shows con-
striction, anxiety, and obsessive compulsive traits. Thus Miss
Black is able to conform with the environment, while Mrs.
White is rigid and not capable of dealing with her hostility.

*Personality dynamics:* A comparison of the projective tests indicates repression in Mrs. White and regression in Miss Black.
The dual personality appears to be the result of a strong desire
to regress to an early period of life, namely the one before
marriage. Miss Black is actually the maiden name of Mrs.
White. Therefore, there are not two different personalities
with completely dissimilar ideation, but rather one personality
at two stages of her life. As is characteristic for this type of
case, the predominant personality is amnesic for the existence,
activities, or behavior of the secondary or subordinate system,
while the secondary personality is aware and critical of the
predominant personality's activities and attitudes. The latter
reaction is quite similar to the ego-conflict in obsessive compulsive disturbances.

Mrs. White admits difficulty in her relation with her
mother, and her performance on the Rorschach and drawings
indicate conflict and resulting anxiety in her role as a wife
and mother. Only with strong conscious effort can she compel
herself to subject herself to these roles. The enforced subjection
results in ever increasing hostility. This hostility, however, is
not acceptable to her, and activates a defense mechanism of
regression to avoid severe guilt feelings, by removing the entire
conflictual situation from conscious awareness. At the same
time, the new situation (in which she plays the role of Miss
Black) permits her to discharge some of her hostility towards
Mrs. White. Miss Black on the other hand has regained her
previous status of freedom from marital and maternal conflicts, and thus has liberated herself from the insoluble situation
in which Mrs. White found herself through her marriage.
In addition, she can avert the—in her conviction—inevitable
spiritual loss of her child. Thus, it is not surprising that she
shows contempt for Mrs. White who permitted herself to

become involved in such a situation because of her lack of foresight, as well as her lack of courage to forcefully solve the dilemma.

Actually the problem started at a much earlier period of life, with a strong feeling of rejection by her parents, especially after the birth of her twin sisters. Mrs. White loves them dearly, Miss Black despises them. In this connection an episode is related by Miss Black. After quitting school to help support the family, she (that is to say Mrs. White) sent home money to be used for overcoats for her twin sisters, denying herself a badly wanted wristwatch. When the money was used to buy them two wristwatches instead of overcoats, she reacted with strong, but repressed, hostility. Significantly, she removed her wristwatch while examined as Mrs. White, stating that she doesn't like jewelry. There are several illustrations of her strong sense of rejection as well as sibling rivalry in her records.

Leopold Winter, Ph.D.
Clinical Psychologist
U.S. Veterans Administration
Hospital
Augusta, Georgia
July 2, 1952

With the circumspect Eve White oblivious of her escapades, Miss Black once recklessly bought several expensive and unneeded new dresses and two luxurious coats. Sometimes she revels in cheap night clubs flirting with strange men on the make. Insouciantly she pursues her irresponsible way, usually amused, sometimes a little bored, never alarmed or grieved or seriously troubled. She has, apparently, been unmoved by any sustaining purpose, unattracted by any steady goal, prompted only by the immediate and the trivial.

Eve White's husband, on discovering the valuable outlay of new clothes, which the other Eve had hidden carefully away, lost his temper and abused his wife for wantonly plunging him into debt. He found no way to accept her innocent denials as genuine but was at length assuaged in wrath by her wholehearted agreement that it would be disastrous for them to run up such a bill, and her promptness in returning all these garments to the store.[3] Eve White

---

[3] Mrs. White apparently failed to produce a satisfactory rationalization. This is true for all of her fugue states. She did tell us she suspected that her husband may have planted the clothes in order to make it appear that she was "insane." She did not, however, seem to come to grips with the problem. Apparently finding it, along with so many other problems, too much for her, she took an attitude in some ways like that of Scarlett O'Hara when the latter would tell herself, "Well, tomorrow will be another day."

has told us of many real and serious incompatibilities with her husband. Even if the two were unmolested by an outsider, it is doubtful if the imperfections of this marriage, its unhappiness, and the threats to its continuation could be alleviated. Adverse acts and influence by an insider have been peculiarly damaging and pernicious. Though Eve Black does not apparently follow a consistent purpose to disrupt the union, or regularly go out of her way to make trouble for the couple, her typical behavior often compounds their difficulties.

"When I go out and get drunk," Eve Black with an easy wink once said to both of us, "*she* wakes up with the hangover. She wonders what in the hell's made her so sick."

Though as a rule only indifferent, passively callous to her alternate's child, Eve Black once in the past became irritated with her and hurt her. Apparently she might have done her serious harm had her husband not restrained her. This act she denied and lied about consistently though the evidence for it through others is strong. Later she flippantly confessed, giving as her reason, "The little brat got on my nerves."

Abstract terms and other descriptive words are not likely to convey much of what one experiences directly of a human being, of a specific personal entity. Nor could any list of ten thousand such items be even near complete. Let us, nevertheless, set down for what they are worth a few points:

| *Eve White* | *Eve Black* |
|---|---|
| Demure, retiring, in some respects almost saintly | Obviously a party girl. Shrewd, childishly vain, and egocentric |
| Face suggests a quiet sweetness; the expression in repose is predominantly one of contained sadness | Face is pixie-like; eyes dance with mischief as if Puck peered through the pupils |
| Clothes: simple and conservative, neat and inconspicuously attractive | Expression rapidly shifts in a light cascade of fun-loving willfulness. The eyes are as inconstant as the wind. This face has not and will never know sadness. Often it reflects a misleading and only half-true naivete |
| Posture: tendency to a barely discernible stoop or slump. Movements careful and dignified | |
| Reads poetry and likes to compose verse herself | |
| Voice always softly modulated, always influenced by a specifically feminine restraint | Voice a little coarsened, "discultured," with echoes or implications of mirth and teasing. Speech richly vernacular and |

*Eve White (cont.)*

Almost all who know her express admiration and affection for her. She does not provoke envy. Her strength of character is more passive than active. Steadfast on defense but lacking initiative and boldness to formulate strategy of attack

An industrious and able worker; also a competent housekeeper and a skillful cook. Not colorful or glamorous. Limited in spontaneity

Consistently uncritical of others. Tries not to blame husband for marital troubles. Nothing suggests pretense on hypocrisy in this charitable attitude

Though not stiffly prudish and never self-righteous, she is seldom lively or playful or inclined to tease or tell a joke. Seldom animated

Her presence resonates unexpressed devotion to her child. Every act, every gesture, the demonstrated sacrifice of personal aims to work hard for her little girl, is consistent with this love

Cornered by bitter circumstances, threatened with tragedy, her endeavors to sustain herself, to defend her child are impressive

This role in one essentially so meek and fragile embodies an unspoken pathos. One feels somehow she is doomed to be overcome in her present situation

No allergy to nylon has been reported

*Eve Black (cont.)*

liberally seasoned with spontaneous gusts of rowdy wit

A devotee of pranks. Her repeated irresponsibilities have cruel results on others. More heedless and unthinking, however, than deeply malicious. Enjoys taunting and mocking the Siamese alternate

All attitudes and passions whimlike and momentary. Quick and vivid flares of many light feelings, all ephemeral

Immediately likable and attractive. A touch of sexiness seasons every word and gesture. Ready for any little, irresponsible adventure

Dress is becoming and a little provocative. Posture and gait suggest light-heartedness, play, a challenge to some sort of frolic

Never contemplative; to be serious is for her to be tedious or absurd

Is immediately amusing and likable. Meets the little details of experience with a relish that is catching. Strangely "secure from the contagion of the world's slow stain," and from inner aspect of grief and tragedy

Reports that her skin often reacts to nylon with urticaria. Usually does not wear stockings when she is "out" for long periods

It is not possible here even to summarize the history of each personality that emerged and accumulated over the months, or to describe the varied and multiplex complications that arose to tax, and often to baffle and overwhelm, the therapist's efforts. Let us note briefly a few scattered items.

In contrast with the interesting case reported by Erickson and Kubie (6), the secondary personality, Eve Black, has shown anything but a regular desire to help the other with her problems. The considerably submerged and dissociated manifestations referred to by Erickson and Kubie as Miss Brown apparently expressed themselves only through the medium of automatic writing. And this writing was so verbally imperfect and abstruse that considerable interpretation or translation was necessary to promote even limited communication. Nevertheless, whatever the influence designated by the term *Miss Brown* may represent, it consistently worked to aid the accessible personality, Miss Damon. It was a therapeutic influence (6).

Efforts to interest Eve Black in taking a similar role met with grim obstacles. Many of these, as can be imagined, were not unlike what impedes and frustrates the psychiatrist who tries to help a typical psychopath deal more constructively with his own problems, to find real goals and to develop normal evaluations. New toys or games can sometimes serve to arouse briefly the interest of a capricious child. So, too, the therapist occasionally was able to enlist Eve Black's support in some remedial aim directed towards the problems of her body's coinhabitant. Sometimes attaining in her even an attitude of neutrality was of value. What helpful acts or abstentions she could be induced to contribute have, however, been prompted, it seems, only by fleeting impulses such as casual curiosity, the playful redirection of a whim towards some pretty novelty. Often she has, by ingenious lies, misled the therapist to believe she was cooperating when her behavior was particularly detrimental to Eve White's progress.

No real or persistently constructive or sympathetic motivation has yet been induced in the irresponsible Eve, but one valuable means of influencing her is in the hands of the therapist. Though Eve Black has apparently been able since childhood to disappear at will, often doing this suddenly to leave the conscientious Eve with unpleasant consequences of misconduct and folly not her own, the ability to displace Eve White's consciousness and emerge to take control has always been limited. Sometimes she could "get out" and sometimes not. Since Eve White during treatment

learned of the other's existence it has become plain that her willingness to step aside and, so to speak, to release the imp plays an
important part in this alternate's ability to appear and express
herself directly. Eve White cannot keep the other suppressed permanently or count with certainty on doing this for some given
period. Her influence, and indirectly that of the therapist, have,
however, been sufficiently strong to use for bargaining with Eve
Black for better cooperation. If she will avoid the more serious
forms of misconduct she is rewarded with more time "out."

Even when invisible and inaccessible she, apparently, has means
of disturbing Eve White. She tells us she caused those severe headaches that brought the latter to us as a patient. Her unsuccessful
struggle to get out often produces this symptom in the other. So
too, she explains that the hallucinatory, or quasi-hallucinatory,
voice which Eve White heard before the other Eve disclosed herself
to us was her deliberate work.

From the two Eves during many interviews and from her husband
and parents, we in time obtained a great deal of information
about the patient. Having concluded we had a reasonably complete and accurate history of her career since early childhood, we
were astonished by the report of a distant relative who insisted that
a few years before she met her present husband a previous marriage had occurred.

Eve White denied this report and has never yet shown any
knowledge of it. To our surprise Eve Black also maintained that we
had been misinformed, insisting that Eve White had married only
once, that she herself had never and would never consider mar-
rying any man.

Finally, under the persistent pressure of evidence, Eve Black
gave up her position, admitted that the relative's report was correct, that she herself and only she had been the bride. This event
she told us occurred several years before Mrs. White's marriage.
While the other Eve was employed in a town some distance from
her parents' home she had come "out" and gone to a dance with a
man she scarcely knew. After a night of merriment, something was
half-jokingly mentioned about the pair getting married more or
less for the hell of it. This apparently struck her fancy.

She has recounted many details of outlandish strife and hardship
during several months when, apparently, she had lived with this
man. No record of a legal union has been obtained but considerable evidence indicates she did co-habit during this period with

such a man as she describes, perhaps under the careless impression that a marriage had really occurred. She insists that some sort of "ceremony" was performed, saying that it was not formally recorded and admitting it may have been a ruse. During this time when she regarded herself as wed, Eve Black enjoyed her longest periods of uninterrupted sway. She was predominantly in control, almost constantly present. Apparently she had no desire for sexual relations but often enjoyed frustrating her supposed husband by denying herself to him. He in turn, she says, was prone to beat her savagely. She claims to have succeeded in avoiding most of the pain from this by "going in" and leaving the other Eve to feel the blows.

This last claim immediately impressed us both as extremely implausible. If Eve White experienced the pain and humiliation of these beatings, why did she not remember them? She has consistently denied any memory of the entire marital or pseudomarital experience reported by Eve Black. Our unreliable but convincing informant maintains that she herself remained in control or possession nearly all the time during this adventure. She furthermore insists that she can, by exerting a considerable effort, often "pick out" or erase from Eve White's reach certain items of memory. "I just start thinking about it very hard," Eve Black says, "and after a while she quits and it doesn't come back to her anymore." All awareness of the beatings she claims so to have erased from the other's recollection. Such a claim, obviously, was subject to testing by the therapist. Several experiments indicated that it is correct.

After approximately eight months of psychiatric treatment Eve White had apparently made encouraging progress. For a long time she had not been troubled by headaches or "blackout." The imaginary voice had never been heard again since the other Eve revealed herself to the therapist. Mrs. White worked efficiently at her job and had made progress financially through salary raises and careful management. The prospect of returning to her husband and of working out a bearable relation was still blocked by serious obstacles, but, having achieved more personal security and financial independence, she had become more hopeful of eventually reaching some acceptable solution. Though sadly missing the presence of her child, she found some comfort in her successful efforts to provide for her. She had made friends in the once strange city and with them, despite many worries and responsibilities, occasionally enjoyed simple recreations.

Meanwhile Eve Black, though less actively resisted in emerging, had in general been causing less trouble. Being bored with all regular work, she seldom "came out" to make careless and costly errors, or indulge in complicating pranks while the breadwinner was on her job. Though in leisure hours she often got in bad company, picked up dates, and indulged in cheap and idle flirtations, her demure and conventional counterpart, lacking knowledge of these deeds, was spared the considerable humiliation and distress some of this conduct would otherwise have caused her.

At this point the situation changed for the worse. Eve White's headaches returned. They grew worse and more frequent. With them also returned the "blackouts." Since the earlier headaches had been related to, perhaps caused by, the other Eve's efforts to gain control, and the "blackouts" had often represented this alternate's periods of activity, she was suspected and questioned. She denied any part or influence in the new development. She did not experience the headaches, but, surprisingly, seemed now to participate in the blackouts, and could give no account of what occurred during them. Apparently curious about these experiences, she said, "I don't know where we go, but go we do."

Two or three times the patient was found lying unconscious on the floor by her roommate. This, so far as we could learn, had not occurred during the previous episodes reported by Eve White as "blackouts." It became difficult for her to work effectively. Her hard-won gains in serenity and confidence disappeared. During interviews she became less accessible, while showing indications of increasing stress. The therapist began to fear that a psychosis was impending. Though this fear was not, of course, expressed to Eve White, it was mentioned to her reckless and invulnerable counterpart. The fact was emphasized that, should it be necessary to send Eve White to an institution, the other, too, would suffer the same restrictions and confinement. Perhaps, the therapist hoped, this fact would curtail her in any unadmitted mischief she might be working.

Since it has for long been presumed that so-called dual personalities arise from a dissociation of an originally integrated entity of functioning and experience, efforts were naturally exerted from the first to promote reintegration. Attempts were made with each Eve to work back step by step into early childhood. With Mrs. White hypnosis was sometimes used to regain forgotten events or aspects or fragments of experience. It was hoped that some link or bridge might be found on which additional contact and coalition could grow or be built. Under hypnosis she occasionally re-experienced considerable emotion in recalling events of her childhood. We have never been able to hypnotize Eve Black.

It soon became possible for the therapist to evoke either personality at will. During the first few weeks a transition from Eve White to Eve Black was more easily achieved by hypnosis. Shortly afterwards it became possible to simplify the procedure. Permission and the promise of cooperation were obtained from the lady present. Then the other was called by name and invited or encouraged to emerge. With repetition, and with deepening emotional relations between patient and physician, this process became after a while very easily accomplished. In the very early stages of treatment an effort was made, perhaps a too naive effort, to promote some sort of blending, or at least a liaison, by calling out both personalities at once. To this attempt Eve White reacted with violent headache and emotional distress so severe that it was not considered wise to continue. When the experiment was reversed, with the apparently invulnerable Eve Black manifest, much less agitation was observed. After one unsuccessful trial, however, she bluntly refused to go further. In explanation she said only that it gave her "such a funny, queer, mixed-up feeling that I ain't gonna put up with it no more."

Sometime after the return of headaches and blackouts, with Eve White's maladjustment still growing worse generally, a very early recollection was being discussed with her. The incident focused about a painful injury she had sustained when scalded by water from a wash pot. As she spoke her eyes shut sleepily. Her words soon ceased. Her head dropped back on the chair. After remaining in this sleep or trance perhaps two minutes her eyes opened. Blankly she stared about the room, looking at the furniture and the pictures as if trying to orient herself. Continuing their apparently bewildered survey, her eyes finally met those of the therapist, and stopped. Slowly, with an unknown husky voice and with immeasurable poise, she spoke. "Who are you?"

From the first moment it was vividly apparent that this was neither Eve White nor Eve Black. She did not need to tell us that. The thousands of points distinguishing the two Eves have grown more clear and convincing as we acquire additional experience with each. So this new woman with time and study has shown herself ever more plainly another entity. Only in a superficial way could she be described as a sort of compromise between the two. She apparently lacks Eve Black's obvious faults and inadequacies. She also impresses us as far more mature, more vivid, more boldly capable, and more interesting than Eve White. It is easy to sense in her a capacity for accomplishment and fulfillment far beyond that of the sweet and retiring Eve White, who, beside this genuinely impressive newcomer, appears colorless and limited. In her are indications of initiative and powerful resources never shown by the other. This third personality calls herself Jane, for no particular reason she can give. In her it is not difficult to sense the potential or the promise of something far more of woman and of life than might be expected from the two Eves with faults and weaknesses eliminated and all assets combined.

Some weeks after Jane emerged to make a group of three patients, electroencephalographic studies were conducted.

### Report of Electroencephalogram

This tracing consists of 33 minutes of continuous recording including uninterrupted intervals of 5 minutes or more of each personality as well as several transpositions. The record was made with a Grass Model 111 EEG machine (8 channels) under conditions standard for this laboratory.

Each personality shows intervals of alpha rhythm interspersed with periods of diffuse low voltage fast activity. Intervals of L. V. F. are presumably associated with periods of mental tenseness, which the patient admitted experiencing. Although it is possible that these periods occurred at random, tenseness is most pronounced in Eve Black, next in Eve White and least of all in Jane. Several EEG's would be needed to show this to be a constant relationship.

When alpha rhythm occurs (relaxation), it is steadily maintained at 10½ to 11½ cycles per sec. by Eve White and by Jane. Eve Black's alpha is increased in rate of 12 or 13 cycles per sec.—generally at 12½. This increase is significant and falls at the upper border of normal limits approaching an F1 category. It is interesting to note that F1 records are fairly common in psychopathic personality although no consistent correlation has yet been demonstrated. In addition to the increased rate there is evidence of restlessness and generalized muscle tension during Eve Black's tracings which are not observed in the other two personalities.

Transposition is effected within a few seconds. It is usually accompanied by artifact from eye movements and slight body movements. Alpha rhythm is frequently blocked for several seconds during and following transposition. Alpha blocking was most pronounced in passing from Eve White to Eve Black. It did not occur at all in transposition from Eve Black to Eve White. This might possibly suggest that transposition from Eve

Black to Eve White is easier to effect. However, only two such transpositions are recorded.

No spikes, abnormal slow waves or amplitude asymmetries are recognized.

### Summary

All three personalities show alternate periods of alpha rhythm and low voltage fast activity, presumably due to alternate periods of mental relaxation and mental tenseness. The greatest amount of tenseness is shown by Eve Black, Eve White next and Jane least. Eve Black shows a basic alpha rate of 12½ cycles per sec., as compared with 11 cycles per sec. for Eve White and Jane. This places Eve Black's tracing on the border line between normal and slightly fast (F1). Slightly fast records are sometimes (but not consistently) associated with psychopathic personality. Eve Black's record also shows evidence of restlessness and muscle tension. Eve Black's EEG is definitely distinguished from the other two and could be classified as border-line normal. Eve White's EEG probably cannot be distinguished from Jane's—both are clearly normal.

J. Manter, M.D.
EEG Laboratory
Medical College of Ga.
Jan. 5th, 1953.

For several months now there have been three patients to interview and work with. Jane has awareness of what both Eves do and think but incomplete access to their stores of knowledge and their memories prior to her emergence upon the scene. Through her reports the therapist can determine when Eve Black has been lying. Jane feels herself personally free from Eve White's responsibilities and attachments, and in no way identified with her in the role of wife and mother. Apparently she is capable of compassion, and, we feel likely, of devotion and valid love. She has cooperated with sincerity, and with judgment and originality beyond that of the others. Though it took her a while to learn what was quite new to her, she has already taken over many of Eve White's tasks at work and at home in efforts to relieve and help her. Her feelings towards Eve's little girl appear to be those of a wise and richly compassionate woman towards the child of a family not her own, but still a child in emotional privation.

Her warm impulses to take a more active role with this little girl are complicated by the deep conviction that she must not in any way act so as to come between the distressed mother and her only child. During the few months of her separate existence Jane has, one might say, become stronger and more active. Despite her fine intelligence she began without experience, or at least without full access to the experience of an adult. As time passes Jane stays "out" more and more. She emerges only through Eve White, never yet having found a way to displace Eve Black or to communicate through her. Almost any observer would, we think, find it obvious that Jane, and she only of the three, might solve the deepest problems that brought the patient we call Eve White to us for treatment. Could Jane remain in full possession of that integrated human functioning we call personality our patient would probably, we believe, regain full health, eventually adjust satisfactorily, perhaps at a distinctly superior level, and find her way to a happy life.

Should this occur is seems very unlikely that Mr. White's wife would ever return to him. On the other hand it is little more likely that Eve White, even if she becomes free of all that she has known as symptoms, could or would ever take up her role again as wife in that marriage. Should she try to do so, it is difficult to foresee much happiness for her or the husband. The probability of deep and painful conflict is apparent, also the real danger of psychosis.

Were we impersonal arbiters in such a matter it would be easy to see, and to say, that the only practical or rational solution to this astonishing problem is for Jane to survive, and Jane only. A steadily prevailing Eve Black would indeed be a travesty of woman. The surface is indeed appealing, but this insouciant and likable hoyden, though perhaps too shallow to become really vicious, would, if unrestrained, forever carry disaster lightly in each hand.

The sense of duty, the willingness for self-sacrifice, so strong and so beautiful in Eve White, might bring her back repeatedly into this marital situation which she lacks the emotional vigor to deal with, and in which it is not likely she could survive. Jane, whose integrity, whose potential goodness, seems not less than that of Eve White, has rich promise of the power to survive, even to triumph against odds.

It is perhaps unnecessary to point out that we have not judged ourselves as wise enough to make active decisions or exert personal influence in shaping what impends. It is plain that, even if we had this wisdom, the responsibility is not ours. Would any physician order euthanasia for the heedlessly merry and amoral but nevertheless unique Eve Black? If so, it is our belief, it could not be a physician who has directly known and talked for hours with

her, not one who has felt the inimitable identity of her capricious
being.

A surviving Jane would provide for Eve White's half-lost little
girl a maternal figure of superb resources.[4] Perhaps in time she
could give the child a love as real and deep as that of the mother
herself. Perhaps. But would those feelings be the actual and unique
feelings that have sustained the frail and tormented Eve White in
her long, pathetic, and steadfast struggle to offer the child a chance
for happiness? It may be said that this is foolish and tedious quib-
bling, that Jane after all, *is* the girl's real mother. Was she not born
of her body? All awareness of her as a daughter ever experienced
by Eve White is recorded on the electrochemical patterns of Jane's
brain. True indeed. But *is* she her mother? Those who have known
Eve White personally will find it hard to accept simple affirmation
as the whole truth. What this whole truth is can be better sensed in
direct feeling than conveyed by explanation.

At a distance bridged only by printed or spoken words these
"beings" may appear as factitious abstractions. In the flesh, though
it is the flesh of a single body, one finds it more difficult so to
dismiss them. Final decisions, or choices in the course of involuntary developments must, we have decided, be offered freely to
something within our patient, perhaps to something beyond any
levels of contact we have reached with Eve Black, with Eve White,
or with Jane.

Jane, who appears to have some not quite articulate understanding or purblind grasp of this whole matter, not available to

---

[4] A question of the psychotherapist's responsibility has been raised. Morton Prince
has been accused by some, particularly by McDougall, of taking too active a part
in "squeezing out" Sally. Our experience made us feel very keenly the wish not to
exert pressures arbitrarily and perhaps play a part in the extinction of qualities
possibly of real value if they were integrated into more responsible patterns of
behavior. We believe there is some choice open to the psychiatrist as to which
personality he will try to reinforce, but that he must be tentative and work along
with developments within the patient (or patients?) rather than make full and
final judgments.

We feel that therapy has played a part in the emergence of Jane, but we do not
consider her merely our creation. Our influence seems to have been more catalytic
than causal. Psychotherapy has not been directed according to an arbitrary plan.
Although we have persistently investigated early experiences through all three
manifestations of our patient, and have encouraged emotional reaction to them,
we have sought to avoid insistence on any of the popular theoretical forms of
interpretation.

Jane continues to grow in influence, to be out more and more. She has established contact with some events in the early life of Eve White, and seems more
rooted in a past. We cannot predict with any great confidence the outcome, but
we are hopeful that some reasonably good adjustment will work out through the
capacities contributed by Jane.

either of the Eves, shares our sharp reluctance about participating in any act that might contribute to Eve White's extinction. Unlike Eve Black, Jane has profound and compassionate realization of Eve White's relation to her child. The possibility, the danger, of a permanent loss of all touch with reality has occurred to Eve White. Through this we have found a better appreciation of her feelings as a mother. Too restrained ordinarily by modesty to speak about such a matter, after hypnosis she offered in quiet tones of immeasurable conviction to accept this extinction if it might win for her daughter Jane's presence in the role she had not succeeded in filling adequately for her child.

It has been said that a man must first lay down his life if he is to truly find it. Is it possible that this mother may, through her renunciation, somehow survive and find a way back to the one and dearest thing she is, for her child's sake, ready to leave forever? That we do not know. Long and intimate personal relations with this patient have brought us to wonder if in her we have blindly felt biologic forces and processes invisible to us, still uncomprehended and not quite imaginable.

Recently Eve White, anything but a physically bold or instinctively active person, was challenged suddenly by an event, for her momentous. Of this Jane, deeply moved, wrote to the therapist:

> Today she did something that made me know and appreciate her as I had not been able to do before. I wish I could tell her what I feel but I can't reach her. She must not die yet. There's so much I must know, and so very much I must learn from her. She is the substance of, *this above all to thine own self be true.* In her, too, *the quality of mercy is not strained.* I want her to live—not me!
>
> She saved the life of a little boy today. Everybody thought him to be her child, because she darted out in front of a car to pick him up and take him to safety. But instead of putting him down again, the moment his baby arms went around her neck, he became her baby—and she continued to walk down the street carrying him in her arms.
>
> I have never been thus affected by anything in my four months of life. There seemed only one solution to prevent her possible arrest for kidnapping. That was for me to come out and find the child's mother. In the end I had to give him to a policeman. Later tonight when she had come back out, she was searching for her own baby. She had her baby again for a short while this afternoon; and I'm so happy for that. I still can't feel Eve Black. I can't believe she's just given up. *I feel inexpressibly humble.*

DISCUSSION

What is the meaning of the events we have observed and reported? Some, no doubt, will conclude that we have been thoroughly hoodwinked by a skillful actress. It seems possible that such an actress after assiduous study and long training might indeed master three such roles and play them in a way that would defy detection. The roles might be so played for an hour, perhaps for a few hours. We do not think it likely that any person consciously dissimulating could over months avoid even one telltale error or imperfection. Though this does not seem likely to us, we do not assume it to be impossible. Let us remember, too, that in plays the actors are given their lines, and their roles are limited to representations of various characters only in circumscribed and familiar episodes of the portrayed person's life. The actor also has costume and make-up to help him maintain the illusion.

Have we, others may ask, been taken in by what is no more than superficial hysterical tomfoolery? We would not argue that the psychopathology presented here has nothing in common with ordinary hysterical conversions and dissociations. We do believe that here there is also something more, and something different. If one is to regard these three manifestations of personality as products of disintegration, could such a presumed disintegration be schizophrenic, or perhaps incompletely schizoid? If the process is akin to the processes of schizophrenia, it must still be noted that none of the three products, not one of the three personalities, shows anything suggesting the presence of that disorder. Are we justified in postulating a once unified whole from which our three performers were split off? Or is it possible that the functional elements composing each, as we encounter them at present, have never in the past been really or completely unified?

The developmental integration of what we call personality appears to be a complex process of growth or evolution, a not-too-well comprehended unfolding of germinal potentialities. Let us compare such a process with the zygote's course from microscopic unicellular entity to adult human being. Reviewing the biologic course of identical twins we come at length to cellular unity in the single zygote. Perhaps we must assume in the multiple personalities at least a primordial functional unity. If so, is it possible that some division might have begun far back in the stage of mere potentialities, at preconscious levels of growth not accessible to us except in surmise or theory? If so, what chance is there that an adequate integration may occur?

One might from our verbal account easily see, or read into, the character Jane some fusion of, or even a mere compromise between, the diverse tendencies of the two Eves. If she has, indeed, been formed of their substance it is difficult for us to assume that the process was merely additive. If all her elements derive from the other two, this union, like that of hydrogen and oxygen to make water, seems to have resulted in a product genuinely different from both the ingredients from which it was formed.

Have we in our many hours of enthusiastic work with this patient gradually lost ourselves, and our judgment, in an overdramatization of the subject? Are we reporting what is objective, or chiefly the verbal forms of our surmises and speculations? It is not for us to give the final answer to these questions. We are aware that the only terms available to indicate what we think is valid carry also many connotations that we do not assume or believe to be supported by fact (27).

Obviously the differing manifestations we have observed in one woman's physical organism do not, in all senses of the term, indicate three quite separate people. Our words referring to the possible disappearance or permanent extinction of one of the personality manifestations perhaps imply we regard this as an equivalent, or at least an approximation, of death. Are we guilty of a misleading exaggeration? No heart would stop beating should this occur. No eyes would permanently close. No flesh would undergo corruption. Such an extinction would not fulfill the criteria by which death is defined. Yet, if we may ask, would his immediate replacement by an identical twin invalidate for a bereaved widow the death of her husband? This analogy is not precise. In some respects it is misleading. It does not give us an answer to the question we raise. Perhaps it may, nevertheless, accurately reflect some of our perplexity.

For these and for many other questions that have confronted us in this study we have no full or certain answers. We ask ourselves what we mean by referring to that which we have observed by such a term as *multiple personality?* Immediately we face the more fundamental question: What is the real referent of this familiar word *personality?* In ordinary use we all encounter dozens of unidentical referents, perhaps hundreds of overlapping concepts, all with vague and elusive areas extending indefinitely, vaguely fading out into limitless implications (28).

Any day we may hear that John Doe has become a *new man* since he quit liquor three years ago. Perhaps we tell ourselves that Harvard actually made a *different person* of that boy across the street who used to aggravate all the neighbors with his mischievous depredations. Many religious people describe the experience of being *converted* or *born again* in terms that to the skeptical often seem chiefly fantastic.

With considerable truth, perhaps, it may be stated that after her marriage Mary Blank *changed*, that she has become *another woman*. So, too, when a man's old friends say that since the war he hasn't been the *same fellow* they used to know, the statement, however inaccurate, may indicate something real. We hear that an acquaintance when drinking the other night was *not himself*. Another man, we are told, *found himself* after his father lost all that money. Every now and then it is said that a certain woman's absorption in her home and children has resulted in her losing her *entire personality*. Though such sayings are never taken literally, there is often good reason for them to be taken seriously.

Are they not exaggerations or distortions used to indicate very imperfectly what is by no means totally untrue but what cannot be put precisely, or fully, into words? The real meaning of such familiar statements, however significant, helps us only a little in explaining what we think we have encountered in the case reported. Some relation seems likely, as one might say there is some relation between ordinary vocal memory or fantasy and true auditory hallucinations.

Though often distinguished from each of the other terms, "personality" is sometimes used more or less as a synonym or approximation for "mind," "character," "disposition," "soul," "spirit," "self," "ego," "integrate of human functioning," "identity," etc. In common speech it may be said that John has a good mind but no personality, or that Jim has a wonderful personality but no character, etc. Often this protean word narrows (or broadens) in use to indicate chiefly the attractiveness, or unattractiveness, of some woman or man. In psychiatry its most specific function today is perhaps that of implying a unified total, of indicating more than "intelligence," or "character," more than any of the several terms referring with various degrees of exactness to various qualities, activities, responses, capacities, or aspects of the human being. In the dictionaries, among other definitions, one finds "individuality," "quality or state of being a person," "personal existence or identity."

There is, apparently, no distinct or whole or commonly understood referent for our word "personality." It is useful to us in psychiatry despite its elasticity, often because of its elasticity. If they are to be helpful all such elastic terms must be used tentatively. Otherwise they may lead us at once into violent and confused disagreement about what are likely to be imaginary questions, mere conflicts of arbitrary definition (14). Bearing this in mind we feel it proper to speak of Eve Black, Eve White, and of Jane as three "personalities." Perhaps there is a better term available to indicate the manifestations of this patient. If so we are indeed prepared to welcome it, with enthusiasm and with relief.

Our study has raised many questions. Even for us it has settled few if any. The relatively slight or inconclusive differences between the personalities of our patient noted electroencephalographically, and in psychometric and projective tests, are not particularly impressive beside the profound and consistent differences felt subjectively in personal and clinical relations. A well-qualified expert examined for us the handwriting performed by each Eve. Though considerably impressed by consistent and significant differences between the two productions, it is his opinion that those with adequate professional training could regularly establish sufficient evidence to show both were done by the same human hand. After a detailed investigation this conclusion was expressed by our consultant:

> As a conclusion of the opinions derived from analysis of the various handwritings of this multiple personality patient, it is believed that the handwriting does not undergo complete subordination to each marked change of personality, even though each group exhibits evidence of emotional instabilities. It readily appears the handwriting of each personality is of a different person. Such apparent or discernible variations may lead the untrained observer to believe that the handwriting of each personality is completely foreign to the other. However, extensive investigation of these handwriting materials establishes beyond any doubt that they have been written by one and the same individual. Nothing was found to indicate a wilful and conscious intent to disguise writings executed within a personality or between the first and second personalities.

> Ward S. Atherton, Captain, Military Police Corps, U.S.A.
> Chief, Questioned Document Section,
> Army Provost Marshal General's Criminal Investigation Laboratory, Camp Gordon, Georgia.

Though unable at present to add anything significant to the hypotheses that were offered in the past by those who have worked with similar patients, we find ourselves singularly stimulated by our direct experience with this case. If we have not so far devised final or even fresh answers we have at least been prompted to ask ourselves a number of questions. A few of these, even when put in verbal forms outwardly familiar, we find to our surprise have somehow become new to us and peculiarly stimulating.

Though long acquainted in a general and indirect way with Morton Prince's celebrated studies, we both deliberately refrained for months after beginning work with our case from reading *The Dissociation of a Personality* (23) and *Clinical and Experimental Studies in Personality* (24). We hoped, in this way, to avoid projecting the conclusions and conceptions of another into what we encountered.

After having noted what is recorded here, we compared our experience with what Prince observed and discussed in cogent detail approximately fifty years ago. The popular terminology and theory of psychiatry today differ considerably from the explanations and hypotheses of behavior offered by the physician who wrote so impressively of Miss Beauchamp and of other matters.

Most of us believe, no doubt, that psychiatry and psychology have advanced marvelously since the turn of the century. In many respects this belief is unchallengeable. In many respects, yes; but in all?

In this half-century of progress have we not also developed some habits of thinking that may confuse us? Have we perhaps unwittingly enshrined as sacred dogma many concepts that obscure or distort more than they reveal? Long sanctified verbal constructs, flabby theoretical abstractions are manipulated with a bold flourish in many of our treatises and monographs, persumably in the name of science. In tedious polysyllabic jargon we read today of electrochemical libidos undergoing gelatinization (15), of parental imagos cannibalistically devoured per os and sadistically expelled per annum (7). Such terms as "proved," "so-and-so has established," "clearly demonstrated," etc. have become in our time more popular as synonyms for fantasy and speculation than Morton Prince found them (3, 7, 15, 21).

How much can we congratulate ourselves on having advanced in the last fifty years if many of our leading authorities still find themselves bound to write in ponderous volumes of "actual neuroses" and solemnly contrast these revered artifacts with "psychoneuroses" (7). Is it progress if we establish the universality of castration fear, and its supreme significance, by redefining "castration" to mean all parental and social forces that tend to restrict or direct genital activity (5)? By this method any point of doctrine regarded as too holy for questioning could indeed be proved valid. But, who will say that thereby we have revealed anything not already well known to a twelve-year-old moron? So, too, we can immediately demonstrate that all women are to a remarkable extent homosexual if we piously agree that no impulse to activity, no courageous response, can be classified as other than purely masculine (10, 18). In recent issues of a reputable medical journal we read how an adult's dream "proves" intrauterine emotional trauma, and demonstrates profound personal relations between embryo and placenta. The investigators warn the reader that "resistance" may cripple his ability to evaluate the plain evidence presented, may disqualify him from scientifically appraising these discoveries (8, 21, 22). Is it not our responsibility as psychiatrists to examine frankly such developments as these and to ask ourselves what sort of progress we are making?

Who can doubt that since the case of Miss Beauchamp was so carefully studied reliable knowledge in the field of psychiatry has accumulated. Psychologic theory, "dynamic" interpretation of personality disorder, has moved to points far more ambitious than those reached by Morton Prince. One need not deny that much of this progress has been helpful, a genuine advance, to wonder if the movement has not also sometimes veered considerably from the direction of what is true or even plausible, and even occasionally spent much of itself in enthusiastic but circular expeditions about areas scarcely distinguishable from dianetics and other swamplands of veritable nonsense (12).

Be this as it may. We suggest that further direct study of multiple personality and careful reappraisal of Morton Prince's generally neglected formulations may yet yield to workers in our field some promising clue still overlooked, a clue perhaps to possible discoveries that may eventually yield insight we need but lack today.

## REFERENCES

1. Alexander, F. *The psychoanalysis of the total personality* (New York and Washington: Nervous and Mental Disease Publishing Co., 1930).
2. Allen, C., *Modern discoveries in medical psychology* (London: Macmillan, 1937).
3. Bergler, E. *The basic neurosis* (New York: Grune and Stratton, 1949).

4. Brady, M. E., "The strange case of Wilhelm Reich," *New Republic*, 1947, CXVI, pp. 20–23.
5. Brown, J. F., *The psychodynamics of abnormal behavior* (New York: McGraw-Hill, 1940).
6. Erickson, M. H., and Kubie, L. S., "The permanent relief of an obsessional phobia by means of communications with an unsuspected dual personality, *Psychoanal. Quart.*, 1939, VIII, pp. 471–509.
7. Fenichel, O., *The psychoanalytic theory of neurosis* (New York: Norton, 1945).
8. Fodor, N., "The search for the beloved," *Psychiat. Quart.*, 1946, xx, pp. 549–602.
9. Freud, S., *Collected papers*, Vol. IV (London: Hogarth Press, 1946).
10. Freud, S., *An outline of psychoanalysis* (New York: Norton, 1949).
11. Henderson, D. K., and Gillespie, R. D., *A textbook of psychiatry*, 6th Ed. (London: Oxford Univer. Press, 1947).
12. Hubbard, L. R., *Dianetics* (New York: Hermitage House, 1950).
13. James, W., *Psychology* (Cleveland: Fine Edition Press, 1948).
14. Korzybski, A., *Science and sanity* (Lancaster, Pa.: Science Press, 1941).
15. London, L. S., *Libido and delusion* (Washington, D. C.: Mental Therapy Publications, 1945).
16. McDougall, W., *An outline of abnormal psychology* (London: Methuen, 1926).
17. Morgan, J. J. B., *The psychology of abnormal people* (New York: Longmans, Green, 1932).
18. Mullahy, P., *Oedipus, myth and complex* (New York: Hermitage Press, 1948).
19. Muncie, W., *Psychobiology and psychiatry*, 2nd Ed. (St. Louis: C. V. Mosby Co., 1948).
20. Noyes, A. P., *Modern clinical psychiatry*, 3rd Ed. (Philadelphia: W. B. Saunders, 1948).
21. Peerbolte, M. L., "Psychotherapeutic evaluations of birth-trauma analysis," *Psychiat. Quart.*, 1951, XXV, pp. 589–603.
22. Peerbolte, M. L., "Some problems connected with Fodor's birth-trauma therapy," *Psychiat. Quart.*, 1952, XXVI, pp. 294–306.
23. Prince, M., *The dissociation of a personality* (New York: Longmans, Green, 1906).
24. Prince, M., *Clinical and experimental studies in personality* (Cambridge, Mass.: Sci-Art Publishers, 1929).

25. Reich, W., *Character analysis* (New York: Orgone Institute Press, 1949).
26. Strecker, E. A., Ebaugh, F. G., and Ewalt, J. R., *Practical clinical psychiatry,* 7th Ed. (Philadelphia: Blakiston, 1951).
27. Taylor, W. S., and Martin, M. F., "Multiple personality," *J. abnorm. soc. Psychol.,* 1944, XXXIX, 281–300.
28. Whaley, C. C., "A case of multiple personality," *Amer. J. Psychiat.,* 1933, LXXXIX, pp. 653–688.

# The Three Christs of Ypsilanti

MILTON ROKEACH

The three Christs met for the first time in a small room off the large ward where they live. The date was July 1, 1959. All three had been transferred to Ward D-23 of Ypsilanti State Hospital a few days before and had been assigned to adjacent beds, a shared table in the dining hall, and similar jobs in the laundry room.

It is difficult to convey my exact feelings at that moment. I approached the task with mixed emotions: curiosity and apprehension, high hopes for what the research project might reveal and concern for the welfare of the three men. Initially, my main purpose in bringing them together was to explore the processes by which their delusional systems of belief and their behavior might change if they were confronted with the ultimate contradiction conceivable for human beings: more than one person claiming the same identity. Subsequently, a second purpose emerged: an exploration of the processes by which systems of belief and behavior might be changed through messages purporting to come from significant authorities who existed only in the imaginations of the delusional Christs. These purposes were intimately connected with my own special field of interest in psychology. I am not a psychiatrist or a psychoanalyst, whose primary concerns are psychopathology and psychotherapy. My training is in social psychology and personality theory, and it is this background that led me to my meeting with the three Christs.   I began the meeting by saying that for the next few months we would all be working together in the hope that they would feel better and that each of them would come to a better understanding of himself. Pointing to the tape recorder, I asked if they had any objections to its use. They offered none; all of them were familiar with it from prior interviews.

The room in which we were meeting was a high-ceilinged, rectangular antechamber off the main recreation hall of D-23, one of several ordinarily used by patients to receive visitors. Arranged against the four bare walls were a dozen or so heavy wooden straight-backed chairs, and a matching wooden table, which we

From *The Three Christs of Ypsilanti,* by Milton Rokeach. © Copyright 1964 by Milton Rokeach. Reprinted by permission of Alfred A. Knopf, Inc.

had moved from its position in the center of the room to give us more space. Two shadeless windows, the lower portion of which could be opened slightly for ventilation, looked out on the paved, tree-lined street that runs the length of the hospital grounds. Directly across the street one could see another brown-brick building which looked like the mirror image of D building.

I suggested that we identify ourselves one by one, and to break the ice I introduced myself first. Next my research assistants—who were to be the three Christs' constant companions from early morning until bedtime—offered their names. Then, turning to Joseph, I proposed that he introduce himself.

Joseph was fifty-eight and had been hospitalized for almost two decades. Of medium height and build, bald, and with half his front teeth missing, he somehow gave the impression of impishness. Perhaps this was due to the fact that, along with his wide grin, one noticed his bulging shirt and pants pockets filled to overflowing with various and sundry belongings: eyeglasses, books, magazines, letters, large white rags trailing from his pockets (he used them for handkerchiefs), cigarette papers, tobacco, pens, pencils.

"My name is Joseph Cassel."

*—Joseph, is there anything else you want to tell us?—*

"Yes. I'm God."

Clyde introduced himself next. He was seventy and had been hospitalized for seventeen years. Clyde was over six feet tall and, despite the fact that he was all but toothless, stated, whenever asked, that he was in excellent health—and he was. He spoke indistinctly, in a low, rumbling, resonant voice. He was very hard to understand.

"My name is Clyde Benson. That's my name straight."

*—Do you have any other names?—*

"Well, I have other names, but that's my vital side and I made God five and Jesus six."

*—Does that mean you're God?—*

"I made God, yes. I made it seventy years old a year ago. Hell! I passed seventy years old."

Leon was the last to introduce himself. Of the three, he looked the most like Christ. He was thirty-eight and had been committed five years before. Tall, lean, of ascetic countenance and intensely earnest expression, he walked silently, erectly, and with great dignity, often holding his hands in front of him, one hand resting gently on the other, palms up. When sitting, he held himself upright in his chair and gazed intently ahead. In his white coat and white trousers, he was indeed an imposing figure. When he spoke, his words flowed clearly, unhesitatingly, and often eloquently. Leon denied his real name vigorously, referring to it as his "dupe" name, and refusing to co-operate or have anything to do with anyone who used it in addressing him. We all called him Rex.

"Sir," Leon began, "it so happens that my birth certificate says that I am *Dr. Domino Dominorum et Rex Rexarum, Simplis Christianus Pueris Mentalis Doktor.* [This is all the Latin Leon knows: Lord of Lords, and King of Kings, Simple Christian Boy Psychiatrist.] It also states on my birth certificate that I am the reincarnation of Jesus Christ of Nazareth, and I also salute, and I want to add this. I *do* salute the manliness in Jesus Christ also, because the vine is Jesus and the rock is Christ, pertaining to the penis and testicles; and it so happens that I was railroaded into this place because of prejudice and jealousy and duping that started before I was born, and that is the main issue why I am here. I want to be myself. I do not consent to their misuse of the frequency of my life."

—*Who are "they" that you are talking about?*—

"Those unsound individuals who practice the electronic imposition and duping. I am working for my redemption. And I am waiting patiently and peacefully, sir, because what has been promised to me I know is going to come true. I want to be myself; I don't want this electronic imposition and duping to abuse me and misuse me, make a robot out of me. I don't care for it."

—*Did you want to say something, Joseph?*—

"He says he is the reincarnation of Jesus Christ," Joseph answered. "I can't get it. I know who I am. I'm God, Christ, the Holy Ghost, and if I wasn't, by gosh, I wouldn't lay claim to anything of the sort. I'm Christ. I don't want to say I'm Christ, God, the Holy Ghost, Spirit. I know this is an insane house and you have to be very careful."

"Mr. Cassel—" Leon tried to interrupt.

But Joseph continued: "I know what I've done! I've engineered the affairs of the stronghold in a new world here, the British province. I've done my work. I was way down, way down. I was way, way up. I've engineered, by God! I've taken psychiatrics. And nobody came to me and kissed my ass or kissed me or shook hands with me and told me about my work. No, sir! I don't tell anybody that I'm God, or that I'm Christ, the Holy Spirit, the Holy Ghost. I know what I am now and I know what I'm going to be. This is an insane house."

"Don't generalize . . ." Leon interrupted.

"I know who I am and I haven't got a hell of a lot of power

right now," Joseph went on. "Christ! I do my work. The only thing I can do is carry on. I know what I am."

"Mr. Cassel, please!" Leon said. "I didn't agree with the fact that you were generalizing and calling all people insane in this place. There are people here who are not insane. Each person is a house. Please remember that."

"This is an insane hospital, nevertheless," Joseph insisted.

"My belief is my belief and I don't want your belief, and I'm just stating what I believe," Leon said.

"I know who I am."

"I don't want to take it away from you," Leon said. "You can have it. I don't want it."

*—Clyde, what do you think?—*

"I represent the resurrection. Yeh! I'm the same as Jesus. To represent the resurrection . . . [mumbling and pausing] I am clear . . . as saint . . . convert . . . you ever see. The first standing took me ten years to make it. Ah, forty cars a month. I made forty Christs, forty trucks."

*—What did you make them out of?—*

"I think that means forty sermons, I think that that's what it means," Clyde answered.

*—Well, now, I'm having a little trouble understanding you, Mr. Benson.—*

"Well, you would because you're probably Catholic and I'm Protestant up to a saint."

*—Did you say you are God?—*

"That's right. God, Christ, and the Holy Spirit."

"I don't know why the old man is saying that," Joseph interrupted. "He has it on his mind. He's trying to discharge his mind. It's all right, it's all right as far as I'm concerned. He's trying to take it out of his mind."

*—Take what out of his mind?—*

"What he just said. He made God and he said he *was* God and that he was Jesus Christ. He has made so many Jesus Christs."

Clyde yelled: "Don't try to pull that on me because I will prove it to you!"

"I'm telling you I'm God!" Joseph was yelling, too.

"You're not!" Clyde shouted.

"I'm God, Jesus Christ and the Holy Ghost! I know what I am and I'm going to be what I am!"

"You're going to stay and do just what I want you to do!" Clyde said.

"Oh, no! Oh, no!" Joseph insisted. "You and everybody else will not refrain me from being God because I'm God and I'm going to be God! I was the first in the world and I created the world. No one made me."

"There's something in you, all right," Clyde said. "I'm the first now to this bank, and Jesus the second. There's two sides there. I'm on the testament side and the other the old Bible side, and if I wasn't I couldn't make, I couldn't make my credits from up there."

As the session ended, Leon—who had been sitting attentive but motionless during the outburst between Joseph and Clyde—protested against the meeting on the grounds that it was "mental torture." He announced that he was not coming to any more meetings. We had decided in advance that we would not try to make the men do anything against their will, even if it meant abandoning the research project. I hoped Leon would reconsider, however, because the first encounter had served only to arouse my curiosity. The confrontation had turned out to be less stormy than I had expected. Despite Leon's remark and despite the differences of opinion which had emerged, the three Christs did not seem to be particularly upset as we adjourned. Perhaps they did not fully grasp the extraordinary nature of this confrontation—at least, not in the way we did.

The next day when I entered the ward and informed the three men it was time for another meeting, Leon offered not the slightest protest. Like Clyde and Joseph, he followed me willingly. To open the session I proposed we resume the discussion where we had left off yesterday, and Clyde responded by repeating substantially what he had said the day before. Then Joseph picked up with a new thread, gesturing toward Clyde.

"He raised me up," Joseph said. "He raised me up in England."

—*What does that mean—he raised you up?*—

"Well, I died and I was reproduced by him."

"Oh, you're a rerise?" Clyde asked, in wonderment.

"Yes."

"Well, I didn't know that!" Clyde said. "See now, he is a rerise from the cemetery and I didn't know that."

—*Now, Joseph, as I understand what you said yesterday, you're God, Christ, and the Holy Ghost. You created the world. Nobody made you, because you're God.*—

"That's correct."

—*That means everybody was made by you?*—

"Right!"

—*Clyde, did you make the world, too?*—

"Well, I'm going to hold it now. I shoot—I shoot quicker than the devil. Now I'm in business. I won't monkey with any patients."

"I don't care," Joseph interrupted. "I know what I am."

"I don't think you do," said Clyde. "I take all the credit. It takes a lot to rock my sanity. Why, there's money coming from heaven and from the old country and from the sea of heaven. The carloads, trainloads, and boatloads. It's seventy-seven hundred cars a mile and that runs from Upper Stock Lake. . . . God marked eight of our trails himself."

*—Rex, what do you think of all this business?—*

"Sir, I sincerely acknowledge that they are hollowed-out instrumental gods," Leon answered. "That's my sincere belief."

*—Are you an instrumental god, Joseph?—*

"There is only one."

"Sir, according to what the book says, it states that there are two types of god: God Almighty who was spirit without a beginning and without an end—" Leon said.

"Well, that is the right one."

"Sir, I was interrupted," Leon continued. "I was going to say— there are two types of god. God Almighty, the spirit, without a beginning and without an end. Nobody created God, the God Almighty. Then there are creatures who are instrumental gods. There are some who aren't hollowed out and there are some who are hollowed out."

"As far as your talk—it's all right," Clyde said. "Your psychology is all right."

"There are two types of psychology," Leon went on. "I understand your situation pertaining to dying the death and making the person a hollowed-out instrumental god. You are correct there. As far as my understanding from what I have read, and from practical experience, it is that I am a creature and I have a beginning. A human spirit has a beginning and his body has a beginning, pertaining to its life as such; therefore, I cannot say that I am God Almighty, because if I do, I am telling myself a falsehood, and I don't believe in telling myself a falsehood. I'm a creature, just a human spirit created by God before time existed."

*—You are a creature, but you are also Christ?—*

"Yes, sir," Leon answered. "I am the reincarnation of Jesus Christ of Nazareth, the first human spirit."

"I think it is one of those things to laugh off," Joseph said. "All this saying that one is God, one is Jesus Christ, just a matter of laughing about it."

Leon looked perplexed and anxious. "Sir, it so happens that I am the person who was the first human creature created, and then he insinuates that he was there beforehand. It's injustice as far as I'm concerned, but I do respect these gentlemen."

*—Why do you respect them?—*

"Because they are instrumental gods. It is my belief to respect the devil too, for what he is."

*—Are you a god, too?—*

"An instrumental god, and so are you, Doctor, as I stated before, sir."

Clyde tried to interrupt with unintelligible mumbling, but Leon went on: "Jesus Christ! Let me get a word in, will you, please? I respect them as Jesus Christ."

"I AM HIM!" Clyde shouted. "See? Now, understand that!"

"Man! maybe this is Jesus Christ," Leon said. "I'm not denying it, sir."

"Well, I know your psychology," Clyde said, "and you are a knick-knacker, and in your Catholic church in North Bradley and in your education, and I know all of it—the whole thing. I know exactly what this fellow does. In my credit like I do from up above, that's the way it works."

"As I was stating before I was interrupted," Leon went on, "it so happens that I was the first human spirit to be created with a glorified body before time existed."

"Ah, well, he is just simply a creature, that's all," Joseph put in. "Man created by me when I created the world—nothing else."

*—Did you create Clyde, too?—*

"Uh-huh. Him and a good many others."

At this, Clyde laughed.

"That doesn't sound right to me," Leon said. "I believe his habeas corpus in front of his face, that living cosmic parchment, states a person is what he is, and why he is what he is. That is my habeas corpus, sir."

*—I would like to interrupt to ask a question: Why do you gentlemen suppose you were brought together?—*

Leon said: "Sir, I sincerely understand pertaining to reading between the lines, and stay behind the scenes. And I realize that those people who bring patients together to have one abuse the other through depressing—is not sound psychological reasoning deduction. Meaning a person who is set in his way, there is nobody on earth ... God cannot change a person, either, because God Almighty respects free will; therefore, this man is so-and-so and I'm so-and-so, and on those merits to try to brainwash, what they call it, organic cosmics through the meeting of patients one against the other—that is not sound psychological deduction also. Therefore I give credit to those gentlemen where credit is due, and when a person speaks the truth it makes that person free. Meaning the other person cannot go against that person and try to take away a righteous conscience."

—*Now are we all, are you, speaking the truth?*—

"Yes, sir, I definitely am," Leon answered.

—*Is Joseph speaking the truth?*—

"Sir, he is an instrumental god. I respect him for that because I know he is a creature and a creature cannot be God Almighty."

—*And Clyde?*—

"Sir, pertaining to his experience as being, of becoming, hollowed out, but becoming an instrumental god six times and Jesus Christ six times, that I admit."

"That don't mean anything," Clyde said "I'm not hollowed out. Not hollowed out at all!"

"Mr. Benson, sir," Leon said, "you're afraid to face the fact that on the merit you think I am taking something away from you whereas I'm not. I'm giving you something that is a reality in itself."

"I know what *I* am," Joseph said. "I'm God, Christ, the Holy Ghost. If there is any opposition it's just a matter of—just laugh it off—to laugh the opposition off."

—*Joseph, why do you think we are all here together?*—

"Well, it's just a matter to assemble and a discussion about my being God, and then to laugh it off, to laugh the opposition off."

—*Is that why you think you were brought together?*—

"This is a hospital," Joseph answered. "This is a visiting stronghold, and it's for the purpose of what I just said, that I'm God and the opposition is being laughed off."

—*Clyde, why do you think you were brought here together?*—

After mumbling about ranches, kingdoms, riches, Clyde answered: "I own the hospital—the whole thing."

Meanwhile, Leon had been holding his head as if in pain.

—*Do you have a headache, Rex?*—

"No, I don't, sir, I was 'shaking it off,' sir. Cosmic energy, refreshing my brain. When I grab cosmic energy from the bottom of my feet to my brain, it refreshes my brain. The doctor told me that's the way I'm feeling, and that is the proper attitude. Oh! Pertaining to the question that you asked these two gentlemen, each one is a little institution and a house—a little world in which some stand in a clockwise direction and some in a counterclockwise, and I believe in a clockwise rotation."

—*Do you all believe in the same things or in different things?*—

"I stated my belief, sir, and we all disagreed accordingly."

The discussion then turned to the question of resurrection. It was pointed out that they all believe they had been resurrected. How many Christs had been resurrected?

"Only one. Just myself," Joseph said.

*—Are we all in agreement that there was just one Christ who was resurrected?—*

"By God Almighty, that is correct," Leon answered.

*"I'm* one—not you," said Clyde. "There's something wrong with you."

"I am the reincarnation of Jesus Christ of Nazareth," Leon said. "My birth certificate says so; my habeas corpus says so."

*—Is it possible that there is more than one reincarnation of Jesus Christ?—*

"There is only one that I know of," Leon stated, "and I am the reincarnation of Jesus Christ of Nazareth, and I was baptized as such, sir, and I have my baptismic certificate, sir, and it's also in Dr. Yoder's office if you care to look at it. I believe the others are instrumental gods, the hollowed-out person who became a Jesus Christ through being hollowed out as such."

"He is a rerise, he is a hick," Clyde said. "He is next to me."

"I do not approve of duping to get prestige or material or popular gains in all directions," Leon went on, "and it is also possible that some instrumental false ideas and false instrumental gods got struck dead by my uncle, or they will kill through heart attacks or through duping."

"No!" Clyde said. "There is no false one in my body that has been raised. I got the spirit, the head."

"Here I am now and if there are any oppositions the only thing I can say is that I'm going to laugh it off," Joseph put in.

"Joseph, I want to give you some information," Leon said. "The fourth of July is coming, Joseph, and there will be a big fireworks, and there's going to be a lot of dung carried out of this place. It's a lot of bodies—disfigured bodies—that are going to be carried out of this place."

"Well, I'm going to get out of here," Joseph said. "I'm going to be dismissed from here and go back to England, and I'll be awfully glad, because I know I belong to England. I'm from England originally. I want to go back there. I've done enough work here. I came here the twentieth of March, 1940, and now it's 1959. I've been here nineteen years. I certainly deserve to be dismissed from this here hospital. I want to go back to England. You can deport me to England to a hospital. They have a hospital in London, don't they? I worked for England right along. Darn right!"

And Leon added: "I do not care to discuss any further on the merits that, pertaining to personality, I have cited my side of the story and I do not care to repeat and repeat, but pertaining to truth it pays to repeat. You are a dupe person against me."

—*Nobody is against you.*—

"Sir, the indirect psychology—with that I agree," Leon said.

"Awfully nice!" Joseph commented.

"Sir, I will not compromise," Leon went on. "I believe that right is right and wrong is wrong. That's why I do not care to discuss further, because I have already told the truth pertaining to these gentlemen. That's my sincere belief. You don't need any further discussion on my part, sir."

"Well, that's who I am," Joseph put in. "I know I'm God, Christ, the Holy Spirit. Joseph Cassel, House of England. I worked for England, the English, and I saved the world. It's all right; there's nothing wrong. It's nice, sweet, swell!"

"On the merits that interferences through duping and electronics are against me," Leon said, "and that's been going on ever since I was conceived—I found out that I died the death in 1953. In the six years I've been here, sir, I know what's going on. I know what the finality is, how it's going to terminate. And my uncle promised me that he is going to do the fireworks in a few days and I believe it is very possible that it will be on July fourth, and I've been waiting for my redemption for a long time. I know that after he strikes me dead I will be dead for three and a half days. God Almighty will raise me from the dead. That's the promise I have been given better than six years ago."

—*Do you still want to be Christ again after you die the death?*—

"I'm still He, and I'm still going to try my enemies through death, sir," was Leon's answer. "Sir, if you will excuse me, I do not care to sit in on any more dicussions."

# Lisa and David

THEODORE I. RUBIN

*This is a love story of two exceptional children.*

*The place is a residential treatment center.*

*The time, one year after admission, is a crucial period in their lives during which communication becomes possible.*

*September 15, 1959–September 15, 1960*

"A big fat sow, a big black cow—and how and how and how.

"A big fat cow, a big black sow—and how and how and how.

"A cow, a cow; a sow, a sow—big and fat, big and fat; so they sat—so they sat, they sat; so they sat."

She hopped around the room, first on one foot, then on the other. On her left foot she always said, "sow," and on her right foot, "cow." She sat down on the floor each time she said, "They sat, they sat." But in seconds she was up again—hopping around the room and, in a loud, clear, high-pitched voice, saying, "A cow, a cow; a sow, a sow—black, black, black, black, black, black, black, black." Her voice changed. She was shrieking now. Then she sat down, held her head with her hands, and moved it up and back, moaning softly. "Dark, dark, dark, dark, dark—so, so, so, so dark."

"Fuddy-dud-dud, fuddy-dud-dud-duddy—fud-fud-duddy fud-fud.

"Scudy-rud—rud-scud, rud-scud; duddy-scud fud rud, duddy scud fud rud."

She sat in the corner and repeated the sequence over and over again. John tried to engage her in a sensible conversation—but to no avail. She listened to him, looked at him, and repeated the sequence again and again.

David listened and wondered what she meant. He finally gave up and thought about a big calendar clock he had seen a year ago.

That night before he fell asleep he had a fantasy. The sky was absolutely clear of clouds, the air cool, crisp, and dry. Thousands upon thousands of stars were visible. Planets could be seen, and the sun and moon, too. Beyond it all there were other suns and planets, other universes. They all moved perfectly, precisely, in exact relation to one another. The universes and galaxies and universes beyond them had all become part of a huge mechanism. It was the Universal Time Clock, and it measured Universal Time. He lay back and smiled, for after all he, David Green, was The Universal Timekeeper—or, better yet, Keeper of *the* Time—all Time.

He made sure the cover was tucked about him perfectly. He lay still—and fell asleep, his right hand clutched around the ancient teddy bear ear under his pillow. The light remained on all night.

"John, John, begone, begone—enough, enough of this stuffy stuff."

"Are you angry with me, Lisa?"

"Angry, angry—bangry, wangry,—be gone, John; John, be gone."

"I guess you are angry. What is it that makes you so angry?"

"You foo, you foo—it's you, it's you—it's you, you foo; foo you, foo you."

She suddenly broke into a wild screaming laugh. She screamed and laughed continuously, imperceptibly inhaling air to laugh some more. After five minutes he interrupted her. "You're still angry, aren't you, Lisa?"

She stopped abruptly.

"You louse, louse—John is a louse, a big fat louse on a little gray mouse."

She looked up at the big man and grinned—an inane, foolish kind of grin. Her mood changed suddenly. The expression on her face became one of utmost seriousness. She suddenly charged away from the man and ran to the other side of the large reception room. She faced the wall and talked to herself in a barely audible whisper.

"He won't give me anything. He's big and fat and mean and why won't he give Lisa the crayons? He would give them to Muriel. He likes the Muriel me—but today I'm Lisa me, Lisa me."

Then she broke into a hop-skip-and-a-jump, quickly running around the walls of the room.

"Lisa, Lisa, is my name—today I'm the same—the same—the same, the same."

"May I speak to you, John?"

John turned to the tall, thin, teenage boy. David wore horn-rimmed glasses, was fastidiously dressed in a gray tweed suit, and conveyed the impression of utmost seriousness and dedication to intellectual pursuit. His pinched, thin, white face seemed too small for his long body. He spoke with the utmost precision.

"Why, yes, David. What would you like to say?"

"Thank you for your indulgence. Of late it has become increasingly difficult to find ears for my words. I've been studying your patient, or, since you are not a physician, shall I say student. I have come to several conclusions, which I feel time and further study by your staff will validate. Lisa is schizophrenic and is a child—I would say approximately twelve years of age. Therefore, my diagnosis would be childhood schizophrenia, undoubtedly of the chronic variety. However, diagnostic work is no challenge to me. I prefer to study the dynamic aspect of a particular case. Do you follow me?"

"Yes. Yes, indeed I do." John shook his head affirmatively.

"Good. Then I will continue."

Lisa was still hopping and skipping around the room, now periodically emitting a loud war whoop.

David chose his words carefully, the effort graphically demonstrated by his eyes and mouth. "Lisa has a most difficult time with authority or authoritarian figures. It is therefore extremely important that you adopt an attitude of complete permissiveness in your relationship with her. You must realize that this child has utmost difficulty with her emotions. Now, it is my belief that this difficulty is related to her obsession with speaking in rhymes. The rhyming serves as a decoy or camouflage for what she actually feels. I therefore think that you should not have refused her the crayons, even though she marked the wall."

Lisa stopped skipping and walked over to them.

"John, John, don't be gone—don't be gone."

"I'll see you later, David." He patted David on the shoulder.

The boy lurched away and screamed, "You touched me, you boor, you unmitigated fool—you touched me! Do you want to kill me? A touch can kill—you bastard, you rotten bastard!" His face was contorted with rage. He turned and left them, muttering to himself, "The touch that kills, the touch that kills," and carefully examining his shoulder.

"Can we sit down and talk a while?"

"Dr. White, I submitted to extensive testing, interviewing, and other such nonsense when I first came here, a year ago. I also spoke to you on occasion after that. Somehow I thought I'd go along with the routine here. New place—all right, I'd go along with the indignities. But there's a limit, even to cooperation—and, frankly, I don't care for more interviewing."

"You felt, New place, get off to a new start."

"Well, I suppose you could say that."

"David, it's not more interviewing I'm interested in. It's talking things over so that perhaps I can help you. After all, that's what we're both here for."

"You call me David—but I call you Dr. White."

"You don't have to."

"What do you mean?"

"You can call me Alan."

"All right, Alan." He smiled. "Let me think about it. When I'm ready, we'll talk."

"Suits me—You know where to find me; I'll be available."

"Suits me too." He walked out of the day room to the library.

She walked to where he was standing and placed herself directly in front of him. She looked up into his eyes and didn't budge. He stared back at her. In a completely serious voice she said, "Hello, hello, kiddo, kiddo."

He smiled. "Kiddo, hello; hello, kiddo."

She felt encouraged—and smiled ever so slightly at him.

"Me, the name; Lisa, the same."

For a minute he was puzzled, but when she repeated, "Me, the name; Lisa, the same," he realized she was asking him a question and then he caught on and answered.

"Me, the same; David, the name."

This time she smiled fully, and it wasn't a silly smile.

She passed David working at his table. On it was a large drawing of a clock.

Then she skipped about the room, chanting in a loud voice.

"Dockety dock, clock, clock; dockety dockety, clock clock clock.

"Hockety clock, dockety hock. Hock, hock; dock, dock."

Then she skipped over to John, who was sitting at the other end of the room. First she just stood in front of him. After a few minutes she slowly rocked from foot to foot. Five minutes later she rocked and chanted, this time in a low voice that only John could hear.

"Rockety rock, clock clock—
dickety—rickety—lock lock."

John started to say something, but she ran off on a tour around the room.

He spent days pouring over books. There were physics books, math texts, engineering manuals, and books on horology. When he wasn't reading, he spent hours at a drawing board, making elaborate plans of watch and clock mechanisms.

Alan made several attempts to discuss his work with him, but David remained seclusive. At times he ignored Alan. At other times he said, "You're not really interested," or, "You wouldn't understand."

Then one day he picked up the plans he had drawn and locked them in his foot locker. From that time, he began to make more frequent visits to the day room.

# YOUTH AND PROTEST

*. . . Public opinion always is in advance of the law.*

Galsworthy

The world we live in can be characterized by a condition of turbulence and unrest. This universal state has caused many youth to respond with great sensitivity. On the domestic scene, for example, many incidents continually illustrate a rejection of the *status quo.* Strikes, demands, marches, and even contemporary song lyrics illustrate this fact. College campuses and major cities have become arenas of protest. The cries have been for peace, relevancy, and no racism. Studies emanating from sociologists and psychologists indicate that college activists come from an advantaged group with above-average intelligence, and comfortable homes, and are second- or third-generation college students. On the other hand, students most likely to be nonactivists come from financially hardpressed families and are first-generation college students.

In this section we will deal with the causes, classifications, and evaluations of the contemporary protest movement. The first reading, by Solomon and Fishman, analyzes a massive student peace demonstration in 1962 in Washington, D. C. This abridgment of *Youth and Peace: A Psychosocial Study of Student Peace Demonstrators in Washington, D. C.* has been considered one of the most thorough and accurate investigations of its kind. The staff of *Trans-action* brings into focus the characteristics of the student protesters. Their data is summarized in the article *Which Students Protest, and Why.* The third article, *Psychological Aspects of the Civil Rights Movement and the Negro Professional Man* by Beisser and Harris, presents an interesting dimension of the civil rights movement. The final article, *Rejection and Protest,* is from the Koerner Report, which was presented by the National Advisory Commission on Civil Disorder in an attempt to understand the reasons and causes of racial disturbance. Included in this article are Chapters 4 and 7 of that report.

# Youth and Peace: A Psychosocial Study of Student Peace Demonstrators in Washington, D.C.

FREDRIC SOLOMON AND JACOB R. FISHMAN

## A. INTRODUCTION

On February 16 and 17, 1962 more than four thousand[1] student demonstrators came to Washington, D.C. from colleges and high schools in various parts of the country for the purpose of picketing the White House and Soviet Embassy and meeting with government officials. Most students (75%) were members of various peace organizations whose leaders had joined together under the banner of "Turn Toward Peace" in order to coordinate the demonstration. A variety of executive and congressional offices were visited by groups of students who expressed the following viewpoints: (a) the belief that the arms race was inevitably leading to nuclear war; (b) opposition to civil defense measures; (c) opposition to a resumption of atmospheric nuclear testing by the U.S.A. (an issue of national interest at that time); and (d) their proposals for unilateral peaceful "initiatives" by which the U.S.A. could begin working toward a "disarmed world under international law."

On the second day of the demonstration, the peace pickets were "counter-picketed" by approximately 200 young people from various "conservative" groups in the Washington area. The authors were able to obtain some data from these students for comparative purposes, although the formal part of the study concerned itself with the "peace" demonstrators.

This is a report of the findings of an "on-the-spot" research project which was carried out during the two-day demonstration.

From the *Journal of Social Issues*, XX, No. 4. Copyright by The Society for the Psychological Study of Social Issues. Reprinted by permission of Fredric Solomon and The Society for the Psychological Study of Social Issues.

[1] Four thousand demonstrators were registered at the "headquarters"; but many students began picketing without pausing to register, and one set of observers counted 8,000 marching. It was reportedly the largest demonstration for any cause Washington had seen in a decade (1).

The formal research tools were a short-answer questionnaire and a 1½ hour individual interview. Informal observations were made, and group interviews were conducted with peace demonstrators as well as with some of the opposing counter-pickets from conservative student groups. Eighteen months later a follow-up questionnaire was sent to some of the peace demonstrator sample; results of the follow-up study are summarized in Appendix B.

Some of the leading findings of the study of the 1962 peace demonstrators include

(1) The demonstrators were quite young (18½ was the mean age).

(2) By and large they had no well-formed, comprehensive political ideology.

(3) Many students (though not usually those in leadership positions) expressed themselves moralistically about the cold war and nuclear weapons—this in spite of there being little or no personal religious commitment evident in the majority of demonstrators. In their statements and actions there seemed to be a moralistic quality of "striving for purity," a combination of idealism and protest.

(4) There is suggestive data to the effect that the age period in which first feelings for social or political "causes" is most likely to develop is 12 to 15.

(5) The majority of students came from politically liberal families, but they were "rebelling" in going far beyond parental experience in the realm of public action. About one-fourth of the students characterized their homes as politically conservative or reactionary. Some demonstrators appeared to display a quality of simultaneous rebellion against and identification with parental images.

(6) The older demonstrators, in their middle twenties, seemed to form a separate psychosocial population from the younger students.

(7) The opposing counter-pickets from conservative student groups differed markedly from the peace demonstrators on many parameters of belief and behavior. Particular attention is drawn to the psychosocial dimensions of trust and distrust in comparing the two groups.

## B. METHOD AND PROCEDURE

The sample consisted of 247 participants which represented approximately 6 per cent of the total number of registered demonstrators (4,000). Two hundred and eighteen demonstrators filled out short-answer questionnaires, and twenty-nine other subjects were interviewed "in depth" for periods of 1½ to 2 hours each.

The questionnaires were distributed by a group of medical student research assistants who were instructed to choose subjects randomly at various times and in various areas of activity. Most questionnaires were filled out in the registration and resting area in the church which was serving as demonstration headquarters. Some forms were completed by demonstrators in or near actual picketing locations. The research assistants (who were paid for each completed questionnaire) stood near the respondents during the 15 to 30 minutes which it took to complete the forms, in order to discourage formation of informal groups making collective responses to the individual questionnaires.

Subjects for interviews were selected at the headquarters area by the five interviewers (four psychiatrists and one psychologist) who then conducted private interviews utilizing an outline prepared in advance.[2] The authors also did some group interviewing under fairly informal circumstances. The whole research team met subsequently to discuss and compare various observations and data on group phenomena.

## C. RESULTS AND DISCUSSION

### 1. SOCIAL DATA

Let us begin by discussing some of the social characteristics of the demonstrators as revealed in our questionnaire sample. They were, by and large, a group in their early college years. They had come to Washington by bus, train and car from 57 different colleges and universities, mostly in the East and Midwest, but also from as far away as Seattle and Florida. Eleven per cent of the students were still in high school. Thirty per cent were college freshmen; fifteen

---

[2] There does not appear to be any systematic bias in the sampling of either the "questionnaire group" of subjects or the "interview group" of subjects except for the following two factors: (1) There were proportionately more "older" (mid-20's) demonstrators in the group which was interviewed than there were in the questionnaire sample; (2) Any students who were excessively suspicious would, obviously, have refused to participate in our study at all—so perhaps we sampled only the more trusting or less alienated segment of the demonstrators. We would emphasize, however, that the reason given by those who refused the questionnaire was almost invariably that of being too busy at the moment, with a promise to cooperate later. Furthermore, the questionnaire was anonymous, with a space for optional identification for the purpose of future follow-up studies. Fifty-eight per cent gave their names and addresses and 42 per cent did not do so.

percent were sophomores; fifteen percent juniors; and eleven percent were seniors. Only 6 percent identified themselves as graduate students in a university. About 12 percent apparently were not enrolled as students at the time of the demonstration. The mean age of the demonstrators was 18½, with *45 percent of the sample being either 18 or 19 years of age.* Twenty percent were 17 and under; only 14 percent were over 22. Almost all of the organizers of the demonstration and its spokesmen in Washington were undergraduate college students. . . .

The sex distribution of the sample was 3:2, Male:Female. Approximately three-fourths of the sample had their homes in urban areas, with 19 percent coming from the New York City area. By and large, students came from small middle-class families with four or more children. Excluding the only children, it is interesting to note that 45 per cent of all demonstrators were the eldest in their families, whereas only 15 percent were the youngest. Seventy-five per cent of all demonstrators were the oldest child of their sex in their families.

One interesting finding concerned major field of study and vocational plans. Of those who gave answers to questionnaire items pertaining to academic vocational areas, two-thirds (66%) were majoring in the humanities or social sciences, with relatively few in the physical or biological sciences, and very few in pre-professional courses (this occurring at a time of intensified national interest in scientific space research). Career plans were often indefinite and were predominantly centered in teaching, social service and research. This finding stands in marked contrast to the career goals of the "counter-pickets" from student conservative groups. These young people were typically very definite about careers in business or law, and were taking appropriate pre-professional courses of study (see below).

The subjects were asked to indicate their religious affiliations and those of their parents. With over 90 per cent of the sample responding, the largest number (51%) reported that they had no religious preference; this included 10 per cent who claimed to be atheists.[3] Fourteen per cent indicated affiliation with "liberal" Protestant sects (Unitarian and Quaker) and 13.5 per cent with other Protestant groups (Lutheran, Episcopalian, Methodist, etc.).

---

[3] The 51 per cent of demonstrators with "no religion" was composed of the following sub-groups, with regard to religion of their families or origin: 14% from families with no religion; 4% (9 students) from Roman Catholic families; 15% from Protestant homes; 14% from Jewish families; and 3% giving no response to the item on family's religion.

Twenty per cent stated that they were Jewish, and only one student (0.5%) was a member of the Roman Catholic Church.

These statistics on religion have not been compared with those which one might find in a general cross-section of American college students in 1962, or in contrasting political or social groups. Therefore, inferences beyond the immediate statistical breakdown cannot be justified at this time. It was noted, however, that the conservative counter-pickets were largely from Catholic universities in the Washington area; this stood in apparent contrast to the low degree of participation by Catholics in the Peace demonstration.[4]

## 2. PERCEIVED GOALS OF THE DEMONSTRATION

When asked what they saw as the concrete goals of this particular demonstration, the majority of peace demonstrators were quick to point out that they did not really expect any change in policy or in the attitudes of government officials to occur as a direct result of their efforts. However, most students mentioned *some* sort of political goal (e.g., some small effect on the government via "balancing off the right-wing").

Secondly, almost everyone hoped that the publicity given the demonstration would somehow result in increased public arousal and awareness of the issues. By influencing the grass roots in this way they hoped to perhaps eventually change the course of national policy. In this respect, there was much talk of future campaigning for political candidates who would incorporate some of these goals into their platforms.[5]

A third goal very frequently mentioned was the strengthening and expansion of the student peace movement itself. Surprisingly, among those interviewed this goal was named more frequently than any of the political objectives. The emphasis was often placed on expression of *student* solidarity and effectiveness as a group, rather than simply supporting a point of view. For example, one demonstrator commented, "This is the first attempt of young people to conduct such a demonstration and show their strength."

---

[4] Recent communications from leaders of leading conservative and liberal student organizations indicate that since 1962 there has been considerably more mixing of religious group representation in both "movements." On the Right, there has been more substantial participation by people from Jewish backgrounds, (7) and, on the Left, there has been increasing participation by young Catholics and members of more conservative Protestant churches. (8)

[5] A few months later, many of these students did in fact get involved in the 1962 election campaigns in Massachusetts, Vermont, and New York where "Peace candidates" were running for Congress.

3. PERSONAL MOTIVATIONS TO PARTICIPATE

What was the range of *personal* motivations identified by interviewed students as being important factors in bringing them to
Washington for this particular demonstration?

*A. To Reduce Isolation.* First of all, students regularly perceived the
various peace organizations to which they belonged as being small
in size and relatively isolated on their college campuses, carrying
little weight with either the student body or the school administration. Indeed, many felt that a rather negative or hostile attitude
from the rest of the college existed toward their activities. The
students reported, therefore, that being part of this demonstration
served to reduce feelings of isolation and alienation—both in political and personal terms—as well as to revive and strengthen enthusiasm for activities back home.

*B. To Combat Helplessness, Anxiety and Uncertainty about Future.* On a
second personal level, many students emphasized the need to take
some clarifying action on an issue which otherwise has become
surrounded by helplessness, futility, and inadequacy. One 19-year-
old young man said: "I'm scared to death. There isn't much hope,
but you have to try. Maybe something will happen." This student
was typical in that this action was a means of avoiding depression
and anxiety about the future, although he was rather pessimistic
and expected things to work our poorly. He saw the government as
"frozen" in its position and feared an accidental war.

A possible inference from students' comments about the future is
that there is considerable overlap between (a) the uncertainty and
inability to master one's fate vis-à-vis the nuclear arms race and
(b) some more typical late adolescent concerns regarding personal
choices for the future. Our study does not permit either the conclusion that the threat of nuclear war is preventing some students
from making firm plans for the future or the conclusion that the
more uncertain students are those who are most drawn to peace
activities. However, both conclusions are probably true to some
extent.

*C. Desire for Political Action.* A third sort of personal motivation
mentioned in several interviews was a fairly straightforward desire
for assertion and expression—a need to take action rather than
merely use words. "If I believe strongly in these goals, I should try
to do something to achieve them." Another student said, "Personally, it's just a nice feeling walking in front of the White House for

something you think is right." Others also indicated that they were "trying to take the idea of pressure groups seriously" or, at least, taking fairly literally an American tradition of vigorous political participation by citizens. Their pessimism about their probable effectiveness is rather noteworthy in this context.

*D. Sense of Guilt over Inactivity.* There were still other reasons given for expressing themselves in this way, regardless of whether or not it would be effective in changing anything. One cluster of responses centered around guilt and other unpleasant feelings which would have occurred if the participant had stayed at home. "I have certain guilt feelings. Even if the situation is hopeless I want to have done something to at least have tried to have stopped war," said one 22-year-old male leader.

*E. Striving for Purity.* A 19-year-old girl gave quite articulate expression to the fifth and perhaps most central of the personal motivations identified in this study. It is difficult to give this a name. It seems to be a kind of striving for purity of humanitarian principles, a combination of idealism and protest. She saw the purpose of the Washington project as follows: "To demonstrate that we as students and future intellectual leaders of our communities feel *there is a better way to live,* mankind can live in peace. . . . If I feel there's another way aside from war and bombs, it's my duty to tell others." She added that in her view, "the leaders of the country are going about it all wrong." A 20-year-old boy from Massachusetts spoke in a similar vein: "The students are here trying to correct what they think is *inhuman.*" He personally felt "an obligation to be here. Every man has an obligation to look out for people's benefit, regardless of the effect on himself of the effort."

This sort of orientation is one which includes the vision of a world to be someday governed more by love than by hate. Students were not necessarily denying the existence of conflict between nations but were anxious to oppose the destructiveness and—by their view—madness symbolized by The Bomb. Racial prejudice and various kinds of commercialism were also seen as examples of hypocrisy, sham, compromise, and inhumanity. This striving for purity and uncompromising humanism seemingly provides the idealistic-moralistic side of much of today's youthful involvement in such activities as civil rights action projects, peace demonstrations, and volunteer service in the Peace Corps.

The affirmative idealism is interwoven with protest in all these "movements," but often the onlookers are able to see only the protest. This was illustrated in Washington in the reactions to the peace demonstrators of several policemen and of a Board member in one of the churches where demonstrators were lodged. These observers became irate about the beards, loose-fitting clothes, lack of make-up, and otherwise apparently offensive appearance of some individual demonstrators. Ideas, issues, and political programs were irrelevant to the Board member and the policemen— their emotions were aroused by what they viewed as a hostile attempt to be "different." Although the self-differentiating aspect of non-conformist wearing apparel would seem to account for some of its appeal to undergraduates, the authors feel that the boys' unshaven faces and the girls' uncurled hair and lack of lipstick can also be seen as part of an attempt to build a less "commercial," more "pure, uncontaminated" image of the self, and, coincidentally, of the world around the self.

### 4. PERCEPTION OF RISK

Half of the questionnaire sample felt that there was a definite risk in their participation. It was felt by many that government agents (CIA or FBI) were observing and that identities of students were being recorded and might well be used later in denying government jobs to applicants who had participated. It was thought that such action would not be limited to highly classified jobs; many believed that the notion of security risk is interpreted very broadly and loosely in government circles. Although we are certainly not in a position to evaluate the validity of such a perception it is of more than passing interest that a great number of students perceive the workings of the government in this manner.

A small number of students felt that there was a significant risk of social ostracism by fellow students back at the campus resulting from their participation. Very few students felt a substantial personal risk from academic lost time, from school disapproval, or from family disapproval. None reported a fear of possible physical harm (in contrast to the kinds of risks perceived by students in desegregation demonstrations (9)).

### 5. FAMILY ATTITUDES

The attitudes of the students' families toward their coming to Washington to participate in this demonstration received special attention in both the interview and the questionnaire. Most students were able to state clearly what their parents thought of their participation, although a large number could not respond with certainty because they had come to Washington without mentioning it to their parents. Close to 50% of all demonstrators sampled felt their parents to be in support of their participation. About 22 per cent reported overt opposition from their parents. Another 22 per cent were unable to state a parental point of view—sometimes because of parental apathy to all politics, but more often because the student could not gauge his parents' reaction. This latter group came almost exclusively from the questionnaire sample. In an interview, any student who said he didn't know how his parents would feel about his coming to Washington was then asked to imagine what the reaction would be. Most often, the student would have expected opposition or a mixed reaction.

Regarding mixed reactions, a small but articulate group of interviewed respondents described their parents' attitudes toward demonstrating in such terms as: "They agree in principle but not in method" or "They disapprove and are fearful in case I might get arrested or somehow jeopardize my future, but they made no attempt to stop me and deep down I think my Father is quite sympathetic" or "Mother said I couldn't go, but really felt otherwise. She finally wished me luck." These perceptions of mixed reactions, as well as perceptions of opposing views *between* the parents came out in about one-fifth of the interviews, but less frequently in the less probing questionnaires.

A related item on the questionnaire evoked some interesting written responses. The question was, "Do any members of your family seem inconsistent in their attitudes toward your activities?" Although almost two-thirds of the students responded "No," there were 23 per cent who found inconsistencies worthy of specific description. The most common response in this latter group was the perception that their parents were "for the same ideas but against doing anything about them." Other descriptions included, "They are Christians but they don't worry about peace"; "They are largely unconcerned. They have their life to live and fallout is much like rainfall—you just can't tell"; "They want me to grow up, but only in their way"; "They don't speak of relevant issues but only of job security or other dangers"; "Demonstrating is 'O.K.' only if you win"; "After church 'O.K.,' before church 'No' "; "They have humanitarian instincts but are petty"; and so on.

On the questionnaire students were asked to note family opinions on several political issues of the day (unrelated to feelings about demonstrations *per se*). Measures of agreement and disagreement with various family members, including siblings, were also included.

In the interview sample, it was possible to place the 29 families in broad categories of political outlook and activity. We found that 16 of the 29 came from homes which they described as more or less "liberal." Nine of the 29 came from "conservative" homes. Two students had families with no political views or involvement whatever and two other students came from homes where definite splits in outlook existed within the family. Only 7 of the 16 "liberal" sets of parents had been active in anything like election campaigns, public meetings or other sorts of political participation more vigorous than merely voting. Only the parents of one student had ever picketed in peace demonstrations. On the "conservative" side, only 2 of the 9 sets of parents could be characterized as having ever been "active" politically.

In those cases where some disagreement with parents was reported by students, the father was the family member usually identified as objecting to his child's views—more than twice as many fathers as mothers were listed as being in conflict with students on political issues. One might speculate that this is because men are more likely to have better-formed opinions on such matters, with which to agree or disagree. Another possibility is that women in America are more concerned about the threat of nuclear war.

In summary, more than half of the demonstrators seem to have come from homes with fairly "liberal" outlooks on domestic and foreign matters. A smaller but quite significant group (20–30%) were ideologically in rebellion against politically conservative families. Parental inconsistency or ambivalence was apparent to a number of the students. Where students were in disagreement with family members about politics, the sharpest disagreement was usually with the father. And, no matter what the family politics were, the students were generally taking a far more active part in a public controversy over national policy than their parents ever had taken.

6. PRESENT AFFILIATIONS AND PAST INVOLVEMENT IN SOCIAL ISSUES

Three demonstrators out of four came to Washington as members of some organization participating in "Turn Toward Peace." The Student Peace Union (SPU) was by far the largest organization represented in our sample. Other well-represented groups included the American Friends Service Committee (AFSC), Student SANE, Tocsin (a local Harvard group), and the Young People's Socialist League (YPSL). Numerous smaller peace groups which were local to individual campuses were also well represented. Even though one-fourth of the demonstrators stated that they were not "with" any organization, only 3 per cent of our sample were totally alone in that they knew nobody else in the demonstration. Indeed, the vast majority of students reported having six or more "friends" who also had come to demonstrate in Washington.

Only a very small proportion of the total sample were members of dedicated pacifist groups such as the Committee for Nonviolent Action and the War Resisters' League. Among these were several veterans of numerous pacifist and anti-nuclear demonstrations (polaris submarine demonstrations, hunger strikes, vigils at a germ warfare center, etc.). Numerically speaking, this small group was greatly overbalanced by the 28 per cent of students who had had *no* experience whatever with action for any "cause" prior to this demonstration.

Of those students *with* previous experience in social or political action (72%), it is of interest to note that about half of them had participated in civil rights activities. In fact, 18 per cent of the entire sample had had previous experience with civil rights protest but *no* involvement with "peace action" prior to the Washington project. These data, along with many comments in our interviews, strongly suggest that the development of the student civil rights movement (starting with the sit-ins of 1960) has had a profound influence on the nation's campuses in mobilizing the potential for student social action, in demonstrating the possibility of such action being effective, and in focusing attention on the techniques of nonviolent public action and civil disobedience.

Data was gathered in interviews not only on students' first activities for political or social "causes," but also on their memories of the first time they had any *feelings* or *serious* thoughts about political and social "causes." This question was presented in order to leave open the widest possible interpretation, which could include political issues, feelings of sympathy for the poor, charitable inclinations, feelings about racial issues, war, international affairs and the like. Sixty per cent of the group interviewed reported their earliest feelings or "desire to do something" regarding a social issue to have occurred between the ages of 12 and 15, in early adolescence. Twenty per cent of the group reported their first feelings and action during their freshman year at college, when they were eighteen. Only two (7%) reported their "first" after the age of eighteen, but four (13%) pinpointed their feelings between four and six years of age. It is interesting to note that this latter group came entirely from strongly liberal families or families which were very much involved in the subject matter of the early experience, at that time; for example, parents very much involved in religious ideas and activities of a social service nature.

The heavy concentration of earliest remembered experiences in the 12- to 15-year-old age range is quite striking in the interviews and consistent with similar findings by the authors in interviews with Negro desegregation demonstrators (2) (3). In the latter group, this particular age coincided with the occurrence of the Supreme Court's desegregation of schools decision. In the group of peace demonstrators under study (almost entirely white), there appears to be a much broader range of earliest social "cause" experiences, which perhaps is not surprising since the range of focal issues is wider for the white population than for the Negro for whom segregation represents such an intense and immediate issue.

This concentration in the early adolescent period might also be related to what is known of the strivings for identity and assertion which accompany the physiological, social, and psychological changes ushered in by adolescence (10, 11, 12). It does suggest a period of heightened vulnerability to the influence of social and political ideology and "causes," an understanding of which would seem to be of crucial importance to educators and social planners in many different kinds of situations. Our limited data cannot be definitive, of course, about the strength of a determinant or the "choice" of a particular path or direction for one's social feelings at any one time. . . .

To summarize, it would seem that with students involved in political or social action there might be three developmental periods of increased susceptibility to the acquisition of social and political awareness (or awareness of "injustice") and the motivation to do something about it. These are the periods of ages 4 to 6, 12 to 15 and the freshman year at college (age 18). Psychodynamic influences and social implications for these periods may well differ, and each may represent the ushering in of new social, sexual, and intellectual vistas at points of intense individual change. It also would seem that social crises and political events occurring coincidentally during those periods may have a profound effect or perhaps be selectively chosen for internalization by other contributing psychosocial influences (e.g., identification with or rebellion against parental values).

In students who came from politically liberal homes, their sense of social or political "identity" seems to involve a synthesis of identification with and rebellion against parental patterns. Indeed, this process of rebellion within a framework of identification seems widespread among young people we have seen who are involved in various kinds of contemporary social or political action. We have already described this in Negro and white student sit-in demonstrators, and have used the term "pro-social acting out" in connection with certain aspects of this phenomenon (2) (3). In striving for a sense of autonomy, these young people will focus their rebellion around "independence," rather than overt hostility toward (or feelings of oppression by) their parents. In so doing, the students often identify—consciously or unconsciously—with the roots of parental ideology and identity, while going far beyond their parents in the sphere of action. Thus, a student in the peace demonstration might: (1) agree with his parents about certain "issues" like nuclear testing; (2) be in conflict with them about the advisability of demonstrating in Washington; (3) go ahead and demonstrate anyway; (4) cite Thoreau and an old American tradition of public protest, and (5) be quite respectful toward officials in Washington and eager for a good "image" in the news media.

## 7. THE LEADERS, THE "RANK AND FILE," AND THE OPPOSITION: SOME IDEOLOGICAL CONTRASTS

With certain exceptions, an absence of broad and firm political ideology was characteristic of the large bulk of peace demonstrators—leaders and followers alike. This phenomenon was remarked upon particularly by several observers who recalled student activist days of the 1930's and 1940's when comprehensive ideology played such an important role among the "socially conscious." This is consistent with our previous studies of student civil rights demonstrators, in which we found that the vast majority focused on the issue of desegregation but differed fairly widely in their attitudes toward other political issues; they appeared interested primarily in the "work at hand," the immediate action to be taken.[6] Indeed, many peace demonstrators spoke directly of the civil rights movement as their model for political action.

The position generally held by all the demonstrating peace groups was that the United States should begin a program of unilateral initiatives (not identical with unilateral disarmament)

---

[6] Since 1962 there have been trends in the civil rights movement (13), the peace movement (5) and other student movements (14) (15) which indicate growing student concern about broader issues now felt to be interrelated.

designed to inspire similar peace-promoting moves by the Communist Bloc. Typically, the rank and file demonstrator justified this position in highly moralistic terms, relying heavily on the emotions of: (a) *fear* of the direction of the nuclear arms race, (b) *trust*, insofar as this can be inspired in international relations, and (c) *indignation* at the government's alleged insensitivity to "evils" like radioactive fallout or the loss of human life in nuclear war.

The demonstration *leaders* typically talked about the issues quite differently from the rank and file. Rather than referring to Bertrand Russell or Gandhi, for example, the leaders might discuss cold war strategy in the "hard-nosed" language of Charles Osgood or Herman Kahn. Thus, in advocating the withdrawal of U.S. missile bases from Italy, Turkey and England they could describe how the cumbersome fueling system for these particular missiles made them useful only for a first-strike and useless for retaliatory purposes, and how, therefore, the government could well afford to evacuate these bases as a step toward reducing Cold War tensions.[7] Government-oriented rhetoric such as this seemed to be almost an "ideology" in itself. The leadership group tended to dress more conservatively than the rank and file and vigorously deplored the bearded and guitar-playing segment of the demonstrator population. The spokesmen tried to influence government officials via persuasive argument and via careful cultivation of good press relations. The rank and file included more of the frankly "humanistic" or "moralistic" young people (although these tendencies were not absent in the leaders—especially when they were seen off guard).

During the Peace Demonstration some 200 counter-pickets from various conservative student groups marched with picket signs across the street from the White House. Although they had not been expected and we were unprepared to gather systematic data, it was possible to observe the group and to conduct several group and individual interviews with ten pickets (5% of the demonstrators). It then became possible to contrast data on general characteristics and attitudes of the group with those of the peace demonstrators.

These demonstrators, too, were mostly college freshmen, age 18 to 19. They had been hastily recruited from the local Washington area campuses primarily by leaders of the Young Americans for Freedom (YAF) in an attempt to "respond to the Peaceniks." The students were generally preparing for careers in business, law or

---

[7] Several months later, the Kennedy Administration did take this step, though not as a publicly stated "peaceful initiative."

foreign service; all of them were white, and the group was predominantly Catholic.

The political attitudes in this group, as might be expected, were in stark contrast to those of the peace pickets, although there were attitudes that represented a fairly wide range—this time of the "right." The contrast was found succinctly and vividly summarized in the slogans of the picket signs carried by both groups (Appendix A).

Their general premises began with an intense distrust of the Soviet Union, partly based on what they described as past performance and partly on an intense antipathy toward the "evils" of Communism, which has as its goal world domination, one way or another. They saw the Russians as cynical and quick to take advantage of any sign of weakness on our part. Their concern was primarily with being strong, and thus unilateral initiatives toward *increased* armaments and toward "pushing back Communism" were the only kinds of unilateral actions which they would countenance. The group seemed to be relatively well equipped with data about past behavior of the Russians and poorly informed about armaments, nuclear testing and nuclear warfare. They tended to view the possibilities of nuclear war in the same political terms as conventional war—in marked contrast to many of the Peace demonstrators who felt that most political issues were very much secondary to the "new realities" of nuclear warfare and destructiveness.

The group supported civil defense as one means of increasing the strength of our stance and our ability to withstand Russian threats and attacks. Shelters were seen as a means of making victory more likely and less costly in the event of war. However, the group was surprisingly unenthusiastic about the whole shelter issue, in contrast to the peace group which was very strongly involved (in opposition) with this issue. None of the interviewed conservative students had ever seen a bomb shelter, built one, or were even thinking about building one. A simple explanation might well be that on one level shelters may be perceived as part of a cowardly withdrawal, not as a vigorous weapon. The qualities of encapsulation, isolation, and withdrawal which a well-stocked and deeply buried shelter suggests are probably quite repugnant to this group which puts so much emphasis on action, potency, and aggression.

The contrasting approaches to the issues of War and Peace, both *between* the two opposing picket groups and *within* the "peace" group, seem only partially related to rationally formulated positions. Much of the world outlook of which these positions are a part seems related to basic psychosocial attitudes. These attitudes apparently include such coordinates as trust-distrust; cowardice-bravery; caution-foolhardiness; dependency-self-reliance; strength-weakness; nationalism-internationalism; vulnerability-invulnerability; passivity-assertion; sacrifice-survival. The process by which formulation of their attitudes, ideology and action takes place would appear to be an intriguing area for further research.

## APPENDIX A

*Picket Sign Slogans (Feb. 17, 1962)*

### *Peace Demonstration*

Total Disarmament
2 + 2 = 5: Arms Race
Peace with Freedom
Peace Race
"Truce to Terror" (Pres. K.)
Strong U.N.
J.F.K.: We Support your Words—Let us Support your Actions
Peace Won't Contaminate Our Milk
Every Test Kills
Deeper the Shelter, Bigger the Bomb
I'd Rather *BE*
Peace The Only Shelter

### *Counter-Pickets ("Conservatives")*

Strike for Strength
Isn't Freedom Worth Defending?
Give me Liberty or Death
Peace not Appeasement
Total Victory over Insidious Ideology
Goals of International Communism have not changed
Peace without Security Isn't Peace
Fallout or Sell-out, Choose!
They Test, We Test
Missiles Not Missives
Khrushchev Backs the SPU
This is a Pacifist (picture of baby pacifier)
Pacifism is Cowardice
No Unilateral Suicide
Purchase Life at the Expense of Slavery?
Pacifism Leads to Communism
K says "Pacifism for you, not for me"
They're Not *Red*, They're YELLOW
When have the Reds Compromised?
TEST SI, Disarm NO
BAN THE BUM (K)

APPENDIX B

*Summary of follow-up study of student peace demonstrators*

The post-demonstration history of the organizations and of the student political leaders involved in the February, 1962 Washington project has been described elsewhere (5) and cannot be reviewed here. Those familiar with members of the movement have reported a general impression of a transition away from pure "peace issues" and toward community action issues such as civil rights. The "elitist" orientation toward influencing government decision-makers via persuasive arguments reportedly has diminished, and the more "moralistic" approach has gained in stature since the demonstration. To test these generalizations and in order to further illuminate the "natural history" of youthful involvement in social action, a modest follow-up study was undertaken.

Of those students filling out questionnaires in the original Peace Study, 128 (58%) signed their names for follow-up purposes. Eighteen months after the Washington project, follow-up questionnaires were mailed to these 128 individuals. Nineteen follow-up questionnaires were returned undelivered; the remaining 109 were presumed to have been received by the subjects. A total of 45 follow-up questionnaires were completed and returned for analysis. The respondents thus comprised 35 per cent of the follow-up sample and 21 per cent of the original questionnaire group from the 1962 demonstration.

The respondent group accurately represents the total questionnaire sample on several important dimensions. (For example, positive history of social action *prior* to the 1962 demonstration was found in 71 per cent of the respondent group and 72 per cent of the total questionnaire sample.) The respondent group was, however, somewhat older than the general sample population and somewhat more weighted with males.

Forty of the 45 respondents (89%) were still actively engaged in some sort of political and social action at the time of the follow-up survey. A host of "off-campus" social action issues were listed by the respondents in addition to the one which had brought them together originally in Washington. Several students did draw a sharp line between issues and were still working solely for peace. But for the majority of respondents, peace and disarmament had apparently slipped from the top of the hierarchy of action issues—being surpassed by civil rights.

The factors influencing this shift were varied. Some students had "relaxed" about the threat of war, partly because of the test ban treaty. On the other hand, because of the lack of apparent "progress," many students had come to feel *more* discouraged about peace efforts, and therefore had abandoned them. The majority of students had condemned the Kennedy administration's handling of the Cuban missile crisis. This incident and their subsequent feelings often led them to a "multi-issue" view similar to that expressed by the following respondent: "It made me realize that 'peace' could not be considered separately from political-ideological issues. In the long run the Cuban crisis was the product of the clash of Soviet and American attitudes toward social revolution." Other students emphasized the feelings of personal effectiveness obtainable via involvement in the student civil rights movement, as compared to that gained in the peace movement. Several students thought that the peace movement might be re-invigorated by using more "direct-action" techniques such as those employed in civil rights activities.

Of special interest among the 45 respondents were those ten students for whom the 1962 demonstration had been an "initiation"—their first experience with public action for a social goal. Eight of these "newcomers" followed up their experience in Washington with continued participation in picketing, public meetings, etc., for various "causes"; the other two had returned to their former inactivity.

Those students who had shunned political and social action since the February 1962 demonstration gave various "reasons" for their behavior, ranging from disillusionment with one's own former naïveté (the government may have "known best" after all) to a return to individual interests (pursuit of intense program of graduate studies).

A somewhat surprising index of the depth of opposition to contemporary military policy was found in the original questionnaire sample when 30 per cent stated that they either intended to register as conscientious objectors or would urge others to do so. An additional 40 per cent replied "maybe" to the same item on the 1962 questionnaire. The responses to the follow-up questionnaire indicated an ongoing concern about the "C.O." question. Two-thirds of the males had been giving consideration to registering as conscientious objectors; two of the 31 males had actually done so, and five others definitely anticipated doing so. Eight males who had responded *negatively* to the inquiry about conscientious objection in 1962 had changed their minds in the next eighteen months and were giving serious consideration to "C.O." status for themselves. Two such students were definitely planning to become conscientious objectors.

REFERENCES

1. The Washington Post, February 17, 1962, p. 1.
2. Fishman, J. R., and F. Solomon, "Youth and Social Action: I. Perspectives on the Student Sit-In Movement," *The American Journal of Orthopsychiatry*, XXXIII, No. 5 (Oct. 1963), pp. 872–882.
3. Solomon, F., and J. R. Fishman, "Youth and Social Action: II. Action and Identity Formation in the First Student Sit-In Demonstration," *The Journal of Social Issues*, XX, No. 2 (April 1964), pp. 36–45.

. . . . . . . . . . . . . . . . . . . . . .

5. Gitlin, Todd, "The Student Political Scene, 1960-3," report prepared for the Howard University Conference on Youth and Social Action (October 1963).

. . . . . . . . . . . . . . . . . . . . . .

7. Jones, David (Executive Director, Young Americans for Freedom), personal communication (August 1963).
8. Gitlin, Todd (President, Students for a Democratic Society), personal communications (August 1963, March 1965).
9. Solomon, F., and J. R. Fishman, "The Psychosocial Meaning of Nonviolence in Student Civil Rights Activities," *Psychiatry*, XXVII, No. 2 (May 1964), pp. 91–99.
10. Jones, Ernest, "Some Problems of Adolescence," *Papers on Psychoanalysis*, 5th edition (London: Balliere, Tindall and Cox, 1923), pp. 389–406.
11. Freud, Anna, *The Ego and the Mechanisms of Defense* (London: Hogarth Press, 1936).
12. Erikson, Erik, "The Problem of Ego Identity," *Journal of the American Psychoanalytic Association*, 1956, IV, No. 1, 56–121.
13. Solomon, F., *et al.*, "Civil Rights Activity and Reduction in Crime Among Negroes," *Archives of General Psychiatry*, XII (March 1965), pp. 227–236.
14. Trillin, Calvin, "Letter from Berkeley," *The New Yorker*, March 13, 1965, pp. 52–107.
15. Powledge, Fred, "The Student Left: Spurring Reform/The New Student-Left: Movement Represents Serious Activities in Drive for Changes," *The New York Times*, March 15, 1965, p. 1, Col. 7 and p. 26, Cols. 1–8.

# Which Students Protest, and Why

On Dec. 2, 1964, more than 1000 students occupied Sproul Hall on the campus of the University of California at Berkeley, protesting new university restrictions on their freedom of speech. In May of 1966, 500 University of Chicago students sat-in at the main administration building on campus demanding that the university stop releasing class rankings to the Selective Service. Last October Harvard students held prisoner a recruiter from Dow Chemical, damning both a company that makes napalm and a university that allows that company to recruit employees on campus. In short, where college students in the 1950s were berated for their political apathy, the campus of the 1960s seems to seethe with student revolt. The *Journal of Social Issues* (July 1967) has devoted an entire issue to examining the roots of this protest.

All of the contributors to the issue agree that the actual number of student protesters is quite small. They also agree that the activists are among the most intelligent students at the best colleges and universities.

James W. Trent and Judith L. Craise of the Center for Research and Development in Higher Education of the University of California at Berkeley document the intellectual superiority of the protesters. The two compared the responses on an Omnibus Personality Inventory from 130 members of the Berkeley Free Speech Movement, active enough to have been arrested; from 92 ordinary Berkeley seniors; and from a portion (1185) of a national sample in college.

The F.S.M. activists, on a scale measuring interest in intellectual inquiry and tolerance for ambiguity, placed highest (a mean standard score of 66). Other Berkeley students were a bit behind, scoring 54. The national sample of college students scored 51. On the measure of independent thought, F.S.M. students scored 67; the Berkeley sample, 61; the national sample, 53. Free Speech activists also outdistanced the other two samples in interest in abstract thinking about art, literature, music, and philosophy; in concern with esthetics; in freedom and imaginativeness of thinking; and in religious liberalism. They were also more anxious than the other students, which may be the price for their greater intellectual and social commitment. Finally, the study reports that activists tended to be students of the humanities and the social sciences.

Other characteristics of activists have been pinned down by Richard Flacks of the University of Chicago. Activists, he and other researchers have found, are rarely financially hard pressed. They are also rarely first-generation college students. Instead, activists come from the most advantaged group on campus; their fathers are professional men, and family income is high; the activists are also the second or third generation to go to college.

Flacks has conducted two studies of students that illuminate this aspect of the student protest. The first study entailed extensive interviews with samples of student activists, nonactivists, and their parents. The second study entailed interviews with a random sample of 65 supporters of the anti-ranking sit-in at Chicago; with a random sample of 35 signers of an *anti*-protest petition, and with a group of 60 randomly selected students of the university.

Both studies showed that activists come from high-status families. In the general sample, for instance, half of the 24 students reporting family incomes above $15,000 participated in the sit-in. Only two of 23 students reporting income below $15,000 sat-in. The fathers of activists tended to be professionals (college faculty, lawyers, doctors) rather than businessmen, white-collar employees, or blue-collar workers. The mothers of activists are more likely to be employed, and to have "career" employment. Many activists are Jewish (45 percent, in the anti-ranking sample, compared with 25 percent of nonactivists). A very high percentage, both of Jewish and non-Jewish background, report that neither they nor their parents have a personal religious commitment.

Student activists, Flacks also found, are *not* rebelling against the political attitudes of their parents. Instead they are pushing an already-liberal political view somewhat further. Father-son attitudes on current issues, for instance, were somewhat similar. Flacks found that both the activists and their fathers disapprove of the bombing of North Vietnam (only 9 percent of the activists approve vs. 27 percent of fathers). And 73 percent of the nonactivists approved of the bombing, along with 80 percent of their fathers. Some 97 percent of the activists approved of civil disobedience in civil-rights protests, and 57 percent of their fathers went along with them. These percentages are a great deal higher than those for nonactivists, where only 28 percent approve of civil disobedience—a view consistent with their fathers' view (23 percent).

Flacks also found that students learned their activism, in essence, from other parental values. Both activists and their parents, for instance, believe intellectual and esthetic pursuits are more important than material success, and that humanitarian concerns and an opportunity for free expression are the really important things in life.

On the basis of these data and his impressions from interviews, Flacks makes several hypotheses:

—that student activists come from secure, upper-middle-class homes where the discipline is permissive and the parents stress values other than achievement;

—that youngsters raised in these homes find it difficult to put up with the authoritarian demands of large organizations (like the multiversity);

—that these youngsters are distressed by the differences they perceive between the values that their parents profess and the way their parents actually live; and

—that these students don't have the usual incentives for conformity—need for income and status—because they can afford to be unconventional.

Activists, then, are irritating, undisciplined, and usually talented students who can and sometimes do turn a university campus upside down. But, as Edward E. Sampson of the University of California at Berkeley put it somewhat wistfully in the introductory article:

"Speaking quite personally, to face a lecture hall filled with these student activists is both an exhilarating and frightening experience. How different this is from the [usual] experience of lecturing to a group of preprofessionals who take in each word as though it were gospel."

# Psychological Aspects of the Civil Rights Movement and the Negro Professional Man

ARNOLD R. BEISSER AND HIAWATHA HARRIS

In order to stir a people to action, leaders must provide them with a means consistent with their psychological makeup as well as with their material reality. A darting guerrilla war was not only tactically effective for the Castro forces in Cuba, but it could capture the imagination and the allegiance of a volatile people. In contrast, the passive resistance movement of Gandhi in India more nearly suited the contemplative Hindu teachings accepted by many of the people.

The genius of the American civil rights movement was in its use of the psychological strength of the American Negro—subservience, learned and practiced over centuries. Had more militant leaders tried initially to incite violent protests and demands for equality, it is doubtful that they would have received the popular support now achieved from the majority of Negroes. Black Americans had learned over the centuries of slavery and postslavery that overt protest led only to speedy retaliation and death. Therefore protests became so subtle and disguised as to make retaliation inappropriate. The Negro often worked slowly or in bungling fashion, seemingly with childlike innocence of the deleterious effect of his actions on commerce. White overlords easily dismissed these subtle tactics as stupidity, for it fit into their own concept of the inferior nature of Negroes. Passive resistance was thus a well-learned characteristic for many American Negroes, a fabled part of what has been called the "Negro character."

Such generalizations, although frequently correct, tend to overlook the uniqueness of the individual and fail to take into account the significant number of Negro Americans who have "made it" on their own. Negro professional men represent such a group. In contrast to passive resistance as a way of life, the Negro professional man chose a different route. Usually through heroic efforts against

Reprinted from the *American Journal of Psychiatry*, CXXIII, pp. 733–737, 1966. Copyright 1966, the American Psychiatric Association.

extremely difficult odds, he achieved a position as a professional man. By so doing, his principal identification was with the white community and could be psychologically labeled as "identification with the aggressor"(5).

Their achievements, moreover, have somewhat set them apart from the majority of Negroes. They have developed meaningful positions within the community of the white majority, creating a mixture of identifications: one with the white community, the other with the Negro community. Their successes have created unique situations for them in the light of the emergence of the Negro in the civil rights movement. Their reactions have, in many respects, been similar to those of the soldier who has been sent home while his buddies remain on the firing line. Although he is relieved at getting away from what is happening, he feels a sense of guilt for having left his buddies behind.

Yet it was these same men who, in many instances, had the courage to initiate protest and civil rights movements. Their own success within the white community gave them the stature and the confidence to try to uplift their people. Their position was like the "leadership from the periphery" which has been described by Kurt Lewin. That is, those who exert leadership within minority groups are often somewhat peripheral members of the group in terms of their loyalty and identification with the minority.

## "THE INVISIBLE MAN"

There has been no really suitable or acceptable identity as a Negro in this country. So extreme has this been that the Negro has been described as "the invisible man" (2). The community at large has pretended that he does not exist. Newspapers would not print pictures of Negroes. Movies and television, including commercials, rarely showed a Negro. When they were shown, they appeared in what Erikson (4) has described as the only complete and successful identification of the Negro—as a slave.

Thus the choices for the American Negro appeared to be the role of near-slave, or to try to be as nearly white as possible. White meant intelligent, economically successful, and symbolically as well as realistically white in color of skin. Erikson has pointed out (4) that many Negroes entertain the fantasy that if they could only clean themselves up, "scrub hard enough," they would be white. Yet, no matter how many educational, economic, or material successes a Negro might achieve, he was always, in reality, black. In many respects, that blackness made him "the invisible man."

A case in point is the Negro physician. Meharry Medical College has graduated more than 50 percent of the Negro physicians in America. This school, in its efforts to elevate the standards of medical care of its graduates, placed emphasis on the denial of Negro-ness. Students were constantly reminded that they were being taught to practice white medicine and not Negro medicine. The former was implicitly good, the latter bad. With this emphasis, it is small wonder that graduates of this school often tended to identify themselves with their Northern undergraduate colleges rather than with the medical school, a reversal of the usual tendency among doctors.

While the Negro physician might strive to become as nearly white as possible, he could never fully be so. Even partial whiteness was achieved at considerable personal expense—the alienation of an important part of himself. One result, which is often seen, is the always correct professional man who seems separated from his feelings and experiences.

## THE CHANGING SOCIAL CLIMATE

In recent years however, especially in the past decade, there has been a change in the social climate towards greater acceptance of the Negro. Perhaps the beginning was with the emergence of the African nations as discrete political entities with their representation in the United Nations. Much publicity was given to these nations and their leaders, creating a new and elevated status for the Negro, who was no longer invisible. The color line in sports has also been broken; today on television or in newspapers one sees Negroes in a great variety of roles. Whatever the sources of the social change, a new dignity has developed in being black. This identity is still somewhat fragmented but now can be legitimately sought.

How, then, does this emergence of a legitimate black identity affect the Negro professional man whose strength has been in his identification with the white aggressor? His potency and his ability to lead and inspire more disadvantaged Negroes had actually come from his identification with the white community. It is evident that the management of such a split in identities, on the one hand being white and on the other being black, both of which now have status, becomes a precarious matter and one which requires a new integration for the individual.

## COMPARTMENTALIZATION OF IDENTITIES

There is a constant struggle in being a Negro and at the same time identifying with a particular professional role. The dilemma is often solved by compartmentalization of identity. While performing functions in one area, the individual denies the existence of the other. He is either a Negro or a professional man, but finds it impossible to be both at the same time. A case in point illustrates this situation.

A Negro judge recently found himself faced with this problem. Before his appointment to the bench, he had been very active in the civil rights movement. As long as 20 years ago, he was active in organizing pickets and protests in Negro areas in an effort to obtain better jobs for qualified Negroes. He was, in fact, president of the National Association for the Advancement of Colored People for two terms.

Then came his appointment to the bench. Because of the area in which he lived, it developed that he was in the position of sitting in judgment in civil rights cases where demonstrators had been arrested.

Here he faced a group with whom he had close identification. If he had not been on the bench, it is not unlikely that he would have been among the demonstrators or even one of the architects of the protest. He stated, "I felt a great deal of pressure because I wanted to be lenient; but at the same time I wanted to execute my duties to protect society as a whole. These guys made it easy for me because they became disrespectful of the court and were unreasonable in their demands. They showed an utter disregard for the law that had nothing to do with their protest."

While in this instance the methods of the demonstrators had somewhat eased the burden of decision, the schism in his identity is evident. His choice was between support of the white establishment or support of the demonstrators. His sympathies were with both. As a judge, he was on the side of the law; as a Negro, he was on the side of civil protest. While he was assuming one identity, the other had to be denied.

Most examples of psychological compartmentalization reveal a part of the individual's personality which is psychologically or socially unacceptable. In this example, however, both identities are acceptable and may be seen as healthy, but at the moment were mutually exclusive. The assumption of the newly legitimate Negro identity is almost completely foreign to some Negroes and it requires a considerable amount of psychological reorientation.

A young Negro physician had grown up in a small white community where, because of his light skin and because his family was the only Negro family in the town and enjoyed a high economic status, he had been quite thoroughly integrated into the community. He had little knowledge of or interest in Negroes other than as a spectator. He had almost no Negro friends or acquaintances and had never attended a Negro school. In fact, his first acquaintance with Negroes was when he went away to college to a well-integrated Northern school.

His identification with the white community was almost complete. Only in a small way did he recognize his difference because of color. He knew little of what it was like to be a Negro and until the emergence of the civil rights movement had been inactive in Negro affairs.

In the past several years he has become increasingly interested in the Negro civil rights movement. This interest has grown to the extent that he now spends only a limited time in his profession while most of his time is spent in his civil rights activity. During this time he underwent a period of considerable emotional crisis characterized by heightened anxiety. He began dressing differently, acting differently, and even trying out different patterns of speech. He began to avoid many of his white friends and spent as much time as possible with Negroes in an effort to get a feel of what it was like to be a Negro. In order to maintain himself in the dominant white community he had, of necessity, utilized the mechanisms of denial and repression. This he had done successfully.

In this case, a process of reidentification with a fraction of the alienated self was necessary. The young Negro physician needed to invest himself fully in the new Negro identity in order to recapture that part of his personality. It was a necessary step in the integration of his whole personality. This may be seen as parallel to the "identity crisis" commonly occurring in adolescence (3). It is unique only in that it emerges in the wake of a new, socially acceptable identity.

## WAYS OF COPING WITH THE CRISIS

The development and perception of the crisis by the individual requires new means of adaptation. These means often include activity, denial, and projection. While some of these mechanisms are ordinarily associated with serious clinical syndromes, here they are more often transitional in the service of achieving a new identity. At the heart of this crisis is the issue of guilt.

Guilt may arbitrarily be divided into two related forms, ontic and neurotic (1). The ontological form, common in some degree to all men, results when we "forget being—by failing to be authentic, by slipping into the conformist anonymity—"(6). The relevance of this disability in being true to one's self is apparent in considering the Negro professional. Of course, social circumstance has created the dilemma, but the individual must shoulder the burden. Neurotic guilt may also develop if the individual does not face and accept this burden but sets it aside with conventional neurotic mechanisms.

For large numbers of Negro professionals, there is a nagging sense of guilt that they should be doing more in the movement. They have a sense of anguish that they have been spared the suffering that others have had. This seems to be further compounded when one finds his white colleagues more involved than he. It is, as has been previously noted, not unlike the feelings experienced by the soldier removed from the firing line while his buddies remain in constant danger.

Three forms of dealing with this guilt have been noted.

*1. By activity.* In this case the Negro professional pours great amounts of his energy and interest into the demonstrations. He takes a creative role in the solution of the problem. He deals with his sense of guilt by turning it into action.

A psychiatrist from the Southwest reported: "You can't be a bystander when you see the chief of the Department of Psychiatry marching in a picket line or sitting in at a lunch counter, or when a famous movie star, who has everything to lose, comes to your city and remains for a long period of time helping the people get organized; you feel that you must get in the mainstream. So, on a weekend, I get up in the morning and tell my wife if I am not home by a certain hour, to come bail me out of jail."

In another instance, a general practitioner stated it in this way: "I got to thinking—when my daughter (who was 18 months old then) is in junior high school and studying history or social studies and asks me, 'Daddy, did you sit in? Did you picket? What was it like?' What am I going to tell her? That's the reason my picture was in the paper and the medical magazine carrying a picket sign protesting Welch speaking to the GPs."

*2. By denial of guilt.* In this instance, he says, in essence, "It's not my problem. I worked hard to get where I am—it was through my own efforts. Let others do the same." While expressing sympathy for the struggles of others, he places his faith in free enterprise.

This attitude has largely become an anachronism because of the growing acceptability of recognizing that there is a Negro problem in the United States at all levels. The culmination of the recognition came with the passage of the 1964 Civil Rights Act. Ten years ago this attitude of denial was prevalent among the Negro professionals; now it is more of a transitional phenomenon that occurs prior to the individual's involvement.

*3. By projection.* The previously rather well integrated Negro, in an effort to deal with his sense of guilt created by his sense of not having done enough, may in some instances project the guilt onto other groups or persons. Where he may have felt that he and other Negroes had been treated in a reasonably fair way before the civil rights movement, he now militantly insists that all persons with white skin are discriminating against him and against other Negroes.

> A Negro professional man had grown up in a Western integrated white community. He had many white friends as close as Negro friends. When he went away to college to study his profession, one of his close white friends and he decided to be roommates. They had been fast friends for years. With the emergence of the civil rights movement, their relationship was disturbed by the insistence of the young Negro that his friend and others had not done enough to forward the causes of the Negro. At times he would make bold accusations of prejudice in the activities of his friend, many of which he himself had engaged in. It would appear that in this case the young man was forced to project his sense of guilt because of the intensity of his discomfort.

## THE PERSONAL INTEGRATION PROBLEM

For the Negro professional a special problem exists in bringing that alienated part of himself into his total personality. The alienated part is that previously invisible black identity. It may be traced dynamically to that stage of psychosexual development when one must choose between black and white, good and bad, right and wrong. For the Negro, this has special meaning beyond that of his white brethren. For if he has "made it" in the white community, it has meant that he has totally shunned an inalienable part of himself which is with him always—his blackness and the fact that he is a Negro. In this instance, the social issue blends indistinguishably with the individual's personality development. To be a whole person, an integrated person, requires the reidentification with all fragments of the self. The civil rights movement has created special problems for that member of the Negro community who has been most successful: the Negro professional. He has had to compartmentalize his identity and use mechanisms of denial in order to survive in a split world.

For the Negro professional the integration issue becomes not only one of social relationships in housing, churches, politics, business, but also concerned with elements of his own personality. We have attempted to show how the Negro professional handles these issues with various mechanisms. We do not advocate that these mechanisms are unique to the professional Negro, and recognize that they were no doubt used by other ethnic groups in their struggle to gain a place in the American melting pot. The Negro minority, however, unlike a white minority, has to overcome the stigma of color in its struggle for acceptance.

## A POSTSCRIPT

The authors of this paper asked a number of well-qualified psychiatrists and psychologists to read the paper for critical comment. The authors were initially dismayed at the comments, for they reflected rather curious attitudes not encountered in such requests for criticism in the past.

The comments generally fell into three categories: (1) The paper implies that there is some illness involved in the subjects described; (2) "It was difficult for me to understand, and I reject many of the premises because I have never recognized differences;" (3) "The paper made me uncomfortable; I'll have to think about it." After the authors considered these comments they became aware that this reflected the same attitudes described in the paper itself.

These varied reactions suggest the kinds of resistances experienced by professional men in our field to examining attitudes of race and culture. The majority of psychiatrists show some degree of identification with the civil rights movement and thus, whatever their color, experience in some degree the same reactions. It is noteworthy that there have been no previous papers in the professional psychological literature describing these phenomena. The authors suggest that this may well reflect the resistances of professional men to examining the problem.

The authors of this paper, one Negro and one white, found their collaboration an interesting experience. Initially, anticipating no difficulties whatever (denial), they encountered a certain degree of awkwardness (anxiety). Views which were originally somewhat different were finally forged into a paper representative of the authors' area of agreement. While there were differences, there was also the common base of long professional collaboration.

To put it another way, the authors together were able to achieve something which parallels the personal integration problem described. To illustrate the nature of crossed identifications, at one point the Negro author facetiously commented that now that his white collaborator had written from the Negro point of view, he would write from the side of the white.

It requires a consistent effort to be open, to examine attitudes and feelings in order to achieve resolution. A continuing dialogue between white and Negro attitudes is necessary. After all, is not the goal of any dialogue an appreciation of differences and similarities?

REFERENCES

1. Buber, M., "Guilt and Guilt Feelings," *Psychiatry* XX (1957), pp. 114–129.
2. Ellison, R., *The Invisible Man* (New York: Random House, 1952).
3. Erikson, E., "Identity and the Life Cycle: Selected Papers," *Psychol. Issues*, I (1959), pp. 103, 113.
4. Erikson, E., *Childhood and Society* (New York: W. W. Norton, 1963), pp. 242–244.
5. Freud, A., *The Ego and Mechanisms of Defense* (New York: International Universities Press, 1946), p. 117.
6. May, R., "Contributions of Existential Psychotherapy," in May, R., E. Angel, and H. Ellenberger, (eds.): *Existence* (New York: Basic Books, 1958), p. 53.

# Rejection and Protest

THE NATIONAL ADVISORY COMMISSION
ON CIVIL DISORDER

CHAPTER 4 / THE BASIC CAUSES

We have seen what happened. Why did it happen?

In addressing this question we shift our focus from the local to the national scene, from the particular events of the summer of 1967 to the factors within the society at large which have brought about the sudden violent mood of so many urban Negroes.

The record before this Commission reveals that the causes of recent racial disorders are imbedded in a massive tangle of issues and circumstances—social, economic, political, and psychological—which arise out of the historical pattern of Negro-white relations in America.

These factors are both complex and interacting; they vary significantly in their effect from city to city and from year to year; and the consequences of one disorder, generating new grievances and new demands, become the causes of the next. It is this which creates the "thicket of tension, conflicting evidence and extreme opinions" cited by the President.

Despite these complexities, certain fundamental matters are clear. Of these, the most fundamental is the racial attitude and behavior of white Americans toward black Americans. Race prejudice has shaped our history decisively in the past; it now threatens to do so again. White racism is essentially responsible for the explosive mixture which has been accumulating in our cities since the end of World War II. At the base of this mixture are three of the most bitter fruits of white racial attitudes:

*Pervasive discrimination and segregation.* The first is surely the continuing exclusion of great numbers of Negroes from the benefits of economic progress through discrimination in employment and education, and their enforced confinement in segregated housing and

From the *Report of the National Advisory Commission on Civil Disorder.*

schools. The corrosive and degrading effects of this condition and the attitudes that underlie it are the source of the deepest bitterness and at the center of the problem of racial disorder.

*Black migration and white exodus.* The second is the massive and growing concentration of impoverished Negroes in our major cities resulting from Negro migration from the rural South, rapid population growth and the continuing movement of the white middle class to the suburbs. The consequence is a greatly increased burden on the already depleted resources of cities, creating a growing crisis of deteriorating facilities and services and unmet human needs.

*Black ghettos.* Third, in the teeming racial ghettos, segregation and poverty have intersected to destroy opportunity and hope and to enforce failure. The ghettos too often mean men and women without jobs, families without men, and schools where children are processed instead of educated, until they return to the street—to crime, to narcotics, to dependency on welfare, and to bitterness and resentment against society in general and white society in particular.

These three forces have converged on the inner city in recent years and on the people who inhabit it. At the same time, most whites and many Negroes outside the ghetto have prospered to a degree unparalleled in the history of civilization. Through television—the universal appliance in the ghetto—and the other media of mass communications, this affluence has been endlessly flaunted before the eyes of the Negro poor and the jobless ghetto youth.

As Americans, most Negro citizens carry within themselves two basic aspirations of our society. They seek to share in both the material resources of our system and its intangible benefits—dignity, respect and acceptance. Outside the ghetto many have succeeded in achieving a decent standard of life, and in developing the inner resources which give life meaning and direction. Within the ghetto, however, it is rare that either aspiration is achieved.

Yet these facts alone—fundamental as they are—cannot be said to have caused the disorders. Other and more immediate factors help explain why these events happened now.

Recently, three powerful ingredients have begun to catalyze the mixture.

*Frustrated hopes.* The expectations aroused by the great judicial and legislative victories of the civil rights movement have led to frustration, hostility and cynicism in the face of the persistent gap between promise and fulfillment. The dramatic struggle for equal rights in the South has sensitized Northern Negroes to the economic inequalities reflected in the deprivations of ghetto life.

*Legitimation of violence.* A climate that tends toward the approval and encouragement of violence as a form of protest has been created by white terrorism directed against nonviolent protest, including instances of abuse and even murder of some civil rights workers in the South; by the open defiance of law and federal authority by state and local officials resisting desegregation; and by some protest groups engaging in civil disobedience who turn their backs on nonviolence, go beyond the Constitutionally protected rights of petition and free assembly, and resort to violence to attempt to compel alteration of laws and policies with which they disagree. This condition has been reinforced by a general erosion of respect for authority in American society and reduced effectiveness of social standards and community restraints on violence and crime. This in turn has largely resulted from rapid urbanization and the dramatic reduction in the average age of the total population.

*Powerlessness.* Finally, many Negroes have come to believe that they are being exploited politically and economically by the white "power structure." Negroes, like people in poverty everywhere, in fact lack the channels of communication, influence and appeal that traditionally have been available to ethnic minorities within the city and which enabled them—unburdened by color—to scale the walls of the white ghettos in an earlier era. The frustrations of powerlessness have led some to the conviction that there is no effective alternative to violence as a means of expression and redress, as a way of "moving the system." More generally, the result is alienation and hostility toward the institutions of law and government and the white society which controls them. This is reflected in the reach toward racial consciousness and solidarity reflected in the slogan "Black Power."

These facts have combined to inspire a new mood among Negroes, particularly among the young. Self-esteem and enhanced racial pride are replacing apathy and submission to "the system." Moreover, Negro youth, who make up over half of the ghetto population, share the growing sense of alienation felt by many white youth in our country. Thus, their role in recent civil disorders reflects not only a shared sense of deprivation and victimization by white society but also the rising incidence of disruptive conduct by a segment of American youth throughout the society.

*Incitement and encouragement of violence.* These conditions have created a volatile mixture of attitudes and beliefs which needs only a spark to ignite mass violence. Strident appeals to violence, first heard from white racists, were echoed and reinforced last summer in the inflammatory rhetoric of black racists and militants. Throughout the year, extremists crisscrossed the country preaching a doctrine of black power and violence. Their rhetoric was widely reported in the mass media; it was echoed by local "militants" and organizations; it became the ugly background noise of the violent summer.

We cannot measure with any precision the influence of these organizations and individuals in the ghetto, but we think it clear that the intolerable and unconscionable encouragement of violence heightened tensions, created a mood of acceptance and an expectation of violence, and thus contributed to the eruption of the disorders last summer.

*The police.* It is the convergence of all these factors that makes the role of the police so difficult and so significant. Almost invariably the incident that ignites disorder arises from police action. Harlem, Watts, Newark and Detroit—all the major outbursts of recent years—were precipitated by routine arrests of Negroes for minor offenses by white police.

But the police are not merely the spark. In discharge of their obligation to maintain order and insure public safety in the disruptive conditions of ghetto life, they are inevitably involved in sharper and more frequent conflicts with ghetto residents than with the residents of other areas. Thus, to many Negroes police have come to symbolize white power, white racism and white depression. And the fact is that many police do reflect and express these white attitudes. The atmosphere of hostility and cynicism is reinforced by a widespread perception among Negroes of the existence of police brutality and corruption, and of a "double standard" of justice and protection—one for Negroes and one for whites.

To this point, we have attempted only to identify the prime components of the "explosive mixture." In the chapters that follow we seek to analyze them in the perspective of history. Their meaning, however, is already clear.

In the summer of 1967, we have seen in our cities a chain reaction of racial violence. If we are heedless, we shall none of us escape the consequences.

## CHAPTER 7 / UNEMPLOYMENT, FAMILY STRUCTURE, AND SOCIAL DISORGANIZATION

### RECENT ECONOMIC TRENDS

The Negro population in our country is as diverse in income, occupation, family composition, and other variables as the white community. Nevertheless, for purposes of analysis, three major Negro economic groups can be identified.

The first and smallest group consists of middle and upper-income individuals and households whose educational, occupational, and cultural characteristics are similar to those of middle and upper-income white groups.

The second and largest group contains Negroes whose incomes are above the "poverty level" but who have not attained the educational, occupational, or income status typical of "middle-class" Americans.

The third group has very low educational, occupational, and income attainments and lives below the "poverty level."

A recent compilation of data on American Negroes by the Departments of Labor and Commerce shows that

The incomes of both Negroes and whites have been rising rapidly.

Negro incomes still remain far below those of whites. Negro median family income was only 58 percent of the white median in 1966.

Although it is growing, Negro family income is not keeping pace with white family income growth. In constant 1965 dollars, median nonwhite income in 1947 was $2174 lower than median white income. By 1966, the gap had grown to $3036.

The Negro "upper-income" group is expanding rapidly and achieving sizeable income gains. In 1966, 28 percent of all Negro families received incomes of $7000 or more, compared with 55 percent of white families. This was double the proportion of Negroes receiving comparable incomes in 1960, and 4 times greater than the proportion receiving such incomes in 1947. Moreover, the proportion of Negroes employed in high-skill, high-status, and well-paying jobs rose faster than comparable proportions among whites from 1960 to 1966.

As Negro incomes have risen, the size of the lowest-income group has grown smaller, and the middle and upper groups have grown larger—both relatively and absolutely.

About two-thirds of the lowest-income group—or 20 percent of all Negroes—are making no significant economic gains despite continued general prosperity. Half of these "hard-core disadvantaged"—more than two million persons—live in central-city neighborhoods. Recent special censuses in Los Angeles and Cleveland indicate that the incomes of persons living in the worst slum areas have not risen at all during this period, unemployment rates have declined only slightly, the proportion of families with female heads has increased, and housing conditions have worsened even though rents have risen.

| Group | Percentage of Negro Families | | | Percentage of White Families |
|---|---|---|---|---|
| | 1947 | 1960 | 1966 | 1966 |
| $7,000 and over | 7% | 17% | 28% | 55% |
| $3,000 to $6,999 | 29 | 40 | 41 | 33 |
| Under $3,000 | 65 | 44 | 32 | 13 |

Thus, between 2.0 and 2.5 million poor Negroes are living in disadvantaged neighborhoods of central cities in the United States. These persons comprise only slightly more than 1 percent of the nation's total population, but they make up about 16 to 20 percent of the total Negro population of all central cities, and a much higher proportion in certain cities.

UNEMPLOYMENT AND UNDEREMPLOYMENT

*The critical significance of employment.* The capacity to obtain and hold a "good job" is the traditional test of participation in American society. Steady employment with adequate compensation provides both purchasing power and social status. It develops the capabilities, confidence, and self-esteem an individual needs to be a responsible citizen and provides a basis for a stable family life. As Daniel P. Moynihan has written:

The principal measure of progress toward equality will be that of employment. It is the primary source of individual or group identity. In America what you do is what you are: to do nothing is to be nothing; to do little is to be little. The equations are implacable and blunt, and ruthlessly public.

For the Negro American it is already, and will continue to be, the master problem. It is the measure of white bona fides. It is the measure of Negro competence, and also of the competence of American society. Most importantly, the linkage between problems of employment and the range of social pathology that afflicts the Negro community is unmistakable. Employment not only controls the present for the Negro

American but, in a most profound way, it is creating the future as well.

For residents of disadvantaged Negro neighborhoods, obtaining good jobs is vastly more difficult than for most workers in society. For decades, social, economic, and psychological disadvantages surrounding the urban Negro poor have impaired their work capacities and opportunities. The result is a "cycle of failure"—the employment disabilities of one generation breed those of the next.

*Negro unemployment.* Unemployment rates among Negroes have declined from a postwar high of 12.6 percent in 1958 to 8.2 percent in 1967. Among married Negro men, the unemployment rate for 1967 was down to 3.2 percent.

Notwithstanding this decline, unemployment rates for Negroes are still double those for whites in every category, including married men, as they have been throughout the postwar period. Moreover, since 1954, even during the current unprecedented period of sustained economic growth, unemployment among Negroes has been continuously above the 6.0 percent "recession" level widely regarded as a sign of serious economic weakness when prevalent for the entire work force.

While the Negro unemployment rate remains high in relation to the white rate, the number of additional jobs needed to lower this to the level of white unemployment is surprisingly small. In 1967, approximately 3.0 million persons were unemployed during an average week, of whom about 638,000, or 21 percent, were nonwhites. When corrected for undercounting, total nonwhite unemployment was approximately 712,000 or 8 percent of the nonwhite labor force. To reduce the unemployment rate to 3.4 percent, the rate prevalent among whites, jobs must be found for 57.5 percent of these unemployed persons. This amounts to nearly 409,000 jobs, or about 28 percent of the net number of new jobs added to the economy in the year 1967 alone and only slightly more than ½ of 1 percent of all jobs in the United States in 1967.

THE LOW-STATUS AND LOW-PAYING NATURE OF MANY NEGRO JOBS

Even more important perhaps than unemployment is the related problem of the undesirable nature of many jobs open to Negroes. Negro workers are concentrated in the lowest-skilled and lowest-paying occupations. These jobs often involve substandard wages, great instability and uncertainty of tenure, extremely low status in the eyes of both employer and employee, little or no chance for meaningful advancement, and unpleasant or exhausting duties. Negro men in particular are more than twice as likely as whites to be in unskilled or service jobs which pay far less than most:

| Type of Occupation | Percentage of Male Workers in Each Type of Occupation 1966 | | Median Earnings of All Male Civilians in Each Occupation 1965 |
|---|---|---|---|
| | White | Nonwhite | |
| Professional, technical, managerial | 27% | 9% | $7,603[1] |
| Clerical and sales | 14 | 9 | $5,532[1] |
| Craftsmen and foremen | 20 | 12 | $6,270 |
| Operatives | 20 | 27 | $5,046 |
| Service workers | 6 | 16 | $3,436 |
| Non-farm laborers | 6 | 20 | $2,410 |
| Farmers and farm workers | 7 | 8 | $1,699[1] |

This concentration in the least desirable jobs can be viewed another way by calculating the changes which would occur if Negro men were employed in various occupations in the same proportions as the male labor force as a whole (*not* solely the white labor force).

| Type of Occupation | Number of Male Nonwhite Workers—1966 | | | |
|---|---|---|---|---|
| | As Actually Distributed[2] | If Distributed the Same as All Male Workers | Difference No. | Percent |
| Professional, technical, managerial | 415,000 | 1,173,000 | +758,000 | +183% |
| Clerical and sales | 415,000 | 628,000 | +213,000 | +51% |
| Craftsmen and foremen | 553,000 | 894,000 | +341,000 | +62% |
| Operatives | 1,244,000 | 964,000 | −280,000 | −23% |
| Service workers | 737,000 | 326,000 | −411,000 | −56% |
| Non-farm laborers | 922,000 | 340,000 | −582,000 | −63% |
| Farmers and farm workers | 369,000 | 330,000 | −39,000 | −11% |

Thus, upgrading the employment of Negro men to make their

[1] Average of two categories from normal Census Bureau categories as combined in data presented in *The Social and Economic Conditions of Negroes in the United States* (BLS #332).

[2] Estimates based upon percentages set forth in BLS #332, page 41.

occupational distribution identical with that of the labor force as a whole would have an immense impact upon the nature of their occupations. About 1.3 million nonwhite men—or 28 percent of those employed in 1966—would move up the employment ladder into one of the higher-status and higher-paying categories. The effect of such a shift upon the incomes of Negro men would be very great. Using the 1966 job distribution, the shift indicated above would produce about $4.8 billion more earned income for nonwhite men alone if they received the 1965 median income in each occupation. This would be a rise of approximately 30 percent in the earnings actually received by all nonwhite men in 1965 (not counting any sources of income other than wages and salaries).

Of course, the kind of "instant upgrading" visualized in these calculations does not represent a practical alternative for national policy. The economy cannot drastically reduce the total number of low-status jobs it now contains, or shift large numbers of people upward in occupation in any short period. Therefore, major upgrading in the employment status of Negro men must come through a faster relative expansion of higher-level jobs than lower-level jobs (which has been occurring for several decades), an improvement in the skills of nonwhite workers so they can obtain a higher proportion of those added better jobs, and a drastic reduction of discriminatory hiring and promotion practices in all enterprises, both private and public.

Nevertheless, this hypothetical example clearly shows that the concentration of male Negro employment at the lowest end of the occupational scale is greatly depressing the incomes of United States Negroes in general. In fact, this is the single most important source of poverty among Negroes. It is even more important than unemployment, as can be shown by a second hypothetical calculation. In 1966, there were about 702,000 unemployed nonwhites in the United States on the average, including adults and teenagers, and allowing for the Census Bureau undercount of Negroes. If every one of these persons had been employed and had received the median amount earned by nonwhite males in 1966 ($3,864), this would have added a total of $2.7 billion to nonwhite income as a whole. If only enough of these persons had been employed at that wage to reduce nonwhite unemployment from 7.3 to 3.3 percent—the rate among whites in 1966—then the income gain for nonwhites would have totaled about $1.5 billion. But if nonwhite unemployment remained at 7.3 percent, and nonwhite men were upgraded so that they had the same occupational distribution and incomes as all men in the labor force considered together, this would have produced about $4.8 billion in additional income, as noted above (using 1965 earnings for calculation). Thus the potential income gains from upgrading the male nonwhite labor force are much larger than those from reducing nonwhite unemployment.

This conclusion underlines the difficulty of really improving the economic status of Negro men. It is far easier to create new jobs than either to create new jobs with relatively high status and earning power, or to upgrade existing employed or partly-employed workers into such better-quality employment. Yet only such upgrading will eliminate the fundamental basis of poverty and deprivation among Negro families.

Access to good-quality jobs clearly affects the willingness of Negro men actively to seek work. In cities with the largest percentage of Negroes in skilled and semi-skilled jobs, Negro men participate in the labor force to the same extent as, or greater than, white men. Conversely, where most Negro men were heavily concentrated in menial jobs, they participated less in the labor force than white men.

Even given similar employment, Negro workers with the same education as white workers are paid less. This disparity doubtless results to some extent from inferior training in segregated schools, and also from the fact that large numbers of Negroes are only now entering certain occupations for the first time. However, the differentials are so large and so universal at all educational levels that they clearly reflect the patterns of discrimination which characterize hiring and promotion practices in many segments of the economy. For example, in 1966 among persons who had completed high school, the median income of Negroes was only 73 percent that of whites. Even among persons with an eighth-grade education. Negro median income was only 80 percent of white median income.

At the same time, a higher proportion of Negro women than white women participates in the labor force at nearly all ages except 16 to 19. For instance, in 1966, 55 percent of nonwhite women from 25 to 34 years of age were employed, compared to only 38 percent of white women in the same age group. The fact that almost half of all adult Negro women work reflects the fact that so many Negro males have unsteady and low-paying jobs. Yet even though Negro women are often better able to find work than Negro men, the unemployment rate among adult nonwhite women (20 years old and over) in 1967 was 7.3 percent, compared to the 4.3 percent rate among adult nonwhite men.

Unemployment rates are, of course, much higher among teen-agers, both Negro and white, than among adults; in fact about one-third of all unemployed Negroes in 1967 were between 16 and 19 years old. During the first nine months of 1967, the unemployment rate among nonwhite teenagers was 26.5 percent; for whites, it was 10.6 percent. About 219,300 nonwhite teenagers were unem-ployed.[3] About 58,300 were still in school but were actively looking for jobs.

*Subemployment in disadvantaged Negro neighborhoods.* In disadvantaged areas, employment conditions for Negroes are in a chronic state of crisis. Surveys in low-income neighborhoods of nine large cities made by the Department of Labor late in 1966 revealed that the rate of unemployment there was 9.3 percent, compared to 7.3 percent for Negroes generally and 3.3 percent for whites. Moreover, a high proportion of the persons living in these areas were "underemployed," that is they were either part-time workers look-ing for full-time employment, or full-time workers earning less than $3000 per year, or had dropped out of the labor force. The Depart-ment of Labor estimated that this underemployment is two and one-half times greater than the number unemployed in these areas. Therefore, the "subemployment rate," including both the unem-ployed and the underemployed, was about 32.7 percent in the nine areas surveyed, or 8.8 times greater than the overall unemploy-ment rate for all U. S. workers. Since underemployment also exists outside disadvantaged neighborhoods, comparing the full subem-ployment rate in these areas with the unemployment rate for the nation as a whole is not entirely valid. However, it provides some measure of the enormous disparity between employment conditions in most of the nation and those prevalent in disadvantaged Negro areas in our large cities.

The critical problem is to determine the actual number of those unemployed and underemployed in disadvantaged Negro areas. This involves a process of calculation which is detailed in the note at the end of this chapter. The outcome of this process is sum-marized in the table on the following page.

Therefore, in order to bring subemployment in these areas down to a level equal to unemployment alone among whites, enough steady, reasonably-paying jobs (and the training and motivation to

---

[3] After adjusting for Census Bureau undercounting.

| Group | Nonwhite Subemployment in Disadvantaged Areas of All Central Cities—1967 | | Total Subemployment |
|---|---|---|---|
| | Unemployment | Underemployment | |
| Adult men | 102,000 | 230,000 | 332,000 |
| Adult women | 118,000 | 266,000 | 384,000 |
| Teenagers | 98,000 | 220,000 | 318,000 |
| Total | 318,000 | 716,000 | 1,034,000 |

perform them) must be provided to eliminate all underemployment and reduce unemployment by 65 percent. For all three age groups combined, this "deficit" amounted to 923,000 jobs in 1967.

THE MAGNITUDE OF POVERTY IN DISADVANTAGED NEIGHBORHOODS

The chronic unemployment problems in the central city, aggravated by the constant arrival of new unemployed migrants, is the fundamental cause of the persistent poverty in disadvantaged Negro areas.

"Poverty" in the affluent society is more than absolute deprivation. Many of the poor in the United States would be well-off in other societies. Relative deprivation—inequality—is a more useful concept of poverty with respect to the Negro in America because it encompasses social and political exclusion as well as economic inequality. Because of the lack of data of this type, we have had to focus our analysis on a measure of poverty which is both economic and absolute—the Social Security Administration's "poverty level"[4] concept. It is clear, however, that broader measures of poverty would substantiate the conclusions that follow.

In 1966 there were 29.7 million persons in the United States— 15.3 percent of the nation's population—with incomes below the "poverty level," as defined by the Social Security Administration. Of these, 20.3 million were white (68.3 percent), and 9.3 million nonwhite (31.7 percent). Thus, about 11.9 percent of the nation's whites and 40.6 percent of its nonwhites were poor under the Social Security definition.

The location of the nation's poor is best shown from 1964 data as indicated by the table on the following page.

The following facts concerning poverty are relevant to an

---

[4] Currently $3335 per year for an urban family of four.

| Percentage of Those in Poverty in Each Group Living in Metropolitan Areas | | | | |
|---|---|---|---|---|
| Group | In Central Cities | Outside Central Cities | Other Areas | Total |
| Whites | 23.8% | 21.8% | 54.4% | 100% |
| Nonwhites | 41.7 | 10.8 | 47.5 | 100 |
| Total | 29.4 | 18.4 | 52.2 | 100 |

Source: Social Security Administration

understanding of the problems faced by people living in disadvantaged neighborhoods.[5]

30.7 percent of nonwhite families of two or more persons lived in poverty compared to only 8.8 percent of whites.

Of the 10.1 million poor persons in central cities in 1964, about 4.4 million of these (43.6 percent) were nonwhites, and 5.7 million (56.4 percent) were whites. The poor whites were much older on the average than the poor nonwhites. The proportion of poor persons 65 years old or older was 23.2 percent among whites, but only 6.8 percent among nonwhites.

Poverty was more than twice as prevalent among nonwhite families with female heads than among those with male heads, 57 percent compared to 21 percent. In central cities, 26 percent of all nonwhite families of two or more persons had female heads, as compared to 12 percent of white families.

Among nonwhite families headed by a female, and having children under 6, the incidence of poverty was 81.0 percent. Moreover, there were 243,000 such families living in poverty in central cities—or over 9 percent of all nonwhite families in those cities.

Among all children living in poverty within central cities, nonwhites outnumbered whites by over 400,000. The number of

| Number of Children Living in Poverty (millions) | | | |
|---|---|---|---|
| Age Group | White | Nonwhite | Percent of Total Nonwhite |
| Under 6 | 0.9 | 1.0 | 53% |
| 6-15 | 1.0 | 1.3 | 57 |
| 16-21 | 0.4 | 0.4 | 50 |
| Total | 2.3 | 2.7 | 54% |

[5] Source: Social Security Administration based on 1964 data.

poor nonwhite children equalled or surpassed the number of white poor children in every age group.

Two stark facts emerge:

54 percent of all poor children in central cities in 1964 were nonwhites;

Of the 4.4 million nonwhites living in poverty within central cities in 1964, 52 percent were children under 16, and 61 percent were under 21.

Since 1964, the number of nonwhite families living in poverty within central cities has remained about the same; hence, these poverty conditions are probably still prevalent in central cities in terms of absolute numbers of persons, although the proportion of persons in poverty may have dropped slightly.[6]

### THE SOCIAL IMPACT OF EMPLOYMENT PROBLEMS
### IN DISADVANTAGED NEGRO AREAS

*Unemployment and the family.*   The high rates of unemployment and underemployment in racial ghettos are evidence, in part, that many men living in these areas are seeking but cannot obtain jobs which will support a family. Perhaps equally important, most jobs they can get are at the low end of the occupational scale, and often lack the necessary status to sustain a worker's self-respect, or the respect of his family and friends. These same men are also constantly confronted with the message of discrimination: "You are inferior because of a trait you did not cause and cannot change." This message reinforces feelings of inadequacy arising from repeated failure to obtain and keep decent jobs.

Wives of these men are forced to work, and usually produce more money. If men stay at home without working, their inadequacies constantly confront them and tensions arise between them and their wives and children. Under these pressures, it is not surprising that many of these men flee their responsibilities as husbands

---

[6] For the nation as a whole, the proportion of nonwhite families living in poverty dropped from 39 percent to 35 percent from 1964 to 1966 (defining "family" somewhat differently from the definition used in the data above). The number of such families declined from 1.9 million to 1.7 million. However, the number and proportion of all nonwhites living in central cities rose in the same period. As a result, the number of nonwhite families living in so-called "poverty areas" of large cities actually rose from 1,561,000 in 1960 to 1,588,000 in 1966.

and fathers, leaving home, and drifting from city to city, or adopting the style of "street corner men."

Statistical evidence tends to document this. A close correlation exists between the number of nonwhite married women separated from their husbands each year and the unemployment rate among nonwhite males 20 years old and over. Similarly, from 1948 to 1962, the number of new Aid to Families with Dependent Children cases rose and fell with the nonwhite male unemployment rate. Since 1963, however, the number of new cases—most of them Negro children—has steadily increased even though the unemployment rate among nonwhite males has declined. The impact of marital status on employment among Negroes is shown by the fact that in 1967 the proportion of married men either divorced or separated from their wives was more than twice as high among unemployed nonwhite men as among employed nonwhite men. Moreover, among those participating in the labor force, there was a higher proportion of married men with wives present than with wives absent.

*Unemployment Rate and Participation in Total Labor Force, 25- to 54-Year-Old Nonwhite Men, by Marital Status, March, 1967*

|  | Unemployment Rate Nonwhite | Labor Force Participation (%) Nonwhite |
|---|---|---|
| Married, wife present | 3.7 | 96.7 |
| Other (separated, divorced, widowed) | 8.7 | 77.6 |

*Fatherless families.* The abandonment of the home by many Negro males affects a great many children growing up in the racial ghetto. As previously indicated, most American Negro families are headed by men, just like most other American families. Yet the proportion of families with female heads is much greater among Negroes than among whites at all income levels, and has been rising in recent years.

This disparity between white and nonwhite families is far greater among the lowest income families—those most likely to reside in disadvantaged big-city neighborhoods—than among higher income families. Among families with incomes under $3,000 in 1966, the proportion with female heads was 42 percent for Negroes but only 23 percent for whites. In contrast, among families with incomes of $7,000 or more, 8 percent of Negro families had female heads compared to 4 percent of whites.

| Date | Proportion of Families of Various Types | | | |
|---|---|---|---|---|
| | Husband-Wife | | Female Head | |
| | White | Nonwhite | White | Nonwhite |
| 1950 | 88.0% | 77.7% | 8.5% | 17.6% |
| 1960 | 88.7 | 73.6 | 8.7 | 22.4 |
| 1966 | 88.8 | 72.7 | 8.9 | 23.7 |

The problems of fatherless families are aggravated by the tendency of Negroes to have large families. This is characteristic of poor families generally. The average poor, urban nonwhite family contains 4.8 persons, as compared with 3.7 for the average poor, urban white family. This is one of the primary factors in the poverty status of nonwhite households in large cities.

The proportion of fatherless families appears to be increasing in the poorest Negro neighborhoods. In the Hough section of Cleveland, the proportion of families with female heads rose from 23 to 32 percent from 1960 to 1965. In the Watts section of Los Angeles it rose from 36 to 39 percent during the same period.

The handicap imposed on children growing up without fathers, in an atmosphere of poverty and deprivation, is increased because many mothers must work to provide support. The following table illustrates the disparity between the proportion of nonwhite women in the child-rearing ages who are in the labor force and the comparable proportion of white women.

| Age Group | Percentage of Women in the Labor Force | |
|---|---|---|
| | Nonwhite | White |
| 20-24 | 55% | 51% |
| 25-34 | 55 | 38 |
| 35-44 | 61 | 45 |

With the father absent and the mother working, many ghetto children spend the bulk of their time on the streets—the streets of a crime-ridden, violence-prone and poverty-stricken world. The image of success in this world is not that of the "solid citizen," the responsible husband and father, but rather that of the "hustler" who takes care of himself by exploiting others. The dope sellers and the numbers runners are the "successful" men because their earnings far outstrip those men who try to climb the economic ladder in honest ways.

Young people in the ghetto are acutely conscious of a system which appears to offer rewards to those who illegally exploit others, and failure to those who struggle under traditional responsibilities. Under these circumstances, many adopt exploitation and the "hustle" as a way of life, disclaiming both work and marriage in favor of casual and temporary liaisons. This pattern reinforces itself from one generation to the next, creating a "culture of poverty" and an ingrained cynicism about society and its institutions.

*The "jungle."* The culture of poverty that results from unemployment and family disorganization generates a system of ruthless, exploitative relationships within the ghetto. Prostitution, dope addiction, casual sexual affairs, and crime create an environmental jungle characterized by personal insecurity and tension. The effects of this development are stark:

The rate of illegitimate births among nonwhite women has risen sharply in the past two decades. In 1940, 16.8 percent of all nonwhite births were illegitimate. By 1950 this proportion was 18 percent; by 1960, 21.6 percent; by 1966, 26.3 percent. In the ghettos of many large cities, illegitimacy rates exceed 50 percent.

The rate of illegitimacy among nonwhite women is closely related to low income and high unemployment. In Washington, D. C., for example, an analysis of 1960 census tracts shows that in tracts with unemployment rates of 12 percent or more among nonwhite men, illegitimacy was over 40 percent. But in tracts with unemployment rates of 2.9 percent and below among nonwhite men, reported illegitimacy was under 20 percent. A similar contrast existed between tracts in which median nonwhite income was under $4,000 (where illegitimacy was 38 percent) and those in which it was $8,000 and over (where illegitimacy was 11 percent).

Narcotics addiction is also heavily concentrated in low-income Negro neighborhoods, particularly in New York City. Of the 59,720 addicts known to the U. S. Bureau of Narcotics at the end of 1966, just over 50 percent were Negroes. Over 52 percent of all known addicts lived within New York State, mostly in Harlem and other Negro neighborhoods. These figures undoubtedly greatly understate the actual number of persons using narcotics regularly—especially those under 21.

Not surprisingly, at every age from 6 through 19, the proportion of children from homes with both parents present who actually attend school is higher than the proportion of children from homes with only one parent or neither present.

Rates of juvenile delinquency, venereal disease, dependency upon AFDC support, and use of public assistance in general are much higher in disadvantaged Negro areas than in other parts of large cities. Data taken from New York City contrasting predominantly Negro neighborhoods with the city as a whole clearly illustrate this fact.

| | *Social Distress—Major Predominantly Negro Neighborhoods in New York City and the City as a Whole* | | | |
|---|---|---|---|---|
| | *Juvenile Delinquency*[7] | *Venereal Disease*[8] | *ADC*[9] | *Public Assistance*[10] |
| Brownsville | 125.3 | 609.9 | 459.0 | 265.8 |
| East New York | 98.6 | 207.5 | 148.6 | 71.8 |
| Bedford Stuyvesant | 115.2 | 771.3 | 337.1 | 197.2 |
| Harlem | 110.8 | 1,603.5 | 265.7 | 138.1 |
| South Bronx | 84.4 | 308.3 | 278.5 | 165.5 |
| New York City | 52.2 | 269.1 | 120.7 | 60.8 |

In conclusion: in 1965, 1.2 million nonwhite children under 16 lived in central city families headed by a woman under 65. The great majority of these children were growing up in poverty under conditions that make them better candidates for crime and civil disorder than for jobs providing an entry into American society. Because of the immense importance of this fact—the potential loss to the society of these young people—we describe these conditions in the next chapter.

[7] Number of offenses per 1,000 persons 7-20 years (1965).

[8] Number of cases per 100,000 persons under 21 years (1964).

[9] Number of children in Aid to Dependent Children cases per 1,000 under 18 years, using 1960 population as base (1965).

[10] Welfare Assistance recipients per 1,000 persons, using 1960 population as base (1965).

# ADDICTIVE REACTIONS:
# DRUGS

*... Turn on, Tune in, Drop out.*

Leary

At one time drug abuse was considered a malaise of the lower economic strata of society. Today, however, we recognize that a significant proportion of its users and advocates are from the middle class. The college community, in fact, represents a large part of this proportion. For this reason we have come to realize that the use of drugs is appealing to several segments of society.

Drugs are usually classed as stimulants, depressants, and hallucinogens. These categories include a wide range of drugs: from alcohol to marijuana to coffee. This section focuses on the hallucinogens. Hallucinogens are frequently divided into *psychedelics* (consciousness-expanding drugs), *psychotomimetics* (mimicking psychosis), and *hallucinogens* (causing hallucinations).

The first article, *The "Hang-Loose" Ethic and the Spirit of Drug Use* by Suchman, presents an analysis of the drug movement and some of its philosophical implications. McGlothlin and Cohen's report, *The Use of Hallucinogenic Drugs Among College Students,* offers an insight into the frequency and type of illegal drug usage. Rinkel's editorial overview in his article *Psychedelic Drugs* reflects the views of many members of the American Psychiatric Association. Finally, in *Motivational Factors in Psychedelic Drug Use by Male College Students,* Lipinski and Lipinski illustrate how drug usage serves as a defense mechanism against frustration.

# The "Hang-Loose" Ethic
# and the Spirit of Drug Use

EDWARD A. SUCHMAN

*A cross-sectional, sampling survey of drug use on a college campus reveals the close association between the use of drugs (overwhelmingly marijuana) and adherence to what might be characterized as a "hang-loose" ethic. Use of drugs was more likely to occur among those students whose behavior, attitudes or values, and self-image were indicative of opposition to the traditional, established order. Such differences occurred regardless of those demographic characteristics of the students also related to drug use, such as sex, socio-economic status, and religion. For these students, marijuana was the recreational drug of choice and its use became a central core of their sub-culture.*

Studies of college students made about 15 years ago found that generation of youth to be "politically disinterested, apathetic, and conservative." (3, 4) To an increasing degree, the college student of the current generation is striving to overcome this image of passive conformity and conservativism in order to evolve a new and more meaningful role for himself, both on campus and in the larger community. Reflecting the many social, political, and economic forces that have widened the generational gap between young people and those "over 30," this youth movement is seeking to develop new values and behavior patterns, often in defiance and opposition to those of the established order.

Central to this new world of youth is a whole new range of recreational and psychedelic drugs. Studies of college students in the last generation found alcohol to be the major campus "vice" and alarming reports were published about the "drinking problem of college students." (12) No mention was made of other drugs. In this respect, the students displayed one more sign of their conformity—drinking was also the favorite social pastime, and problem,

From the *Journal of Health and Social Behavior*, June 1968, IX, No. 2, pp. 146–155. Reprinted by permission of the author and the American Sociological Association.

of their parents. Almost as if rejection of the establishment also demanded the development of a different form of "high," the new generation of college students is increasingly turning to other drugs for the relaxation and "kicks" their parents found in alcohol. As described by Simmons and Winograd (11), "The drug scene is the central plaza of happening America . . . it is here, in the drug scene that generational change in America most vividly thrusts itself forward. . . ." And perhaps forgetting their own bouts with the law in the days of prohibition and repressing the serious threat of alcoholism as a major health problem today (14, 8), adults have been almost unanimous in their condemnation of this new and strange intoxicant. As one "over 30" judge recently opined, alcohol is the socially approved drug of choice for the well-adjusted, responsible, hard-working member of society seeking sociability and pleasant relaxation, while the use of marijuana represents the neurotic and antisocial behavior of the juvenile delinquent.

Unfortunately, there is little empirical data about what is taking place in the colleges today. The present study represents an initial attempt to ascertain basic facts about the use of drugs by one college population and to examine those factors, both causes and consequences, associated with the use of drugs. The major assumption is that drug use on the campuses today is largely limited to the occasional smoking of marijuana cigarettes and represents a social form of recreation far removed in nature from the traditional problem of narcotics addiction and, for that matter, alcoholism. (7) Furthermore, the set of hypotheses to be tested is that the use of marijuana will be highly associated with other expressions of a new breed of youth characterized by a "hang-loose" ethic. As described by Simmons and Winograd (11) "One of the fundamental characteristics of the hang-loose ethic is that it is irreverent. It repudiates, or at least questions, such cornerstones of conventional society as Christianity, 'my country right or wrong,' the sanctity of marriage and premarital chastity, civil disobedience, the accumulation of wealth, the right and even competence of parents, the schools, and the government to head and make decisions for everyone—in sum, the Establishment."

METHOD OF PROCEDURE

This study was conducted in November, 1967, at a West Coast university. A representative sample of 600 students out of a student body of 12,200 was selected at random from the registration lists of undergraduate and graduate students. A questionnaire dealing with drug use and various aspects of college life, educational and political values, and current social issues was prepared on the basis of detailed interviews of students, especially so-called "hippies," and observation of student activities, especially so-called "happenings." Interviews and observation were carried out by 125 students enrolled in a course on social research methods.

The questionnaire was administered in two parts of almost equal length. The first part was a personal interview, while the second, which sought information on more sensitive topics, such as sex, drug use and the draft, was filled out by the respondent and placed with the first part in a sealed envelope without identification. The questionnaires were thus kept anonymous to increase the probability of truthful answers. The completion rate of interviews was 81 per cent. The remaining 19 per cent were not interviewed largely because the assigned respondent could not be reached during the week allotted to field work, rather than the refusal to be interviewed (less than 5 percent). A comparison of the sample obtained with available demographic characteristics for the entire population shows no characteristic with a difference beyond what might be expected by chance.

*Conceptual and Operational Model.* Our dependent variable is frequency of drug use as reported by the respondent. Our major independent variable is degree of adherence to the "hang-loose" ethic as determined by a series of questions designed to tap (1) behavioral patterns, (2) attitudes and values, and (3) self-image and personality. The behavioral patterns refer to such acts as taking part in "happenings" and mass protests, and reading underground newspapers. We view such behaviors as indicative of a rejection of traditional society on the part of the student and subject to disapproval by the representatives of that society. The attitudes and values studied are drawn from the educational area (i.e., worthwhileness of college education, student power), the political area (i.e., Vietnam war, the draft), and the social area (i.e., "hippies," the law, sex and life goals). Finally, we study the student's self-image in such respects as conformity, cynicism, anti-establishment and rebellion in an effort to index his own portrait of himself vis-a-vis the established order.

In all three aspects of behavior, attitudes, and self-image, our major hypothesis is that the more the student embraces the "hang-loose" ethic (as opposed to the so-called "Protestant ethic") the more frequently will he make use of drugs.

## FINDINGS

PREVALENCE OF DRUG USE

The following proportions of students reported taking some drug (Question: "How frequently do you take drugs (marijuana, LSD, etc.)?"):

| | |
|---|---|
| About every day | 2.0 |
| Once or twice a week | 6.6 |
| Once or twice a month | 6.6 |
| Less than once a month | 6.0 |
| Do not use drugs | 78.8 |
| Total | 100.0% (N = 497) |

Of the drugs used, marijuana was listed by *all* students taking drugs, with occasional use of LSD mentioned by 18 per cent of those taking drugs (2.2% of the entire population). A wide variety of other drugs (i.e. "speed," Methadrine, peyote) also was listed, none by more than 10 per cent. There can be little question concerning marijuana's being the recreational drug of choice among this college population, one of five admitting its use, despite its illegality. The word "drugs" as used in this report may therefore be equated largely with marijuana.

This figure of 21.1 per cent use is quite similar to the results of surveys at UCLA (33%) (Santa Barbara News-Press, 1967), Harvard (25%), Yale (20%), and Princeton (15%) (15), although a Gallup Poll of 426 college campuses reports only about 6 per cent as having smoked marijuana (9). While this "numbers game" is largely unproductive in the absence of any reliable and valid data, it does seem apparent that marijuana use on the campus is high enough to warrant serious attention.

Most of the students using drugs began in college, 40 per cent in their freshman year, although 22 per cent had smoked marijuana before coming to college. Almost all began to use drugs through the personal influence of a friend who was already smoking marijuana (1). Drug use usually took place at night as a social activity with other people in the student's or a friend's room.

Overwhelmingly, the reaction of the students smoking marijuana is positive. Four out of five report that they have never gotten sick, although one out of four does mention having experienced a bad "trip." Less than 10 per cent want to stop or have ever tried to stop, although 20 per cent report being "somewhat" worried.

There is no evidence in these findings to support the claims that smoking marijuana is a predecessor to the use of other, more than dangerous drugs. Marijuana users may occasionally "cross over" to try other drugs, but this is more of a search for new experiences than "progressive degeneration."

## ALCOHOL AND MARIJUANA

In addition to the question about their own use of drugs, the students were asked, "How frequently do most of the students you know do the following: smoke marijuana, take LSD, drink alcoholic beverages?" They were also asked in relation to these three recreational drugs, "How strongly do you approve or disapprove doing each of the following?" and "How much pressure do you feel to engage in any of the following?" A comparison of their responses to these three aspects of use, attitude, and pressure for marijuana, LSD, and alcohol is given in Table 1 on the following page.

First, we note the higher perception of marijuana use as compared to actual use. While 4 out of 5 students (78.8%) report that they do not use marijuana themselves, only 1 out of 3 (30.7%) estimates that most of the students they know do not smoke marijuana. Almost 2 out of 5 (38.6%) report that most of the students they know smoke marijuana frequently or occasionally.

Second, we see that alcohol continues by far to be most frequently used, with an overwhelming majority of students (84.1%) reporting that most of the students they know drink alcohol frequently or occasionally, as compared to 38.9 per cent for marijuana and 10.0 per cent for LSD.

Third, we note that approval parallels use, with most of the students (70.6%) approving alcohol, some approving marijuana (35.4%), and few approving LSD (4.8%). The ratio of approval to disapproval is 10:1 in favor for alcohol, 1:1 for marijuana and 1:20 against LSD. It would appear that the campus is split on the use of marijuana, but overwhelmingly in favor of alcohol and against LSD.

Fourth, the pressure to use each of these drugs also parallels attitudes and practices. Most students report pressure to drink alcoholic beverages (51.1%), but only 19.5 per cent report feeling any pressure to smoke marijuana, with 4.9 per cent feeling some pressure to use LSD. These findings underscore the highly personal and voluntary nature of marijuana or LSD use. If anything, students are being more highly pressured toward possible alcoholism than drug addiction. The major recreational drug on the college campuses is still alcohol.

The relationship between pressure toward use of drugs and the actual frequency of use is quite high. An individual who reports

*Table 1.* Comparison of drugs according to use, attitudes, and pressures

| Questions | Type Drug | | |
| --- | --- | --- | --- |
| | Alcoholic beverages | Marijuana | LSD |
| **Use*** | | | |
| Frequently | 47.2 | 14.1 | 1.2 |
| Occasionally | 36.9 | 24.5 | 8.8 |
| Seldom | 10.0 | 18.9 | 16.9 |
| Never | 2.4 | 30.7 | 53.8 |
| Don't know | 3.5 | 11.8 | 19.3 |
| **Attitude†** | | | |
| Strongly approve | 11.4 | 5.6 | 1.2 |
| Approve | 59.2 | 29.5 | 3.6 |
| Undecided | 22.2 | 31.5 | 20.9 |
| Disapprove | 5.2 | 20.1 | 25.7 |
| Strongly disapprove | 2.0 | 13.3 | 48.6 |
| **Pressure‡** | | | |
| A great deal | 12.9 | 3.0 | 2.8 |
| Some, but not much | 38.2 | 16.5 | 2.0 |
| Very little | 47.0 | 78.1 | 92.6 |
| No answer | 1.9 | 2.4 | 2.6 |
| Total per cent | 100.0 | 100.0 | 100.0 |
| Total cases | 497 | 497 | 497 |

* Question: "How frequently do most of the students you know do the following?"

† Question: "How strongly do you approve or disapprove of students doing each of the following?"

‡ Question: "How much pressure do you feel to engage in any of the following?"

feeling pressure to smoke marijuana is twice as likely to be a frequent user of marijuana (at least once a week) than one who reports little or no pressure (15.7% vs. 7.2%). A similar relationship exists between pressure to use LSD and actual use (16.6% vs. 8.5%). This finding is supported by the much more frequent use of marijuana among those students who report that most of the students they know also smoke marijuana. As many as 68.6 per cent of those students who report that most of the students they know smoke marijuana frequently do so themselves, as compared to only 0.7 per cent among those whose friends do not smoke marijuana.

A significant reversal between alcohol and drug use occurs in these data. The more the individual knows other students who drink alcohol, and the more pressure he feels to drink himself, the *less* likely is he to use marijuana. This finding would indicate that marijuana is more of a substitute for alcohol than a supplement. For many students it would appear that the use of marijuana represents a preference over alcohol as a source of "high."

The relationship of attitudes toward use and actual use is, not unexpectedly, extremely high. Approval is much more likely to mean use (45.7%), with only a small minority (0.6%) disapproving of smoking marijuana at the same time that they do it. This finding once again attests to the voluntary nature of this act. It is also interesting to note that half of the students who approve of smoking marijuana still do not do so themselves. Most of the students (66.6%) do not feel that "anyone smoking marijuana is foolish" although only a minority agree that "the use of psychedelic drugs should be a matter of conscience and not legal restriction" (34.7%) and that "the university should not cooperate with legal authorities in the enforcement of drug use laws" (23.2%). In all cases, those students having positive attitudes towards marijuana, either in the wisdom of its use or in its freedom from legal restrictions, are much more likely to be users of marijuana.

DEMOGRAPHIC COMPARISONS

The use of drugs varies significantly by sex, social class, marital status, and religion. No differences were found by age, year in college, birthplace or current marital status of parents. Males are almost three times as likely as females to be using drugs (e.g., smoking marijuana) at least once a week (13.9% vs. 4.6%), upper income groups twice as likely as lower income groups (14.1% vs. 7.3%), single students four times as likely as married students (8.9% vs. 2.1%) (but engaged students show greatest use—10.7%), and Atheists and "other religious affiliations" reporting much more use (25.0%) than Protestants (4.9%), Catholics (4.8%), and Jews (4.0%). Similar differences occur in the category "less than once a week."

Social class differences are much more pronounced among the females than male students. Among coeds, the proportion smoking marijuana at least once a week rises rapidly from 1.5 per cent among those who come from families with annual incomes under $12,000 to 13.1 per cent from families with incomes of $20,000 or more. No statistically significant social class differences are found among the male students. In general, our analysis by demographic characteristics would support the findings of others that marijuana smoking is not, like the use of narcotics, linked to a lower income sub-culture.

THE "HANG-LOOSE" ETHIC: BEHAVIORAL CORRELATES

Our primary hypothesis has been that drug use is only one aspect of the more general "happening" scene and reflects a broad range of other "anti-establishment" behaviors. Support for this hypothesis comes from our finding that drug use varies considerably according to such activities as participating in "happenings" (34.3% drug users among those who participate frequently vs. 17.0% among those who do so rarely), reading "underground" newspapers (42.0% users among frequent readers vs. 3.7% among non-readers), and participating in mass protests (45.9% among those who have done so more than twice vs. 15.2% for non-participators). It appears from these results that drug use in the form of smoking marijuana is highly associated with "non-conformist" behavior.

If we look at the student's cumulative grade as an index of his academic behavior, we see that drug use is more likely to occur among the poorer than the better students. Among those with an average grade of 3.0 or higher, only 15.3 per cent report the use of drugs as compared to 31.0 per cent among those with an average of 2.5 or less. This difference in grade probably represents one more manifestation of the rejection of the "hard work-success" ethic of conventional society.

THE "HANG-LOOSE" ETHIC: ATTITUDINAL CORRELATES

Similar differences in frequency of drug use are found in relation to a wide range of educational, political, and social attitudes and values indicative of a rejection of the established order. Drug use is more likely to be reported by those students who are relatively antagonistic to the educational system and who are dissatisfied with the education they are receiving. For example, among those students who disagree with the statement, "American colleges today should place more emphasis on teaching American ideals and values," more than seven times as many are frequent smokers of marijuana than among those who agree (13.8% vs. 1.8%). Similarly, whereas 30.2 per cent of those students who "often" feel that what they are learning is a waste of time smoke marijuana, only 12.9 per cent of those who don't feel this way do so. However drug use does not mean "apathy" toward academic life—more smokers of marijuana are to be found among those students who believe that students should have a more active role in making decisions about student life than among those who do not (28.4% vs. 11.1%).

On the political scene, drug use is much more likely to occur if the student is opposed to the Vietnam war (37.5% among those favoring immediate military withdrawal vs. 3.0% among those supporting President Johnson's policy). Drug users are also more frequent among those who believe that "human lives are too important to be sacrificed for any form of government" (32.0% vs. 12.6%). Opposition to the draft is another political view associated with drug use. Among those who are opposed to military service, 35.2 per cent use drugs as compared to 15.0 per cent among those who are not opposed, and, in fact, for those male students whose decision to attend college was affected by the possibility of being drafted, 41.7 per cent are drug users as compared to 25.2 per cent among those for whom this was not a consideration.

Social attitudes also reflect this "hang-loose" ethic on the part of drug users. Drug users are more likely to be found among those who feel it is all right to get around the law if you don't actually break it (34.6% vs. 13.8%) and who feel that the "hippie" way of life represents a desire for serious change as opposed to an unproductive expression of non-conformism (26.6% vs. 10.5%). The student who reports that he expects to get the most satisfaction out of life by means of his leisure time recreational activities is a much more frequent user of marijuana than the student who values participation in civic affairs or family relations (45.2% vs. 12.5% and 17.0%). An indication of possible family conflict among drug users is given by the higher proportion of drug users among those students who feel that their parents don't respect their opinions (29.2% vs. 15.3%).

One finding in regard to social attitudes appears contrary to many claims made about drug use. A series of four questions designed to index "alienation" (i.e., "These days a person does not really know whom he can count on"; "If you don't watch yourself, people will take advantage of you.") showed no statistically significant relationships to smoking marijuana, despite the claim of Halleck (15) that "Smoking marijuana has become almost an emblem of alienation." Given the large number of significant differences found, this lack of any association between drug use and alienation is impressive. The "hang-loose" ethic, while it may represent antagonism to the conventional world, does not appear to create apathy and withdrawal. Subscribers to this ethic are not so much "anomic" in regard to society in general as critical of the existing "Establishment" in specific.

THE "HANG-LOOSE" ETHIC: PERSONALITY CORRELATES

The more the student's self-image tends to be rebellious, cynical, anti-establishment, "hippie," and apathetic, the more likely is he to smoke marijuana. Conversely, the more his self-image tends to be conformist, well-behaved, moral, and "square," the less likely is he to make use of marijuana. The greatest differences are to be found between those students who regard themselves as "hippies" (39% difference in favor of use) or well-behaved (37% difference against use). The smallest differences occur in relation to apathy (8% difference in favor of use) and cynicism (10% difference in favor of use).

These contrasts in self-image between users and non-users are congruent with the previous findings in relation to behavioral and attitudinal correlates. Such attitudes as disrespect for the law and skepticism about the worthwhileness of college, coupled with such behaviors as participating in mass protests and "happenings," match the self-portrait of the marijuana smoker as anti-establishment, cynical, and rebellious. If we view these traits as indicative of an underlying value system, we can quite readily see the contrast in "Protestant" vs. "hang-loose" ethic between marijuana smokers and non-smokers. These self-characterizations do lend face validity to the general public stereotyping of the marijuana smoker as "deviant" and the marijuana's own stereotyping of those who do not use marijuana as "square."

DEMOGRAPHIC CONTROLS

Each of the major differences in behavior, attitudes, and personality between users and non-users of marijuana was examined separately by sex, income, and religious group. Since, for example, males are more likely than females to smoke marijuana and also to subscribe to the "hang-loose" ethic, the possibility exists that both ethic and drug use are reflections of sex and are not really associated in and of themselves.

Analysis of the demographic control tables shows that this, by and large, is not the case. In almost every instance, the differences in marijuana use occur independently for both the demographic control and the behavioral, attitudinal, and personality correlates of the "hang-loose" ethic. In other words, the "hang-loose" ethic continues to be related to marijuana smoking regardless of the subgroup of the student population being studied.

This is illustrated in Table 2, which presents the relationship between several different indices of the "hang-loose" ethic and

*Table 2.* Relationship between "hang-loose" ethic and marijuana use, according to sex

| "Hang-loose" ethic | (Percent smoking marijuana) | |
| --- | --- | --- |
| | Male | Female |
| **Behavioral** | | |
| Participate in mass protests | | |
| No | 9.9(141) | 3.8(212) |
| Once or twice | 12.5 (48) | 5.9 (51) |
| More than twice | 40.0 (25) | 16.7 (12) |
| Attend a "happening" | | |
| Rarely | 8.6(116) | 2.4(168) |
| Occasionally | 15.5 (58) | 3.7 (82) |
| Frequently | 33.3 (33) | 20.8 (24) |
| **Attitudinal** | | |
| "It is all right to get around the law, if you don't actually break it." | | |
| Disagree | 18.2 (99) | 11.3(168) |
| Undecided | 34.0 (47) | 19.0 (63) |
| Agree | 40.3 (62) | 26.7 (45) |
| "How strongly do you approve or disapprove of students having premarital sexual intercourse?" | | |
| Disapprove | 0.0 (18) | 1.2 (81) |
| Undecided | 26.8 (56) | 11.1 (90) |
| Approve | 33.8(136) | 33.3(102) |
| **Personality** | | |
| "Anti-establishment" | | |
| Not at all well | 18.0(111) | 12.1(182) |
| A little | 32.4 (34) | 13.2 (38) |
| Undecided and well | 46.9 (64) | 32.7 (55) |
| "Well-behaved" | | |
| Very well | 15.6 (32) | 4.6 (65) |
| Fairly well | 21.4(131) | 17.8(185) |
| Undecided and not well | 56.2 (48) | 27.6 (29) |

marijuana use separately for males and females. First, we note that males are more likely than females both to subscribe to the "hang-loose" ethic and to smoke marijuana. Second, we see that for males and females separately, the more the student adheres to the "hang-loose" ethic, either in his or her behavior, attitudes, or personality, the more likely he or she is to smoke marijuana. Thus, we conclude that both sex and ethic contribute independently to marijuana use. This same conclusion appears in general for other demographic variables and for other indices of the "hang-loose" ethic.

We can also see from Table 2, in general, that the relationship between the "hang-loose" ethic and marijuana use is somewhat higher among the males. Also, the differences due to sex are much smaller than those due to variations in behavior, attitudes, or personality. It would thus appear that one's ethic is a more important determinant of marijuana use than one's sex. For example, in all cases, those females who subscribe to the "hang-loose" ethic are much more likely to use marijuana than those males who do not.

ATTITUDE TOWARD USE AND FREQUENCY OF USE BY OTHER STUDENTS

In the same way that we have analyzed the student's use of marijuana according to various correlates of the "hang-loose" ethic, we can also examine his attitudes toward such use and his reports about how many of the students he knows also smoke marijuana. (Since so few students report feeling any pressure to smoke marijuana, this aspect is omitted from the following analysis.) We present the results of this analysis in a summary fashion in Table 3. With

*Table 3.* Relationship between attitude to use of marijuana, frequency of use by other students and selected characteristics

| Student characteristics* | Attitude to use of marijuana† | Frequency of use by other students‡ |
|---|---|---|
| Demographic | | |
| Sex | .14§ | .19 |
| Income | n.s. | .14 |
| Behavior patterns | | |
| Attend "happening" | .17 | .30 |
| Read "underground" newspaper | .30 | .26 |
| Participate in mass protest | .16 | .20 |

\* See previous text for question wording used to determine student characteristics.

† Question: "How strongly do you approve or disapprove of students smoking marijuana?" (Strongly approve, Approve, Undecided, Disapprove, Strongly disapprove).

‡ Question: How frequently do most of the students you know smoke marijuana?" (Frequently, Occasionally, Seldom, Never, Don't know).

§ Coefficients of association as determined by Cramer's V.

| Student characteristics* | Attitude to use of marijuana† | Frequency of use by other students‡ |
| --- | --- | --- |
| **Self-image** | | |
| "Hippie" | .28 | .30 |
| Anti-establishment | .23 | .19 |
| Well-behaved | .23 | .22 |
| **Educational values** | | |
| College a waste of time | .16 | .16 |
| Students active in student affairs | .14 | .13 |
| **Political values** | | |
| Vietnam a mistake | .19 | .20 |
| Human lives not to be sacrificed in war | .12 | .12 |
| Conscientious objection a loophole | .19 | .17 |
| **Social values** | | |
| Approval of pre-marital sex, if consent | .32 | .28 |
| Approval of abortion | .22 | .20 |
| Approval of birth control | .22 | .17 |
| Approval of law-breaking | .15 | .14 |
| **Frequency of other student behaviors** | | |
| Drink alcoholic beverages | .15 | .19 |
| Smoke marijuana | .42 | — |
| Take LSD | .29 | .41 |
| Have sexual intercourse | .30 | .37 |
| **Attitude to student behaviors** | | |
| Drink alcoholic beverages | .25 | .14 |
| Smoke marijuana | — | .42 |
| Take LSD | .33 | .30 |
| Have sexual intercourse | .42 | .31 |

only one exception—the relationship of family income to attitudes to marijuana use—all of the variables listed are significantly related (chi square $p < .05$) to attitudes to use and frequency of use by other students in the same direction as the student's own use of marijuana. That is, the behavioral, attitudinal, and personality correlates of the "hang-loose" ethic also relate to one's attitude toward smoking marijuana and the frequency of marijuana use among the students one knows. These three aspects of attitudes toward use, use by one's friends, and use by oneself, then, all become part of the general picture of marijuana use as such use reflects adherence to the "hang-loose" ethic.

The relative size of the associations (keeping in mind the variations from question to question of the number of answer categories) can be determined in an approximate way from the size of Cramer's V, a coefficient of association (2). Self-image tends to be more highly related than either attitudes or behavior. Sex attitudes are, in general, more highly related than either political or educational values. Very high associations are to be found among attitudes and behaviors in regard to smoking marijuana, taking LSD, having sexual intercourse, and drinking alcoholic beverages, in about that order.

In summary, this table of associations underscores the interrelationships between attitudes and use, and between the various correlates of the "hang-loose" ethic and such attitudes and use. It is quite clear that the more one's behaviors, attitudes, and personality conform to the "hang-loose" ethic, the more likely one will be to approve of smoking marijuana and the more likely is it that one will associate with other students who smoke marijuana.

Finally, in Table 4, we show the mutual effects of attitude toward smoking marijuana and several aspects of the "hang-loose" ethic upon the use of marijuana. By and large, similar differences are found for all other aspects of the "hang-loose" ethic. As hy-

*Table 4.* Relationship between "hang-loose" ethic, attitude toward marijuana use and use of marijuana

| "Hang-loose" ethic | | (Percent smoking marijuana) | |
|---|---|---|---|
| | | Attitude to use of marijuana | |
| | | Favorable | Unfavorable |
| Attend a "happening" | | | |
| | Rarely | 31.3 (83) | 4.5(201) |
| | Occasionally | 51.9 (54) | 11.8 (84) |
| | Frequently | 73.5 (34) | 25.6 (19) |
| "It's all right to get around the law, if you don't actually break it" | | | |
| | Disagree | 37.3 (75) | 4.7(191) |
| | Undecided | 42.2 (45) | 14.3 (61) |
| | Agree | 60.4 (48) | 14.6 (55) |
| "Anti-establishment" | | | |
| | No | 39.8(103) | 6.6(260) |
| | Yes | 54.9 (71) | 19.3 (47) |

pothesized, these two variables are independently related to drug use with the most frequent use occurring among those students who have both a favorable attitude toward the use of marijuana and an adherence to the "hang-loose" ethic. In general, an unfavorable attitude toward the use of marijuana will be equated with the absence of marijuana smoking. However, even among those with an unfavorable attitude, use will be higher with adherence to the "hang-loose" ethic. Similarly, given a favorable attitude toward use of marijuana, actual use is much more likely to take place among those students displaying "hang-loose" attitudes, behavior, and personality.

On the basis of these interrelationships of demographic characteristics, attitudes, behavior, and personality to drug use, the following sequence or chain of events appears quite probable (although it would require a prospective study to test it); adherence to the "hang-loose" ethic is more likely to occur among certain predisposed personality types (i.e., rebellious, cynical) and in certain social sub-groups (i.e., males, non-religious); such adherence is likely to lead to a favorable attitude toward smoking marijuana both for its "high" effects and its symbolism of rebellion against authority; this favorable attitude will be supported by other students who also embrace the "hang-loose" ethic and engage in similar overt and covert expressions of rejection of the established order. Finally, given this climate of opinion and behavior, the smoking of marijuana becomes almost a "natural" act for many students far removed from the public's current efforts to define it either as a legal or a health problem.

## SUMMARY AND DISCUSSION

The data presented in this report strongly support the major hypothesis that the more the student embraces the "hang-loose" ethic, the more frequently will he make use of marijuana. Also supported is the further hypothesis that certain social sub-groups such as males will more frequently both smoke marijuana and adhere to the "hang-loose" ethic, but that regardless of group membership, the "hang-loose" ethic will be related to marijuana use. In regard to attitudes toward use, we find, as hypothesized, that the more the student subscribes to the "hang-loose" ethic, the more favorable will he be toward marijuana use; and the more favorable he is, the more will he actually use marijuana. These attitudes toward use and the "hang-loose" ethic become independent factors in marijuana smoking, reinforcing each other with the greatest use occurring among those students with a favorable attitude who also believe in the "hang-loose" ethic. Finally, the student's use of marijuana is strongly supported when his friends also smoke marijuana.

These findings have significance for both sociological theory and social action. From a theoretical point of view, they support the interpretation of drug use as part of a sub-cultural group way of life. Among students, this sub-culture is strongly characterized by a "hang-loose" ethic which attempts to cut itself loose from the traditional "establishment" and to develop freedom from conformity and the search for new experiences. This culture becomes expressed in such behaviors as attending "happenings," reading underground newspapers, participating in mass protests, avoiding the draft, engaging in sexual intercourse and, very much to the point of this report, smoking marijuana. Such use of marijuana constitutes an important means both of attaining "freedom" from the pressures of society and of expressing antagonism toward the "unfair" laws and restrictions of that society. For such students, marijuana serves much the same function as "social drinking" does for their parents, and their "law breaking" has the same social sanctions as drinking did during Prohibition. And just as "social drinking" is a far cry from "alcoholism," so is smoking marijuana far removed from "narcotics addiction."

The relationship of both social drinking to alcoholism and smoking marijuana to narcotics addiction illustrates a significant interaction between social problems, health problems, and legal problems (13). A social act (e.g., one carried out by members of a group as part of the sub-cultural norm of that group) will be labelled a social problem when it conflicts with the accepted norms of the larger society. In this sense, marijuana smoking among students has become a social problem, whereas drinking alcohol has not. The type of corrective action "legitimatized" by the larger society to meet this problem will then determine whether it is viewed as a health or a legal problem. The more the social problem threatens the "value system" of the society, the more likely is it to be labelled a legal as opposed to a health problem and to be assigned to the police rather than the doctor. Restriction and punishment become the means for handling the problem rather than understanding and treatment.

In the absence of any clear-act evidence that (1) marijuana smoking is physiologically addictive or has serious health effects, and

(2) use of marijuana leads to crime and delinquency or use of other drugs, it seems premature to view it as either a health or a legal problem (6). Our data would strongly suggest that use of marijuana is predominantly a social act favored by a sub-group in our society which happens to be disenchanted with the established order and for whom such use has become simply a normal preference for their own particular recreational drug (10). To crack down on these youth with all of the powerful forces of law and order and to justify such a restriction of freedom in the name of preventing crime or disease seems more an uncontrolled expression of adult moral indignation and righteousness than of human concern or social justice—and, sadly, an ineffective and destructive expression at that (5). While there can be little question that the "hang-loose" ethic is contrary to the Protestant ethic and the spirit of capitalism, and may be socially disapproved for that and other reasons, the issue, it seems to us, should be openly faced and debated as one of conflicting social values and not of crime or health. As formulated by Simmons (10), "It [the marijuana issue] seems to be the pivot around which far deeper conflicts and confrontations are raging—oldsters versus youngsters, hippies versus straight society, administered morality versus personal freedom."

Surely, it should be possible to express one's disapproval of marijuana and to seek its control without making its use a crime against society.

## REFERENCES

1. Becker, H. S., "Becoming a marijuana user," *American Journal of Sociology*, LIX (Nov. 1953), pp. 235–242.
2. Blalock, Hubert M., *Social Statistics* (New York: McGraw-Hill, 1960), p. 230.
3. Goldsen, Rose K., *et al.*, *What College Students Think* (Princeton: D. Van Nostrand, 1960), p. 199.
4. Jacob, Phillip E., *Changing Values in College* (New York: Harper and Bros., 1957).
5. Lindesmith, Alfred R., *The Addict and the Law* (Bloomington: The Indiana University Press, 1965).
6. Mayor's Committee on Marijuana, "The marijuana problem in the City of New York," 1944, pp. 233–360 in David Solomon (ed.), *The Marijuana Papers* (Indianapolis: The Bobbs-Merrill Co., 1966). For an excellent analysis of this report see

David Arnold, "The meaning of the La Guardia report," pp. 111–135 in Jerry Simmons (ed.), *Marijuana: Myths and Realities* (North Hollywood, Calif.: Brandon House, 1967).

7. McGlothlin, W. H., "Toward a rational view of marijuana," 1967, pp. 163–214 in Jerry Simmons (ed.), *Marijuana: Myths and Realities* (North Hollywood, Calif.: Brandon House).

8. Plaut, Thomas F., *Alcohol Problems: A Report of the Nation* (New York: Oxford University Press, 1967).

9. *Reader's Digest* (November 1967).

10. Simmons, Jerry L. (ed.), *Marijuana: Myths and Realities* (North Hollywood, Calif.: Brandon House, 1967), p. 11.

11. Simmons, Jerry L., and Barry Winograd, *It's Happening: A Portrait of the Youth Scene Today* (Santa Barbara, Calif.: Marc-Laird Publications, 1966), pp. 86, 12.

12. Straus, Robert and Seldon D. Bacon, *Drinking in College* (New Haven: Yale University Press, 1953).

13. Suchman, Edward A., *Sociology and the Field of Public Health* (New York: Russell Sage Foundation, 1963), pp. 58–64.

14. Suchman, E., "The addictive diseases as socio-environmental health problems," 1963, pp. 123–143 in H. Freeman, *et al.* (eds.), *Handbook of Medical Sociology* (Englewood Cliffs, N.J.: Prentice-Hall, Inc.).

15. *Time* (May 19, 1967).

# The Use of Hallucinogenic Drugs Among College Students

WILLIAM H. McGLOTHLIN AND SIDNEY COHEN

Several authors have recently voiced concern over the increasing unsupervised use of LSD, psilocybin, morning glory seeds and other hallucinogenic substances, especially by college students (2, 3, 4). The popularity of the milder hallucinogen, marihuana, is also claimed to be on the upswing. To our knowledge, however, there have been no actual surveys on the incidence of hallucinogenic drug use. The selection of subjects (January 1965) for an experiment on the effects of LSD provided the opportunity to obtain data on this question as well as some information on the personality differences between those attracted and those opposed to such behavior.

The subjects were U. S.-born male graduate students at a large urban university who responded to an advertisement for paid experimental subjects. They had no prior knowledge that the study involved LSD, or indeed, that it was a psychological or drug experiment. Prior to learning the nature of the experiment, they were given an interview which included questions on the use of hallucinogens embedded in a larger section dealing with usage of tobacco, alcohol and other stimulants, tranquilizers and sedatives. Of the 121 students interviewed, only four reported experience with the stronger hallucinogens. All four had taken peyote (two once and two twice); one of these had also had LSD (once in an experiment and once unsupervised). Three of the four had had experience with marihuana and two had taken morning glory seeds, although none did so regularly. Of the remaining 117, ten had tried marihuana and two morning glory seeds. Of these, seven reported only a single trial, two twice and three more than twice.

Following this portion of the interview the subjects were informed that the current experiment involved the use of drugs and that one of the drugs they might receive was LSD. They were questioned concerning their knowledge of the hallucinogens and

Reprinted from the *American Journal of Psychiatry*, CXXII, pp. 572–574, 1965. Copyright 1965, the American Psychiatric Association.

their reactions and expectations to the prospect of possibly receiving LSD. Seventeen percent had never heard of LSD; 12 percent had read fairly widely on the subject; the remainder had only casual knowledge acquired from magazine articles or T.V. Seventeen percent were doubtful about participating because of concern about the dangers of LSD; 13 percent were enthusiastic in the sense that they hoped to acquire personal insight or gain some other lasting benefit from the experience; the remainder were simply curious as to what the effects would be and had no expectations of lasting effects, either beneficial or detrimental.

In addition to the interview, the Minnesota Multiphasic Personality Inventory (MMPI) was administered for screening purposes, and Aas' test of hypnotic susceptibility and the Myers-Briggs Type Indicator for matching experimental and control groups. This permitted the comparison of groups with positive, neutral and negative attitudes toward taking LSD from the standpoint of the limited personality variables measured. The Aas test is intended to measure hypnotic susceptibility using questions on naturally occurring hypnotic-like experiences (1). The Myers-Briggs test is based on Jung's theory of type and provides four indices: extroversion-introversion (EI), sensing-intuition (SN), thinking-feeling (TF) and judgement-perception (JP). EI refers to outward- vs. inward-turning personality, SN measures the extent to which intuition or the unconscious is utilized along with the senses in the process of perception, TF refers to preference for thinking or feeling in making judgements and JP indicates a preference for a judging or perceptive attitude in dealing with the environment (5).

The positive, neutral and negative LSD groups are compared on the above variables in the table following.[1] The positive group is made up of the four who had previously taken peyote plus 11 subjects who were strongly desirous of receiving LSD in the hopes of obtaining beneficial effects. The 57 subjects in the neutral group reacted routinely to the question of expectation—the most frequent response being curiosity as to what type of hallucinations they might experience. The negative group includes 17 who withdrew from the experiment and gave as their reason concern over the safety of LSD; also included in this group are nine subjects who indicated doubt for this reason at the time of the interview but remained in the experiment. Most of the subjects who withdrew did not do so

---

[1] Does not include 22 subjects who were eliminated from the experiment because of a history of psychosis in immediate family, presently in psychotherapy, doubtful MMPI profiles and interview impressions.

Personality differences between students with positive, neutral and negative attitudes towards taking LSD

| Variable | Attitude toward LSD | | | F ratio |
| | Positive N = 15 | Neutral N = 58 | Negative N = 26 | |
|---|---|---|---|---|
| Hypnotic susceptibility | 32.4 | 29.6 | 27.5 | 3.26* |
| Myers-Briggs Type Indicator | | | | |
| Extroversion-introversion† | 90.5 | 101.5 | 100.5 | 1.24 |
| Sensing-intuition | 135.4 | 113.7 | 110.1 | 5.30** |
| Thinking-feeling | 96.2 | 90.1 | 82.5 | 1.85 |
| Judgement-perception | 114.6 | 100.2 | 84.8 | 5.24** |
| Percent married | 13 | 36 | 50 | |
| Percent attending church | 0 | 21 | 25 | |
| Percent who have tried marihuana or morning glory seeds | 60 | 5 | 0 | |

\* Significant beyond the .05 level of confidence.

\*\* Significant beyond the .01 level of confidence.

† Scores below 100 are in the extroversion direction, those above 100 in the introversion direction, and similarly for the other three scales.

immediately; rather, they declined after being advised not to participate by wives, physicians, parents or other persons whom they consulted.

The Aas test results show that students who are desirous of experiencing the hallucinogenic drug phenomena tend to score higher on hypnotic susceptibility. An analysis of variance results in an F-ratio which is significant beyond the five percent level of confidence. The results for two of the Myers-Briggs scales (SN and JP) show significant differences beyond the one percent level of confidence. Students with a positive attitude toward taking LSD tend to exhibit higher preferences for the intuition and perception ends of the scales.

Other characteristics of the pro-LSD group are higher proportions of unmarried and nonchurch attenders than are found in the other two groups. Also, virtually all the students who have had experience with marihuana or morning glory seeds are included in the pro-LSD group. Other variables (not shown in the table above) which exhibited little difference between groups were age, undergraduate grade-point average, field of study, income of father and MMPI scores.

## DISCUSSION

The incidence of hallucinogenic drug use in the present sample of male graduate students is quite low compared to the estimated rates among students of certain other universities of comparable size. Of the sample of 121, only three percent had taken the stronger hallucinogens and 12 percent had tried marihuana or morning glory seeds. Of the latter group, the majority had limited their experimentation to one or two trials. No reason is apparent why the university from which our subjects were obtained should differ from others where high hallucinogenic drug-taking behavior has been reported. It does not seem likely that our subjects misrepresented their drug-consuming habits since these questions were asked in a neutral, nonjudgmental manner.

The personality differences found among groups with positive, neutral and negative attitudes towards taking LSD are generally consistent with expectations. Persons desirous of experiencing the hallucinogenic phenomena tend to report a higher than average number of naturally occurring states of altered consciousness. In terms of Jung's theory of types, their perception of the world is more heavily influenced by unconscious or intuitive processes. They are reluctant to make a firm judgment or conclusion, tending to remain open-minded toward the possibility of additional evidence.

## REFERENCES

1. Aas, A., "Hypnotizability as a Function of Nonhypnotic Experiences," *J. Abnorm. Soc. Psychol.* 66: 142–150, 1963.
2. Cole, J. O., and M. M. Katz, "The Psychotomimetic Drugs. An Overview," *J.A.M.A.* 187:758–761, 1964.
3. Farnsworth, D. L., "Hallucinogenic Agents," *J.A.M.A.* 185:878–880, 1963.
4. Ingram, A. L., "Morning Glory Seed Reaction," *J.A.M.A.* 190:1133–1134, 1964.
5. Myers, I. B., *"The Myers-Briggs Type Indicator* (Manual) (Princeton: Educational Testing Service, 1962).

# Psychedelic Drugs

MAX RINKEL

The psychedelic[1] drugs, also known as hallucinogenics, psychotomimetics, dysleptics and psychotoxics, are normal constituents of "magic plants."[2] Originally magic plants were used only in ceremonial or sacred contexts, and some are still so used. The following are major representatives of the psychedelic drugs: LSD (d-lysergic acid diethylamide), derived from ergot fungus; psilocybine, derived from the Mexican "sacred" mushroom, Teonanacatl; and mescaline, derived from the peyote cactus, Lophophora Williamsii.

Exactly how these drugs work in the human brain is still a mystery. Many theories, not yet sufficiently supported, have been advanced, including that of interaction with brain enzyme systems. What is clear is that ingestion causes alterations of the mind, described by some as a "psychedelic experience," i.e., a "journey to new realms of consciousness," an "expanding of consciousness." Known, too, however, is that the nature of this experience may range from celestial ecstasy to pure horror, the feeling of "going mad." Their extraordinary effects upon the mind have been the subject of scientific investigation, of heated controversy and widespread misuse.

The psychedelics were introduced in this country in 1949, and the first organized research with LSD was set up at the Boston Psychopathic Hospital (now the Massachusetts Mental Health Center) for the study of experimentally produced psychopathological phenomena which showed similarities to those of an acute schizophrenic attack. These experiments were soon followed by the experimental study of social-psychiatric problems, such as the group interaction of persons who had taken LSD.

At present psychedelics are legitimately used in research for the purpose of cutting short psychoanalysis and as an aid in

Reprinted from the *American Journal of Psychiatry*, CXXII, pp. 1415–1416, 1966. Copyright 1966, the American Psychiatric Association.

[1] The word psychedelic was coined by Humphrey Osmond; delic is derived from the Greek word, dēlos, which means manifest, evident.

[2] There was an exhibition of "magic plants" at the 1965 annual meeting of the APA in New York by the Committee on Transcultural Psychiatry. The plants are now on permanent exhibition at the Botanical Museum of Harvard University.

psychotherapy for the treatment of alcoholism and some other psychiatric conditions, for example, autism in children.

Psychedelics have been tried in the study of religious experiences. In the Native American Church, peyote is the holy sacrament, and the newly formed Church of the Awakening seems to have as its sole purpose "to provide for those who request it, the opportunity to have a psychedelic experience."

Psychedelics, especially LSD and psilocybine, have been used in an attempt to promote psychological growth and mystic experiences and to enhance creative activity. However, no recognized works of art have yet been produced under the influence of LSD or as the result of an LSD experience. On the contrary, as Rinkel and Bender demonstrated, under the direct influence of LSD the drawings of a famous American painter progressively deteriorated. Years later, when the artist was asked whether the LSD experience had improved his artistic creativity, his reply was in the negative.

Perhaps the most serious controversy could be summarized under the heading of the "LSD Movement." This is a recent development, and unique on the American scene. Its vociferous adherents are composed of artists, writers, painters, musicians and their hangers-on in Bohemia, and of a transcendental group comprised predominantly of psychologists, philosophers, theologians and others. This movement teaches a unified world view with meaning beyond that drawn from empirical reality and obtained by the use of LSD. The cause of this movement is freedom from internal constraints, freedom to explore one's self and the cosmos and freedom to use LSD and other drugs as a means thereto. Followers of this movement believe that everyone, and this includes children as well as adults, ought to take LSD. They base their demands on the belief that LSD is harmless, that it is not a drug but a "food"—a sort of vitamin for the brain—and that the occurrence of psychosis and other harmful effects is not the result of LSD but of the setting.

Quite the contrary is true. Reports in medical journals from here and abroad (see *Amer. J. Psychiat.* 121:238–244, Sept. 1964) provide evidence that dangers are involved even in the legitimate use of these drugs. These dangers are many times multiplied by their illegitimate use. Persons who have taken LSD obtained on the black market become psychotic often weeks or months after the ingestion of LSD. They are being admitted to hospitals in an ever-increasing number. This and the widespread use of "bootlegged" LSD by college and high school students have led to the flood of publicity about the psychedelic drugs in lead articles of national magazines and newspapers and over radio and television. This in turn caused the Food and Drug Administration to outlaw the use of these drugs except for carefully selected and approved scientific experiments. On April 6 this agency sent a letter to 2,000 colleges and universities warning of the marked increase in the illegal use of drugs on campus and urging concerted action lest "an untold number of students suffer permanent mental or physical injury."

In its endeavor to restrict the use of psychedelic drugs, the government has had the full cooperation of Sandoz Pharmaceuticals, the sole legitimate producer of LSD and psilocybine. Sandoz, in conformity with the FDA, will make these drugs available only to the following: grantees of the NIMH (number of grant requested); investigators within the confines of a state psychiatric institution, with a letter of approval from the respective Commissioner of Mental Health; and investigators of the Veterans Administration with approval of the head office.

While some private investigators may protest this action as being negative-minded, the close cooperation of Sandoz and the government is highly commendable in view of the dangers that do exist, particularly for those who believe in self-experimentation with LSD to solve their own problems.

We have heard complaints that the government is restricting if not suppressing LSD research. That is not true. The United States government, through the National Institute of Mental Health, has already allocated a total of half a million dollars for clinical and laboratory research with LSD. It is prepared to spend even more money for research projects which conform to the high standard demanded by this government agency.

The cult aspect of the LSD movement has rendered serious damage to the scientific study of this group of drugs. However, uncontrolled and uncritical experimentation should not be allowed to create a hysterical attitude which will hinder or obstruct legitimate experimentation with LSD, an excellent tool of research in biological psychiatry.

# Motivational Factors in Psychedelic Drug Use by Male College Students

EDWIN LIPINSKI AND B. G. LIPINSKI

The material for this article was gathered over. a period of two years in psychiatric and psychological interview settings with students attending a prominent private university. They sought help for problems related to psychedelic drug use or spoke of psychedelic drug use while seeking help for seemingly unrelated problems. Others were experiencing no problems in drug use, but knew of our interest in the field and hence came in to talk about their experiences. Finally there was a group of students who attended informal seminars for the purpose of presenting general information regarding psychedelic drugs.

In this discussion, psychedelic drugs refers mainly to d-lysergic acid diethylamide (LSD) but also to dimethyltryptamine (DMT), morning glory seeds, psilocybin and mescaline. Occasional reference will be made to marijuana, not because it should be included with the more potent drugs such as LSD, but because similar motivational statements are often made by students who use one or other of the compounds or both. For the sake of convenience, we have treated motivational factors in three major overlapping areas—social or societal, peer group, and individual. It should be stressed at the outset that such division is artificial and merely provides a vehicle for presentation. A single motivational factor rarely accounts for psychedelic drug use. Most students, when provided ample time to consider their motives initially reflected on individual needs or views, and often reflected on peer group influences and almost invariably discussed the social relevance of their behavior.

## SOCIAL OR SOCIETAL FACTORS

### 1. PROHIBITION VERSUS PROMISE

One of the prime aims of university education is to teach problem-solving techniques. Students are taught to seek out objective infor-

From the *Journal of the American College Health Association*, December 1967, XVI, No. 2, pp. 145–149. Reprinted by permission of the authors and the American College Health Association.

mation in a wide-ranging fashion, to evaluate critically, and to
arrive at independent conclusions. Passive mastery of course work
is not enough. "Creativity" is the valued measure of a person. It is
the creative individual who *counts*. Paralleling the development of
problem-solving techniques and creative strivings, most students
are in a period of their development when they are experimenting,
testing and rebelling.

What has this to do with psychedelic drug use? The law, various
social groups, and the student's parents say that the use of
psychedelic drugs is wrong. The prohibitions frequently convey a
moral judgment often supported by poorly gathered data, exaggerated, somewhat hysterical newspaper reports and so forth.
Although the warnings reflect genuine concern and even alarm,
exaggerations are easily discerned by the enquiring student, and the
entire prohibition is viewed as false. In those instances, where the
student does not approach the problem in a methodical, information
gathering fashion, the prohibition encounters the student's developing sense of independence expressed through questioning, testing
and rebellion.

Parental and social sanctions are currently competing with encouragement from a small but highly articulate segment of the academic community which presents the student with a promise. On
some campuses, highly regarded professors hold out the promise of
creativity to be found through the use of psychedelic drugs. The
lay and professional literature abounds with a whole spectrum of
promises. Some examples are

> The CE (i.e., consciousness-expanding) drugs unplug these
> narrow programs. They unplug the ego, the game machinery,
> and the mind (that cluster of game concepts)[1], and

> There is little doubt that psychedelic experiences involve cre-
> ative perception. . . .More and more paintings, poems, films and
> musical compositions are starting to appear as clear and obvi-
> ous psychedelic products.[2]

No matter how carefully the promise is qualified, that is, "the right
circumstances" or "in a controlled setting," the seductive message
remains. The seduction is even extended by many authors who
appeal to a daring, exploring, face-up-to-life motive:

[1] D. Solomon (ed.), *LSD: The Consciousness Expanding Drug* (New York: Putnam,
1966), p. 105.

[2] R. Alpert, S. Cohen, and L. Schiller, *LSD* (New York: New American Library,
1966), p. 68.

Thus what we know for certain implies that these chemicals cannot be used without caution. But this applies equally to antibiotics, whisky, household ammonia, the automobile, the kitchen knife, electricity and matches. No worthwhile life can be lived without risks, despite current American superstitions to the contrary— . . .[3]

or to sportsmanship, humility, etc.:

Those of us who play the game of 'applied mysticism' respect and support good gamesmanship. You pick out your game. You learn the rules, rituals, concepts. You play fairly and cleanly. . . You win today's game with humility. You lose to-morrow's game with dignity. . . .[4]

## 2. THE CONTRADICTORY MESSAGE

Closely aligned with the previous dichotomy of prohibition versus promise is the problem of the contradictory message. On the one hand students feel that they are asked to be adult and to prepare themselves for responsibility and leadership, while, on the other hand, they feel that rules of behavior, areas of competence, and levels of function appear to be predetermined. The message seems to be "act like a responsible, grown up person, but we will tell you what is right and what is wrong." This is seen in campus drinking laws, various rules and regulations regarding dress and appearance, the influence of neighboring communities on the campus, and the determination of many university officials to act as the absent parent. The taking of psychedelic drugs is one way for the student to establish autonomy and undergo an experience and viewpoint which few people in the "Establishment" share.

## 3. WHAT DOES THE LAW MEAN?

A further extension of the first two points is the current preoccupation by many student and nonstudent groups to question the basis for certain laws. Prohibitions regarding marijuana are especially central in this regard. For the student who gathers the facts, it is difficult to respect the legal status of prohibitions regarding marijuana. Relevant and well-documented empirical studies do not support the legal point of view. Public statements by many people with much knowledge in the psychedelic field indicate that current

---

[3] Solomon, op. cit., p. 121.

[4] Solomon, op. cit., p. 118.

legislation regarding psychedelic drugs is precipitant, ill-conceived and unworkable. Students express concern about the philosophy of legislation which provides prohibitions in order to protect the individual from himself. Such basic questions find a receptive climate during an era of direct testing of questionable laws.

## 4. "WELL, WHAT ABOUT - - -"?

In rebuttal to prohibitions regarding the use of psychedelic drugs, students often reply: "Well, what about alcohol, or cigarettes, or . . ." and a list is given of items with proven physiological and psychological deleterious effects.

## PEER GROUP FACTORS

### 1. "IT'S COOL, MAN"

Peer influences can be at once the most supportive and most devastating experiences in a university student's future development. Being able to talk to one's peers about your "high" or explaining the functions of the "ground control" man to a group of curious classmates or freshmen may be a passport to acceptance or to heroic elevation. Extensions on the basic principle are constantly occurring now that psychedelic drug use is more widespread on the campus. Your "high" may not be too interesting any longer. It may require a description of how you took "2,000 micros," or of how you remained "up" for a week, or even a description of your "horrors" or how your friend "freaked out" or "blew his mind."

### 2. CHALLENGE OR DARE

Little explanation of this motive is required. In sophisticated circles a challenge or dare is rarely presented directly. Words like "sincerity," "really communicating," "true humility," and so forth are the vehicles to goad the student to test himself. An unfortunate peripheral development that is occurring with increasing frequency in high school and younger college student groups takes advantage of the suggestibility and cognitive disorganization of the individual who is "high" to suggest a wide variety of things to him which are not happening. The suggestions may act as the precipitating factor for him to "blow his mind" or "freak out."

### 3. PROOF OF FLEXIBILITY

Various professionals who have a wide background in psychedelic drug use, state that the experience provides an opportunity to develop a degree of flexibility of character that results in being able to handle most difficult situations and no longer to indulge in the "games" of society.

> Anger and anxiety are irrelevant because you see your small game in the context of the great evolutionary game which no one can win and no one can lose.[5]

### 4. PROOF OF EMOTIONAL MATURITY AND INTELLECTUAL DEPTH

Many people who have taken LSD report a greater rapport with their fellows and a greater understanding, a giving up of immature games and a general feeling of well-being and strength with respect to daily, trying experiences. Things that once "bugged" them no longer cause  them to be upset. The age-old concepts of proving one's masculinity or strength by direct challenge or demonstrated feats of strength have little place on the modern campus. One proves the same things to others (and himself) in verbal exchange and intellectual understanding. In this respect, intellect and power or strength are almost tautological. Statements such as the following must prove almost irresistible to students concerned about the need to prove themselves:

> We discover that our brain works with a velocity and scope which far surpasses our mental operations. The potential of cerebral association is of the order of thirteen billion to the twenty-five-thousandth power per second. . . . Our present mental machinery cannot possibly handle the cerebral potential . . . Most distressing is this fact: the instrumental inadequacy is not external but internal. The whirling, speed-of-light, trackless processes are properties of our brain, our organ of consciousness itself.[6]

Reports of changes in the area of understanding, deeper communication, sense of well-being, and so forth, act as a powerful selling point to the uninitiated. One student recently reported to us that "I always felt that I was highly perceptive, intuitive and introspective. I thought I was more this way than most. Then these fellows began to say how they became so much more perceptive in just a few hours. I don't mind admitting I became real jealous and decided to give 'acid' a try."

---

[5] Solomon, ibid.
[6] Solomon, op. cit., p. 13.

## INDIVIDUAL FACTORS

### 1. CURIOSITY, EXPERIMENTATION, PERSONAL CHALLENGE

Students most frequently reported that such factors as curiosity, the wish to experiment, or presenting themselves with a personal challenge as opposed to the public, peer-group challenge, were those which led them to try the psychedelic drugs. In most instances, although this was the initial statement, given sufficient time to reflect on their experience, most students saw a variety of underlying motives.

### 2. FEELING OF BEING LEFT BEHIND, OR MISSING SOMETHING

As with the previous point, students often spoke of feelings of having missed out on something, of being an outsider, or being left out. Often such statements reflect a chronic feeling of having been cheated, of having been handed the short end of the stick, of having received less. Sibling and family relationships are often important in understanding these types of feelings. The sense of inadequacy which underlies such feelings often gives rise to the hope for a "one-shot-cure" and the expectation that through psychedelics there will be a sudden bright tomorrow.

### 3. INDIVIDUAL PROOF OF EMOTIONAL MATURITY
### AND INTELLECTUAL DEPTH

The factors involved here are similar to those described under peer group factors except in the individual instance where the student is often somewhat socially isolated or shy with poorly formed peer relationships. He would not likely accept the peer challenge, but poses questions to himself about his strength and adequacy which are translated into concepts such as greater understanding and communication, increased perceptiveness, and so forth.

### 4. SEEKING MEANING

Often, students who speak of seeking "meaning" or "real meaning" in their world around them and in the relationships they form, are grappling with problems of identity. Such students are especially impressed with writings in the psychedelic literature in which the "game" quality of living is described. For example:

> Those of us who talk and write about games of life are invariably misunderstood. We are seen as frivolous, or cynical anarchists, tearing down the social structure. This is an unfortunate misapprehension. Actually, only those who see culture as

a game, only those who take this evolutionary point of view can appreciate the treasure, the exquisitely complex magnificence of what human beings do and have done.[7]

Experiences of this kind underlie some of the great world religions. ... They contradict common sense so violently and are accompanied with such a powerful sense of authenticity and reality (more real than reality is a common description) that men have always wondered whether they are divine revelations or insidious delusions ....[8]

## 5. SEEKING ANSWERS TO PHILOSOPHICAL OR PERSONAL PROBLEMS

Some students are disturbed when they encounter ambiguity in certain areas of life of which they had been confident previously. Examples are religious concepts, the nature of their social relationships, or ultimate meanings of life. They desperately seek to regain confidence and control by amassing information from wide-ranging areas and attempting to integrate the information in an orderly, cohesive, explanatory system. By the very nature of their information-gathering and ensuing discussions, they encounter further ambiguity and an even greater sense of uncertainty. Once more proselytizers of psychedelic drugs appear to offer the answer with statements such as

Now with hallucinogens, there is no reason why we all can't be taught the Eastern skills in a matter of weeks.[9]

## 6. SOLVING PERSONAL PROBLEMS AND FEELINGS OF INADEQUACY

Perhaps the most frequent underlying motive, recognized and unrecognized in the students who told us of their psychedelic experiences, was the hope for the rapid solution to personal problems. Most often these problems were in the area of deep-seated feelings of inadequacy with associated profound feelings of shame. Such feelings were often projected in terms of the "phoney world" or the "insincerity of people." Much energy was expended to reassure themselves of their adequacy, usually as statements of their potentials or capabilities. They seemed to hope for some sort of magical cure for their emotional turmoil without undergoing, as seen through their eyes, the shameful experience of working out their problems in the presence of another person (a therapist) whom they feared would scorn their secret weaknesses. Such students

[7] Solomon, op. cit., p. 118.
[8] Solomon, op. cit., p. 120.
[9] Solomon, op. cit., p. 59.

seemed to live constantly in dread that they would be "discovered" or found out by significant others. The fear was that such discovery would result in alienation, destruction of the relationships and abandonment. At depth, the concept of abandonment seemed to mean a form of exile—being left to die. Psychedelic drugs seemed to offer the hope that one could take a pill and in the turbulence, but privacy of his own "being" (mind) solve his dreadful problems unobserved. Many writers hold out such a hope:

> For many people one or two psilocybin experiences can accomplish the goals of a long and successful psychotherapy, a deep understanding and game-free collaboration between participants plus insight.[10]

> LSD enables *everyone* (italics ours) to become an astronaut of himself.[11]

> For one thing, the tour through the hell of ego was like a quick psychoanalysis.[12]

> LSD should be included in every Do-It-Yourself Personality-Change Kit . . . .[13]

### 7. CLOSENESS TO OTHER PEOPLE

Many students feel isolated and unable to communicate or find meaning in their relationships with others. In their desperate loneliness, a drug which will clear the channels of communication and free them to take part in the interchange of life around them has a vast appeal.

Perhaps the most constantly implied theme is that of magical cure, magical change, instant solution. Such thinking is not new. Throughout history mankind has incorporated in his folklore stories of magic potions, substances which caused immediate transformation or single experiences which resolved life's problems. Most of us have witnessed the appearance of miracle drugs (antibiotics). Everyday modern technology provides us with a new miracle. Magical expectations for psychedelic drugs have not occurred *de novo*. But perhaps, like so many magic potions, for some the transformation is indeed miraculous, most are left unchanged and, for others, the transformation is tragic.

---

[10] Solomon, op. cit., p. 115.

[11] Solomon, op. cit., p. 72.

[12] Solomon, op. cit., p. 75.

[13] Alpert, op. cit., p. 52.

# THE ROLE OF PSYCHOLOGY

*. . . At times truth may not seem probable.*

Boileau

Psychology is an outgrowth of philosophical positions. Controversies of the 1920s centered about such topics as the presence or absence of instincts in man, the dichotomy of mind and matter, and the value of introspection as a scientific tool. Issues such as these are necessary in the development of later theories. Sciences thrive on controversy. The essays in this section deal with two types of issues that are still debated: applied psychology practices and the mental health movement.

Child psychology as a discipline dates back to the early 1920s, yet juvenile delinquency is increasing. Benjamin Spock's essay, *Psychology Can't Substitute for Morality*, is an excursion into some of the current problems of child rearing. Spock contends that children tend to adopt their parents' morality without excessive preaching.

Earl Ubell's article, *Has Psycho-Probing Helped Anyone?* condenses the findings of several investigations challenging the techniques of psychotherapy. His appraisal supports the thesis that neuroses have a limited course even if untreated. Therefore the need for psychotherapy becomes debatable.

Auerback's *The Anti-Mental Health Movement,* an interesting evaluation of this movement, emphasizes its political implications. Szasz' *Mental Illness is a Myth* contends that mental disorders should not be classified as an "illness" but rather as "personal conduct." His viewpoint has evoked much controversy among behavioral scientists. This controversy is seen in the final article, Thorne's *An Analysis of Szasz' "Myth of Mental Illness."* The author criticizes Szasz' terminology as well as his philosophical bases.

# Psychology Can't Substitute for Morality

BENJAMIN SPOCK

Juvenile delinquency has increased markedly since World War II. So has the prevalence of venereal disease in adolescents. Illegitimate births have tripled in 20 years. Youths from well-to-do families have gone out to steal or destroy property for excitement.

I don't think that the picture is all dark. A majority of young people behave responsibly. There are many more serious students in high school and college and graduate school than there have ever been before. But I don't believe we can shrug off the signs of trouble on the assumption that they'll go away by themselves. There's a good chance they'll grow worse, for I see little evidence yet of a corrective reaction.

A lowering of standards of behavior in children presumably reflects either the same process in adults or at least a great uncertainty in parents about what the standards should be. I'm sure that the factors responsible are many and complex. A basic one has been the increasing acceptance of a scientific and naturalistic view of man's place in the world, which was given great impetus by the discovery of evolution a century ago and which has weakened the authority of religious teaching for many, many people. Another quite recent factor has been the postwar prosperity; it is unfortunately true that man generally behaves better in adversity than in affluence.

But I want to single out for comment now certain ideas current in child psychology in the past generation or two that I think have made trouble for parents in their teaching of morality because they have accepted them too literally. The concept that a child naturally wants to be good and will grow up right if he only has parents who show him the right kind of love has made parents feel it was their fault, not the child's, whenever he misbehaved. There's been the fear—mistaken, in most cases—that if a parent is strict, the child will not love him or will be traumatized. There is the oversimplified belief that sexuality is just a wholesome instinct that should not be repressed too severely. There has been the strong American emphasis on social adjustment, which some parents have interpreted to mean that when in any doubt they had better let their child go along with the crowd. There's been the reassuring principle, generally but not always true, that children will absorb their parents' moral standards just by living with them, without having to be preached at all the time. Reinforcing these new concepts has been the drive, which has persisted since the turn of the century, to throw out the prudery, the stuffiness, the insincerity, of the Victorian period.

The emphasis in child rearing in the past 50 years has been so heavily on the psychological factors that it has almost crowded the moral aspects out of sight. The effect of all this has been to make many parents doubt their own standards and to dilute them— quite drastically—as they have passed them on to their children.

There's one aspect of the present relaxation of morals that I can think of as both reassuring and disturbing. Surveys indicate that quite a large percentage of young people consider it not very wrong to cheat on school and college examinations. Many people feel that it is all right to cheat large institutions such as the government and insurance companies. Yet person-to-person honesty and considerateness are still highly valued. Young people in some fraternities and sororities, for instance, have had the courage and humanity to end discrimination, which most of their parents and grandparents accepted quite smugly. Adults in small, stable communities will go a long way to be helpful and generous to neighbors in trouble. Service clubs strive for the same spirit downtown.

What this contrast seems to mean is that some Americans don't have the imagination or the depth of conscience—I don't know which it is—to realize that an organization is made up of or represents real people, and it is hurt by dishonesty just as any individual is. The irresponsibility toward institutions and toward society as a whole might not have become significant if we Americans had continued to live in small towns and rural communities, where morality is quite personal because everyone knows almost everyone else. But the move is all toward the cities, where individuals feel less visible, less significant, less responsible.

You may say that people are entitled to relax their morals if that's what, collectively, they want to do. After all, customs and standards vary widely throughout the world, and they are constantly being modified in each country in response to changes in basic conditions. My own answer would be that we have changed our surface standards too abruptly, not primarily in adaptation to new conditions but in response to new ideas with which we have been fascinated and which we have not fully digested. Also, I think that the basic convictions of most of us have not changed as much as the lowered surface standards would indicate. As a result, there is a cruel discrepancy, for young people who transgress, between the tolerant attitude they believe exists and the reality. The girl who has an illegitimate child or the boy who gets caught in vandalism finds that our customs and laws and a majority of our citizens are almost as stern as they used to be.

The most impressive evidence that standards have slipped in a *maladaptive* way comes from guidance clinics. The children who are growing up with too little restraint, too little sense of moral obligation, are likely to be miserable in childhood, to get into trouble in adolescence and to be unhappy and ineffectual in adulthood.

It is the nature of man, when he grows up in a stable family in almost any culture, to want to share in the aspirations of his community, to cooperate in its work, to have its approval. Conscientious parents have always tried to teach these attitudes. When this rearing process fails to work right, when the individual turns out as an adult to lack a sense of direction or to be impulsive and irresponsible, there is distress in the individual—though he may deny it—and in those who are close to him.

I want to be a little more specific now. But I'm not assuming that there is only one right set of morals. Morals will always be quite different at different social levels, even in the same community, and somewhat different in every family. I'm only encouraging parents to be clear and firm in passing on the set which they themselves believe in.

Though it's true that a child who is loved wants to be good, he also is tempted frequently to get off the narrow path. He needs to be reminded regularly of what is expected, and corrected when he has misbehaved. If his parents feel the guilt instead of making him feel it, he will be stimulated to create more trouble the next time and the next.

When a parent is just in his strictness or punishment, the child is not hurt and he does not turn against the parent. He is made more comfortable in having been kept from wrongdoing or in paying for it. Underneath, he feels grateful to his parent. Naturally he won't say thank you; he grumbles or sulks temporarily; but this doesn't mean he has been disciplined unwisely. All children, being lawyers at heart, will experiment once or twice with trying to make a parent feel guilty for some disapproval or punishment. If the parent is unable to fend off such a reproach, the child will surely bombard him with more—not because he is ruthless but because he can shield himself in this way from guilt.

Parents often find it particularly difficult nowadays to know how much direction to give their children about sexual matters. In this respect it is helpful to keep in mind that sexuality is not a simple instinct in human beings at all. Its roots are strong and primitive. But it is designed to be firmly controlled by the parents' sense of propriety. It is meant to be molded by the idealized image that the child gains of his parents and by the ideals they teach specifically. In this elaborate process a great part of the sexual longing is transmuted into such spiritual attitudes as tenderness, chivalry, altruism, marital devotion, love of children. Through subtle transformations sexuality is also one of the mainsprings of creativity in the arts and sciences, and even of the drive to study. (Many adolescents who married before they were mature in character have experienced an ebbing of their academic ambitions.)

It is generally true that children tend to adopt their parents' morality without excessive preaching. But we've learned in child-guidance work that parents are often more tolerant toward one child than another and that an occasional parent will be surprisingly lax in what he expects of one child without being consciously aware of this. Therefore it clarifies and crystallizes matters for the parents as well as for their children when they speak explicitly of the standards they are setting and of the specific behavior they expect from their children.

At the top of the list of expectations, if it were my child, I'd put a strong sense of obligation to be helpful, generous, honest and gracious—not only toward the people he'll know but also to those he won't know. A child is ready to begin learning consideration at the age of a year, to say thank you, then to run small errands, to give part of his treat to another, later to help with the housework or yard work, to make greeting cards and presents. These may sound like petty gestures. But the child who acquires genuine considerateness is more likely to become the dependable worker, the well-beloved friend, the deeply responsible citizen of the community and of the world.

I'm quite convinced that not only the best-behaved children but also the happiest and most successful ones are those whose parents present their beliefs unequivocally and leave no doubt that they expect their children to live up to them. I don't mean harsh parents. I mean affectionate but firm parents.

# Has Psycho-Probing Helped Anyone?

EARL UBELL

While a man lying on a couch in a psychiatrist's office has his deep troubles, so does the doctor sitting behind him and assiduously taking notes. The physician knows he must help the patient! Yet he also knows his talk-talk methods now bear the weight of heavy criticism that can little longer be ignored.

"Not effective!"

"No proof!"

"The patients heal themselves!"

"Dangerous!"

So run the jibes of other doctors, psychologists, scientists and even fellow psychiatrists who approach mental disease via drugs and biology. They want to see simple scientific proof that couch psychiatry—psychoanalysis—and its variant—psychotherapy—actually ameliorate mental illness.

Even a man as sympathetic to psychotherapy as Dr. Paul Hoch, Commissioner of Mental Hygiene in New York State and a leading research psychiatrist, told me:

"An objective evaluation of psychotherapy is long overdue, but we do not yet have the methodology for making one. We have to try step by step to develop the methods."

At this moment, the practitioners of person-to-person treatment cannot point to a single strictly controlled experiment—an objective evaluation—that proves psychological treatment changes psychological illness for the better.

Dr. Hans Eysenck, professor of psychology at the University of London and the bete noir of the psychotherapists, has repeatedly surveyed the scientific reports for such evidence and found none.

". . . Psychologists and psychiatrists," Dr. Eysenck asserts, "will have to acknowledge the fact that current psychotherapeutic procedures have not lived up to the hopes which greeted their emergence 50 years ago. . . . It would appear advisable . . . to discard the psychoanalytic model. . . ."

From *The New York Herald Tribune*, June 3, 1962, Section II, p. 1. © 1962, New York Herald Tribune, Inc. Reprinted by permission of W. C. C. Publishing Company, Inc.

259

## CONTROLLED TEST

What exactly is this method or really, group of methods, bearing the family name of psychotherapy? The experts cannot agree. One psychologist called it: "... an unidentified technique applied to unspecific problems with unpredictable outcomes. For this technique we recommend rigorous training."

However, they have outlined its main features. It arose from the work of Dr. Sigmund Freud in the years between 1910 and 1915, although it had earlier roots. He divided the mind into three great interacting psychological forces, each unknown to the thinking, conscious individual. Neurosis—with its various symptoms including anxiety, lethargy, fear—arose from the unbalanced conflict of those forces. The imbalance could be traced back to early, childhood psychological experiences.

In psychoanalytic treatment, the physician (or lay analyst if the therapist is not an M.D.) aims to reveal to the patient the unseen struggle of his unconscious mental forces. The method involves talk by the patient and establishment of a relationship between him and the therapist.

Most psychoanalysts assert that their methods, with or without couch, can give a permanent cure of neurosis. In their view, other treatments merely manipulate external signs and never get to the psychological bottom.

In the last 50 years these other therapies have rapidly multiplied, producing almost as many psychotherapeutic species as psychiatrists. They frequently bear the name of their founders: Adler, Jung, Horney, Sullivan, to name but a few. They all have common features.

First, there is an interpersonal relationship between two people: patient and therapist. The latter has been trained in handling such human relationships. The methods are psychological: suggestion, explanation, advice, interpretation of thoughts, dreams and written matter. Behind each therapy there is a theory of the cause of the illness and the structure of the personality. All therapists aim to help the condition for which the patient sought treatment.

Needless to say, this bare outline hides volumes of written matter describing this or that therapy, with the numerous claims made for their effectiveness.

## REPORT SUCCESS

Of course, the psychoanalysts and psychotherapists do have tantalizing hints that their treatments work. They have a constant stream of reports from their fellows reporting cure or help for this or that psychological disorder. They often see with their own eyes the conversion of a miserable patient to a happy one.

In addition, they have an incontrovertible observation that education—a psychological method—does work; people do learn and change under its power. They also see the apparent success of Alcoholics Anonymous, which employs psychological methods to prevent taking "that first drink." And recently there was a report from Dr. Harry Weinstock, of Mount Sinai Hospital, New York, that psychoanalytic treatment prevented the recurrence of ulcerative colitis, a particularly recalcitrant "psychosomatic" disorder of the bowel.

## OUTLINE TESTS

But the scientists clamor for a different kind of test, one that relies less on the psychiatrist's own, and possibly prejudiced, observations that his treatment benefited the patient. They want the treatment applied to patients with known psychological disease; they want another equivalent group of patients to receive no treatment; they want the effects "blindly" and objectively evaluated and compared in the two groups.

As of this writing, every type of test in which psychotherapists applied this controlled method came up with a zero for psychotherapy: the rates of improvement in the treated and untreated individuals remained identical.

One famous study of this kind was carried out on potential juvenile delinquents in the Cambridge-Sommerville area of Boston, between 1937 and 1945. School teachers, police, and settlement workers submitted names of 650 boys between six and 10 they thought likely to become delinquent.

"These boys were individually matched in pairs, according to ... age, intelligence quotient, school grade, delinquency rating, ethnic and socio-economic background and other factors," the scientists reported. "The decision which boy in each pair should be treated was made by a toss of a coin."

The average boy received four years and two months of psychotherapy, some of which was psychoanalytically oriented.

Typically, the psychotherapists reported that two-thirds of the treated boys had "substantially benefited." Half the boys themselves volunteered that they had been "helped."

But then two psychologists checked the court records of the boys. Here's what they found:

Number of boys in court: 96 treated; 92 untreated.

Number of offenses: 264 treated; 218 untreated.

Conclusion: "We submit . . . the data yielded one definite conclusion: that the burden of proof is on anyone who claims specific results for a given form of therapy."

Next: a follow-up study of war neuroses reported by Dr. N. Q. Brill, a psychiatrist, and Dr. G. W. Beebe, a statistician. They tried to find out what happened to a large group of men who had "nervous breakdowns" either in combat or just before getting to combat and who had had various treatments.

The results:

| Treatment | Percent returned to duty |
|---|---|
| Essentially none | 56% |
| Rest and sedation only | 68% |
| Individual therapy | 62% |
| Hospital routine | 48% |

It is clear that individual therapy (psychotherapy) is second to rest and sedation and little better than the other methods.

## CASES TESTED

Again Drs. T. F. Leary and F. Barron, both of San Francisco, tried psychotherapy on 75 psychoneurotics—patients with severe anxiety. Compared with an equal number of untreated patients, the treated individuals show no changes not found in the control group.

Dr. Eugene E. Levitt, a psychologist then at the Illinois Institute for Juvenile Research, and two associates repeated the little drama with 469 emotionally disturbed children. They treated 327 with psychotherapy; another 142 received no treatment. Five years later: ". . . there is no difference at follow-up between the adjustments made by treated and untreated child patients."

Later, Dr. Levitt surveyed 37 investigations involving 8,000 patients given psychotherapy at different clinics. Again, no differences between treated and untreated groups.

Finally, Dr. Jerome Frank, of Johns Hopkins University, tried three different kinds of psychotherapy on three groups of patients. At the end of five years, no single method showed any superiority.

## CONTRADICTORY TESTS

What could account for the contradictory situation in which the therapists report good results and the scientific tests show no differences?

The clew rests in the natural history of emotional illness and particularly neurosis. Dr. Ernest Gruenberg and Dr. M. Shepherd studied psychoneurosis—severe anxiety—among the enrollees of the Health Insurance Plan of Greater New York.

"It is perfectly clear, in the mass," they said, "neuroses have a limited course even if untreated." The average duration was about two years. In other words, most neurotics get better on their own.

Figures from England and elsewhere in the United States reveal that about 70 per cent of neurotics improve within two years; within five years, nine out of 10 show marked improvement.

These reports indicate how a doctor could honestly report that his patients improved. They show how it is possible that a patient actually believes his doctor helped him. They demonstrate forcibly that unless carefully controlled studies are made, individual physicians will not know whether psychotherapy works or not.

Furthermore there is the well-known placebo effect. It derives its name from the harmless sugar pills which some doctors give to their patients merely to please them (hence: placebo, from the Latin: to please). Dr. Henry K. Beecher, an anesthesiologist of Harvard, has shown in several experiments that placebo pills can produce the physical and psychological effects of real drugs. For example, if a patient believes he is getting an anti-histamine, but is really getting a placebo, he will react not only with the anti-histamine effects but with the side effect as well.

The powerful effect of the placebo also gives warning to those psychotherapists who believe they are changing the psyche of their patients by their methods based on involved theories of personality. Their results may be an example of the placebo on the non-pill level.

Nevertheless, if this is the case why does one need extensive training, or complex theories to be a psychotherapist? Does the placebo effect last a long time? Dr. Beecher indicates that it does not. Does it change the patient? Probably not.

## EVADE RESPONSIBILITY

Despite these facts, the psychotherapists capable of performing more specific tests of effectiveness continue to duck the responsibility. Part of their reticence comes from the difficulty of the experiment.

Dr. Lawrence S. Kubie, a leading psychoanalyst, has worried about the problem for two decades. He and others have pointed out the three main obstacles:

1. You can't quite define psychotherapy so that different physicians can apply it in exactly the same way.
2. You can't precisely define the mental disease you're treating, so that you may end up treating different diseases with different treatments.
3. You can't observe nor get precise agreement on success or failure because each doctor looks at the patient with his own prejudice.

In 1956 Dr. Benjamin Pasamanick, professor of psychiatry at Ohio State University, proposed a $100,000 test of psychotherapy involving childhood behavior disorders. He met the problems head on with a careful test design.

"These findings," he said, "are so necessary for the future development of the discipline of child psychiatry that, not only is the expenditure of this amount of money in itself of not little consequence, but it is of utmost immediate necessity. Without such an expenditure, we are doomed to remain practitioners of an art only, not a science."

Suggested at a meeting of the American Academy of Child Psychiatry, the proposal was greeted with derision by the psychotherapists present. One screamed: "Do you think you are in Russia?" The test was never made.

To many doctors, the existence of an unproved treatment in the community presents grave dangers.

## SEE DANGER

1. The treatment itself may be dangerous. Some psychoanalysts assert that for certain patients their treatment may do harm; i.e., it might uncover a psychosis, severe mental illness.
2. The treatment may divert patients away from other, more suitable, therapy. Dr. Nathan S. Kline, of Rockland State Hospital, has accused many psychotherapeutically oriented clinics of preventing patients from getting proper drug treatment.

3. The treatment may take talented doctors and scientists away from more fruitful research.
4. You can't improve a treatment if you have no measure of its effectiveness.

Yet despite these dangers, the number of psychotherapists and the patients undergoing the treatment grows apace. Figures are hard to come by. In all, 200,000 patients a year may be involved in psychotherapy directly and many more indirectly. There are 6,500 psychiatrists, 4,000 psychologists, 10,000 social workers and uncounted family physicians and internists who practice some form of psychotherapy. The total annual bill may be $500 million. It is hardly private entertainment.

What stands out is that people have severe emotional problems (perhaps four out of five may have enough of a problem to want to see a psychiatrist at some time); psychotherapists offer, explicitly and implicitly, cure and amelioration. Who will blame the public for trying it even in the face of poor scientific evidence that psychotherapy works. It might help.

# The Anti-mental Health Movement

ALFRED AUERBACK

Mental disorders have been disturbing occurrences to mankind since earliest recorded history. They have been considered evidence of demons possessing the individual, of punishment by angry gods, even of holiness on rare occasions. The most common social reactions have been hostility, rejection, or withdrawal and, in the not-too-distant past, physical punishment or incarceration for the afflicted individual. Mankind nearly always has looked with fear on the mentally ill individual, a feeling that has associated itself with mental healers down through the ages. This antagonism was compounded by Freud's stressing the sexual components of human behavior. While psychoanalysis has won increasing acceptance, hostility still remains towards many of its concepts, along with some doubt as to its therapeutic effectiveness.

Psychiatry, too, though a branch of medical science, still has not won complete acceptance (1). Whenever criticism has been expressed it has been accepted on the basis that psychiatry is still an inexact science, that we do not yet know the causes of mental illness and that our tools for combatting it are, in large degree, empirical. Yet despite some public and professional criticism, psychiatry and mental health activities generally have been accepted as legitimate undertakings which are continually seeking to perfect themselves.

The last few years have seen major progress in the better understanding of psychiatric needs. This is reflected in the Joint Commission on Mental Illness and Health Report, *Action for Mental Health,* the recommendations of the Governors' Conference of November 1961, and the first Mental Health Congress under the sponsorship of the American Medical Association in Oct., 1962. In Feb., 1963, President Kennedy indicated his personal interest in better care and treatment of the mentally ill and mentally retarded, in his request of Congress for extensive appropriations in this field. Leading to these developments have been the open door policy in mental hospitals, initiation of community mental health

Reprinted from the *American Journal of Psychiatry,* CXX, pp. 105–111, 1963. Copyright 1963, the American Psychiatric Association.

services in many states and more intensive use of varied therapeutic methods for hospitalized patients which have brought new horizons in the mental health field.

In recent years a new form of attack has been mounted against the mental health movement that is reminiscent of the Salem witch-hunting days. In contrast to legitimate criticism of deficiencies or methodology, it imputes deliberately evil intent to the mental health program in general and to those engaged in the field. Directly, but most often by innuendo, it accuses mental health associations and psychiatric groups of being subversive, even conspiratorial. The constant refrain is that the entire mental health program is a subversive racket and anti-American or communistic in nature, established by agents of the Kremlin to subvert and take over the United States. The groups making these charges, while containing a few well-meaning persons, seem to be in large measure made up of rabble-rousing individuals who have been involved in various "right-wing" activities over the years. Being well financed and vociferous, they manage to create public turmoil far out of proportion to their actual numbers. They have become effective pressure groups both at the local level and before state legislative bodies, where they have sown seeds of dissension and confusion. At times this has effectively blocked proposed mental health programs or brought about reduced appropriations for new or existing programs.

*California Survey.* In Sept., 1961, a study of anti-mental health trends in California was made by a small group representing medical and educational organizations concerned with this problem. An analysis was made of 166 samples of attack on psychiatry or on the mental health movement gathered from 38 different communities in California. The major sources were

| | |
|---|---|
| Letters to the editor | 46 |
| News stories and articles | 41 |
| Leaflets and brochures | 21 |
| Newspaper editorials | 17 |
| Newspaper columns | 12 |

Sampling these items revealed a wide range of targets, including the California Department of Mental Hygiene, the Short Doyle Act, mental health associations, the World Health Organization of the United Nations, commitment procedures in California, psychological testing in the schools, and attacks upon psychiatrists, psychologists and social workers in general. A common thread running through all of them was the charge that these agencies, groups, and individuals were subversive and conspiratorial. Repeatedly it was implied that the mental health program was part of a communist conspiracy or that it was set up for the oppression of anti-communists. The theme was that prayer and time were all that was needed to alleviate the human misery and social problems created by mental illness. Typical statements found in these publications were:

"Mental hygiene is a subtle and diabolical plan of the enemy to transform a free and intelligent people into a cringing horde of zombies." "Mental health programs are part of a communist plot to control the people's minds." "Do we want to become a regimented nation, brain-washed and brain-fed through a powerful army of psychiatrists?"

These attacks are irresponsible, offering no constructive suggestions. They do not even evidence concern for the problem of psychiatric illness or for those afflicted. They use mental illness and the mentally ill as scapegoats for purposes which have no relation to mental illness. The issues are never discussed. They are deliberately dodged by attributing "evil motives" to mental health work in general and to those engaged in it. Running throughout are implications that psychiatric clinics are designed solely to probe into people's minds for subversive purposes; that psychological testing in schools is designed to teach children immorality and disrespect for their country. Never are these charges documented; always, they are by innuendo. At times, the "big lie" technique is used, the repeated out-and-out misstatement.

DEVELOPMENT OF ANTI-MENTAL HEALTH TRENDS

The anti-mental health movement is an outcropping of the opposition to all scientific progress, particularly in the field of public health. Nearly every major advance in this field during the past century has been violently opposed. Pasteurization of milk, chlorination of water and immunization against smallpox, diphtheria and other infectious diseases have evoked strong opposition whenever these measures were introduced. There are still pockets of opposition to smallpox vaccination and to Salk vaccine. Antagonism to fluoridation of water has mounted in recent years to the point where 14,000 communities are deprived of this caries preventive (2). Similarly, there has been clamor against the use of animals in laboratory experiments ("vivisection"). The first significant public denunciation against the mental health movement occurred in

1955. It came from a group of some 100 housewives in Burbank, Calif., who called themselves the American Public Relations Forum, Inc. They were studying legislative bills with the announced purpose of exposing subversion and pounced on a proposed community mental health services bill. When the bill was defeated this group claimed credit for a "victory for Americanism." Re-introduction of the California Community Mental Health Services bill in 1957 again brought this group into the fray, but despite its vociferous opposition, the bill passed the legislature. During its stormy legislative course it was exposed to repeated claims that it was communistically inspired. Despite the fact that the bill was drafted by the California Medical Association, many physicians in that state still oppose it on those baseless charges six years after its passage.

In 1956 the 84th Congress appointed a subcommittee to hold hearings in connection with HR6376, a bill providing for the hospitalization and care of the mentally ill of Alaska. During the hearings a motley crew harangued in opposition to the bill. A clever phrase, "Siberia, U.S.A." was coined at this time by a Mrs. Burkeland of Van Nuys, Calif. During the hearings it was worked into such statements as: "This legislation will place any resident of the United States at the mercy of any person with whom they might have a disagreement, causing a charge of 'mental illness' to be placed against them with immediate deportation to 'Siberia, U.S.A.'" And again: "It is entirely within the realm of possibility that we may be establishing in Alaska our own version of the Siberian slave camps run by the Russian government"(3). Soon, "Siberia, U.S.A." was being printed all over the country in right-wing publications, including those of well-known rabble rousers and of groups with high sounding American names, seemingly dedicated to the perpetuation of American freedom. During the congressional hearings, several witnesses switched from "patriotism" to bigotry. They indicated that the mental health movement was a Jewish plot. One witness testified that 100% of all psychiatric therapy was Jewish and that about 80% of the psychiatrists in the United States were Jewish.

The importance of these congressional hearings to the anti-mental health forces lies in the fact that the verbatim text of the hearings was printed by the United States Government Printing Office, and in some cases later read into the Congressional Record. As a result, the wild statements made at that time have been repeated across the country countless times citing the Congressional Record and thereby implying governmental approval.

Interestingly, whenever mental health work is being attacked the phrases used are identical to those first appearing in the period of 1955–1958. Years after Alaska has built its mental hospital the phrase "Siberia, U.S.A." is still in use. Words like "communist-inspired," "anti-religious" and "conspiracy" are still frequent, but no new labels have evolved. No matter where the opposition has appeared the language is the same while documentation or substantiation remain nil. In many cases merely calling the mental health field "subversive" has proved sufficient.

Although the American Medical Association, the American Psychiatric Association and the National Association for Mental Health supported the Alaska Mental Health Bill, one nationwide group of physicians, the Association of American Physicians and Surgeons (AAPS) opposed it. In circularizing its ten thousand physician members the AAPS repeatedly mentioned the bill's "horrendous provisions." Interestingly, the association's congressional adviser quit in disgust when it refused to retract its stand (4). Over the years, many physicians exposed to this propaganda have continued to repeat the hackneyed clichés and frequently have led the attack on local or state mental health activities. Often this thinking has colored the deliberations of state and county medical societies, a fact substantiated by a recent national study of anti-mental health trends made by the writer. In ten or more states physicians or physicians' wives have played prominent roles in these attacks, at times succeeding in winning official or unofficial support of the medical societies. Perhaps the most striking example of this occurred in the San Fernando Valley near Los Angeles, where a professional propagandist, after attacking "The Mental Health Racket," was given a letter of commendation by the district medical society. Only after forceful argument by outraged members including the psychiatrists was this commendation revoked. This near miss led to publication of a booklet, *The Doctors Speak Up* (5), in which psychiatrists of the San Fernando area exposed and refuted the false statements and misrepresentations of the propagandist.

On August 15, 1958, an article entitled "Mental Health—a Marxist Weapon" first appeared in the *Economic Council Letter 437*. According to this right-wing publication, mental health was an inaccurate label for what was really a skillful attempt by communist propagandists to bring about Marxist conformity to the Marxist ideology. According to this publication, "nonconformists" would be in actual peril of being judged insane. The contents of the article have been reproduced in countless other "anti-commu-

nist" publications and have been repeated ad infinitum and ad
nauseam. At about the same time there appeared a booklet entitled *Brainwashing—A Synthesis of a Russian Textbook on Psychopolitics*,
its 64 pages purporting to hold the text of a talk given by Beria,
former head of the Soviet Secret Police, to American students attending classes in "psychopolitics" at Lenin University (6). It contained some of the most bald-faced lies ever directed against the
psychiatric profession. The book has had a tremendous circulation
and has been cited at great length. Quotes crop up in publications
of the Daughters of the American Revolution and in various other
brochures such as "Lifelines," "Common Sense," "Freedom Build-
ers of America," "Freedom Forum," etc. In each it is stated
unequivocally that under the "false name of 'mental health'" a
communist master plan is being put into operation in hundreds of
American cities and that mental health groups are being used to
further the goal of communist conquest of the mind. A sampling of
this treatise on "brainwashing" must be quoted to indicate the
source of phraseology now in frequent use:

> Psychopolitics is a branch of geopolitics concerned with mental
> healing. It is used to produce chaos in the fields of mental
> healing. It is designed to have every doctor and psychiatrist
> act as an unwitting agent of the communist doctrine. Through
> it you achieve dominion over the minds and bodies of the
> nation. Institutions for the insane provide the means of hold-
> ing a million persons without any civil rights or any hope of
> freedom. By use of electric shock or brain surgery you can
> keep these people so they will never again draw a sane breath.
> By making readily available drugs of all kinds, by giving the
> teenager alcohol, by praising his wildness, by stimulating him
> with sex literature, the psychopolitical operator (psychiatrist)
> can create the necessary attitudes of chaos, idleness and
> worthlessness in the teenager. The psychiatrist has no interest
> in cures, hence the greater the number of insane in hospital,
> the greater the number of people under his domination and
> the greater will become the size of his hospitals. Exercises in
> sexual attack on patients can be practiced by the psychiatrist
> to demonstrate the inability of the patient to withstand him
> while indoctrinating the lust for further sexual activities on the
> part of the patient. If a psychiatric ward could be established
> in every general hospital in every city in the nation, it is
> certain that at one time or another leading citizens of the
> nation could come under the ministrations of the psychopoliti-
> cal operator. The attraction of the field of mental healing to
> many people is that it provides unlimited sexual opportunities

and the possibility of complete dominion over the minds and bodies of patients, the possibility of complete lawlessness without detection.

While these statements are ludicrous, the fact remains that millions of Americans are being exposed to them over and over again. In addition to thousands of pamphlets and brochures repeating them there are many radio and television stations across the United States which routinely broadcast this philosophy, although in a more subtle manner. The attack on mental health is coupled with attacks on our educational system, churches, minority groups, and governmental institutions amongst others. It must be recognized that this is part of a well-organized and well-financed campaign against our democratic institutions carried out by groups and individuals making resounding statements about their "patriotism" and "Americanism."

Psychiatrists, generally, assume that educated people pay no attention to such remarks. Regrettably, this is not the case. In the Feb., 1962 issue of *Reader's Digest* (7), with a circulation of 14 million copies, an article entitled "The Tragedy of Sane People Who Get 'Put Away' " indicated that thousands of sane men and women are being "railroaded" into mental hospitals every year. The article further stated: "Only when all men are secure from unjust imprisonment can each of us feel truly free." It considered state hospitals terribly bad places and to be hospitalized in one was comparable to being put in prison. It is too early to measure the damage done by this article but its repercussions will be with us for years.

While the effects of the anti-mental health movement have been felt in Western and Southern states and its influence is spreading across the United States, it has had a profound impact in the southern part of California. In at least a dozen communities mental health activities have been attacked by these groups, in some cases successfully eliminating entire mental health programs. The stand taken by the attacking group or individuals is a rehash of the statements made in connection with the Alaska Mental Health bill or the booklet on psychopolitics. It is somewhat dismaying to find psychiatrists being vilified by other physicians as amoral, fools, knaves, quacks and traitors, to list but a few epithets. Repeatedly these physicians have stated that psychiatric treatment is of little or no benefit, that it undermines moral principles, that psychiatrists are unmindful of individual rights and are violating the Hippocratic oath and medical ethics by conducting worthless or harmful treatments. When the local press has joined the fray against mental health programs in combination with one or more vociferous physicians, free public discussion of the issues has been impossible. Mental health associations have come under such violent fire that leading citizens have resigned from them as the result of intimidation or the fear of being labelled "pro-communist." Many others have been persuaded by the "big lie" that the model Draft Act is a measure to railroad political dissenters into mental hospitals, although in reality it is a recommended model prepared by federal agencies to provide quick help to the mentally ill through commitment procedures protecting their constitutional rights. As a result, states now attempting to pass mental health legislation invariably meet accusations of "railroading" as well as the demand that every mentally ill person should have a trial by jury before being hospitalized. An interesting derivative of this anti-mental health movement is to be seen in the Community Mental Health Act passed in Utah in 1961(8):

> It shall be a felony to give psychiatric treatment, non-vocational mental health counselling, case finding, testing, psychoanalysis, drugs, shock treatment, lobotomy, or surgery to any individual for the purpose of changing his concept of, belief about, or faith in God.

The plan of attack against mental health associations is reviewed in *The Facts . . . a Reply to Anti-Mental Health Critics* (9) published by the National Association for Mental Health in 1962. About the same time the *S K & F Psychiatric Reporter* published an article "Is Mental Health a Communist Plot?"(10). The appearance of such publications would indicate that the increasing virulence of the anti-mental health group no longer permits ignoring them as nonsensical or misguided individuals.

NATIONAL SURVEY

During January 1963, the writer communicated with the officers of the District Branches of the American Psychiatric Association requesting information about anti-mental health tendencies in their states. In addition, inquiries went to many state mental health associations. An interesting pattern developed. In most states the psychiatric society either knew of no anti-mental health trends or was aware of only isolated instances. Shortly thereafter, there might be a follow-up letter in which it was reported, with considerable surprise, that anti-mental health activities *were* under way in that state! Psychiatrists generally do not move in circles where this opposition operates, whereas mental health associations functioning closer to the community do come in contact with it.

Some states have serious problems arising as consequences of this trend. In the State of Washington, anti-mental health forces precipitated a legislative probe of the state hospital system. At least one legislator who strongly supported the state mental health program was defeated for reelection on this issue and other sympathetic legislators have been threatened with similar political fates. In South Carolina a medical society study of *Action for Mental Health* declared (11)

> The field of mental health will likely become within the next 10 to 15 years an enormous federal health empire probably under the direction of the Department of Health, Education and Welfare, which will centrally regulate all the mental health activities in the nation both at a state and community level. Furthermore, by its own statement of intentions, the Joint Commission would place this vast program dealing with one of our greatest health problems largely in the hands of non-medical people. That it would become primarily a political empire seems inescapable.

A graphic expression of anti-mental health trends is reflected in Texas. In this state, a number of well-intentioned, over-patriotic organizations, convinced that anything related to mental health is subversive, have conducted a running campaign against all mental health activities. Organized telephone campaigns and even full page advertisements in the papers attacking mental health work have occurred. As elsewhere, the anti-mental health organizations do not deal openly with the issues but use techniques of harassment and hasty withdrawal when confronted by a challenge to discuss their charges. They avoid libel by verbal inference rather than in written context.

PERSONALITY TRAITS

There is no doubt that some of the individuals involved in this trend have paranoid personalities but this does not necessarily encompass the heterogeneous group. To understand these individuals the best references are the discussions of ethnocentrism in *The Authoritarian Personality* (12) and the article, "Psychodynamics of Group Opposition to Health Programs"(13). The ethnocentric individual feels threatened by groups to which he does not have a sense of belonging. Where he cannot identify, he must oppose. He believes the "in" groups to which he belongs are superior to the "out" groups, which he considers threatening and power-seeking. The ethnocentrists are nationalistic in thinking, strongly opposed to internationalism in every form. Favoring an authoritarian ideology, they are opposed to any philosophy that stimulates critical evaluation or scientific inquiry. As a consequence psychiatry, which directs the individual to study his own motivations and to look critically both at himself and at his environment, is antithetical to the orientation of ethnocentrism.

Marmor and his associates point out that the same group of people are involved over and over again in opposition to widely diverse health programs. The same individuals and organizations that are active in the fight against water fluoridation can be found in the ranks of those opposing mental health measures and compulsory vaccination. To such individuals, purity is equated with security and health with wholeness. They are equally concerned with pure foods, pure morals and pure races. They are excessively preoccupied with fears of sexual attack, bodily poisoning or ideational contamination. Safety lies in what is old and familiar; the new and unfamiliar are threatening. New habits, new foods, new drugs or new ideas are all viewed with suspicion and apprehension.

Since anti-mental health activities stem from many sources there is no simple solution in terms of coping with them. Much of the strong emotional attitude expressed by anti-mental health partisans reflects their own unconscious anxieties. It also reflects a large degree of conscious opportunism on the part of various self-seeking and self-serving individuals and groups. One of them summarized their philosophy as follows (4):

> When you are espousing a right-wing cause you are apt to attract a fairly sizable lunatic fringe which has to be dealt with kindly if for no other reason than to keep them from going over to the enemy. This is just simple realism. There isn't any use denying it, a great many people who are on our side aren't there because of any sound and sincere belief in our principles, but rather because they conceive our side of the argument to be the one that is to their personal and often pecuniary advantage. Nonetheless, when you are in a war you have to take what allies you can find.

The fanaticism of the anti-mental health believer "prevents an appeal to his reason or moral sense. He fears compromise and cannot be persuaded to qualify the certitude and righteousness of his holy cause"(14).

## DISCUSSION

Considering these facts, what can psychiatrists, psychiatric organizations and mental health groups do to combat this spreading trend across the country? Most important is the need for all groups and individuals with any interest or concern in the mental health field to recognize the nature and the extent of this problem. Indications are that in the coming years these attacks will increase rather than diminish in proportion to the tensions of domestic politics and the international situation. Direct attack on these groups or individuals after the fact is fruitless; then it can be only a defensive response because of the insidious nature of their activities. Mental health groups, whether state mental health department, mental health association or psychiatric association, must *anticipate* these situations and be prepared to respond immediately. Too often, they are unprepared, inept and too late.

The psychiatric group in the San Fernando Valley of California when attacked prepared a brochure exposing the nature and techniques of the opposition. The Southern California Psychiatric Society also has prepared a memorandum which is being sent to physicians and other interested groups and individuals in Southern California. This is a fact sheet about psychiatry listing anti-mental health statements with rebuttals. Material of this nature should be sent *beforehand* to members of legislative bodies, newspaper editors and columnists and other influential policy-making members of the community.

When newspapers or magazines print material of an anti-mental health nature a letter to the editor with a dispassionate rebuttal should be sent. Those publications expressing support for the mental health movement should be sent letters of commendation. The issues at stake no longer permit psychiatrists to remain uninvolved.

Psychiatrists generally have avoided the hurly-burly of political activity and involvement, particularly in medical matters. Consequently when they turn to organized medicine for help most other physicians are loathe to join in the battle. Psychiatrists must become more active participants in their county and state medical societies, in their committees and in their work.

Only by becoming more personally involved in community activities can psychiatrists win a feeling of acceptance by the community. For many people the old stereotypes of the psychiatrist still persist. This atmosphere of uncertainty and suspicion regarding psychiatry provides a potential spawning ground for members of the anti-mental health group. Unless psychiatrists and mental health groups can present themselves and their goals to the public and its governing officials in more clearly defined terms, they pose no obstacles to those who seek to present their biased and bigoted ideas.

## SUMMARY

Anti-mental health trends are manifestations of an ideological struggle under way in the United States in recent years. "Right-wing" groups in the name of "patriotism" have been attacking various aspects of our democratic process. Psychiatry and the mental health movement, for historical, sociological and emotional reasons, have been under increasing attack, a trend that will continue. Organizations and individuals connected with mental health activities must anticipate this development and plan to meet it.

## REFERENCES

1. Miller, M. H., and S. L. Halleck, *Am. J. Psychiat.*, CXIX, 1963, p. 705.
2. Flemming, Arthur S., *New Med. Mat.*, III, 1961, p. 37.
3. Washington: U. S. Govt. Printing Office, 1956.
4. Smith, A. Robert, *Reporter Magazine*, XXVII, June 28, 1956.
5. *The Doctors Speak Up* (Los Angeles: Valley M. H. Assoc., 1961).
6. Anonymous, *Brainwashing*, Box 116, Englewood, Colo.
7. Maisel, Albert Q., *Reader's Digest*, XCVII, Feb. 1962.
8. Salt Lake City, Utah: State Printing Office, 1961.
9. New York: National Ass. for Mental Health, 1962.
10. *S K & F Psychiatric Reporter*, V, Sept.-Oct., 1962.
11. Report to Charleston County Medical Society (South Carolina), 1962.
12. Adorno, T. W., *et al.*, *The Authoritarian Personality* (New York: Harper, 1950).
13. Marmor, Judd, *et al.*, *Am. J. Orthopsychiat.*, XXX, 1960, p. 331.
14. Hoffer, Eric, *The True Believer* (New York: Harper, 1958).
15. Los Angeles: Southern Calif. Psychiat. Soc., 1962.

# Mental Illness Is a Myth

THOMAS S. SZASZ

On Feb. 28, 1966, the United States Court of Appeals for the Second Circuit handed down a decision which displaced the time-honored M'Naghten Rule as a test of criminal insanity, and substituted for it a new rule recommended by the American Law Institute.

The M'Naghten Rule dates from 1843, when one Daniel M'Naghten shot and killed a man named Drummond, the private secretary of Sir Robert Peel, whom M'Naghten had intended to kill. At M'Naghten's trial, evidence was introduced showing that he "was laboring under an insane delusion" of being hounded by enemies, among them Peel. The jury found him "not guilty, on the ground of insanity."

*De jure,* M'Naghten was acquitted; *de facto,* he was sentenced to life imprisonment in an insane asylum. He died in 1865, having been incarcerated for the last 22 years of his life.

The new ruling (binding on Federal courts in New York, Connecticut and Vermont) provides that: "A person is not responsible for criminal conduct if at the time of such conduct as a result of mental disease or defect he lacks substantial capacity either to appreciate the wrongfulness of his conduct or to conform his conduct to the requirements of law."

Both of these tests—and others, whatever their semantic differences—rest on the premise that the human mind may become "diseased," and that a person who has a "diseased mind" may, because of it, commit criminal acts unintentionally, not know the difference between right and wrong, or be unable to restrain himself from engaging in conduct prohibited by law. The value of all psychiatric tests of criminal responsibility thus hinges on the soundness of this underlying concept of "mental disease."

But what exactly is mental disease? If it is an illness, what kind is it? And if it is not an illness, what is it and why is it called an illness? Because of the frequency with which issues of mental health and illness arise not only in criminal cases but in matters of everyday life, it is important that we ask these questions and intelligently debate various possible answers to them.

I submit that mental illness is a myth. Bodies are physical objects; minds, whatever they may be, are not physical objects. Accordingly, mental diseases (such as depression or schizophrenia) cannot exist in the sense in which bodily diseases (such as broken bones or ulcerated skins) exist.

My disbelief in mental illness does not mean that I reject any facts of human behavior. "A myth," says the British philosopher Gilbert Ryle, "is not a fairy story. It is the presentation of facts belonging in one category in the idiom belonging to another. To explode a myth is accordingly not to deny facts, but to reallocate them." To say that mental illness is a myth is therefore not to *deny* facts (such as sadness or fear) but to *reallocate* them (from the category of mental illness to the category of personal conduct). Insofar as men are human beings, not machines, they always have some choice in how they act—hence, they are always responsible for their conduct. There is method in madness, no less than in sanity.

As long ago as the early nineteen-twenties, George H. Mead formulated the thesis that social situations—and human behavior in them—are analogous to games which must be played by certain "rules." In life, the games are infinite. As social conditions undergo rapid change, old games are constantly scrapped and new ones started. But most people are totally unprepared to shift from one type of game playing to another. They have early in life learned one set of rules—or, at most, a few—and find themselves forced to play new games by the old rules. This fundamental conflict leads to various problems in living—some severe enough to be commonly diagnosed as "mental illness" or "disease." It is these problems in living that the psychiatrist is usually called on to treat.

"But surely," someone might say, "a dope fiend, a rapist, or a Lee Harvey Oswald is not a *normal* person. What difference does it make whether we call him sick or something else?"

It makes, of course, all the difference in the world, for what we call things, and especially people, will shape our attitudes and justify our actions toward them. For example, when socially threatening behavior is called "witchcraft," it is handled by means of theological sanctions; when it is called "crime," it is handled by means of judicial sanctions, and when it is called "mental illness," it is handled by means of psychiatric sanctions.

The practices of modern American psychiatrists originate from two principal sources: hospital psychiatry and psychoanalysis.

Institutions for the care of the insane have existed since antiquity. However, the systematic confinement of madmen in buildings labeled "hospitals" did not begin until the middle of the 17th century. For about 250 years, from 1650 to 1900, the psychiatrist worked almost exclusively in the mental hospital. The alienist, as he was then called, was employed by an institution—a private or, more often, a public insane asylum.

The historical model and social prototype of the modern mental hospital is the French Hôpital Général. According to the distinguished medical historian George Rosen, the purposes of this institutional system were three-fold: "In part they were economic: to increase [the] manufacture [of goods], provide productive work for the able-bodied, and to end unemployment; in part social: to punish willful idleness, restore public order, and rid Paris of beggars; and in part, religious and moral: to relieve the needy, the ill and suffering, to deal with immorality and antisocial behavior, and to provide Christian instruction."

A few years after its foundation, the Hôpital Général of Paris alone contained 6,000 persons, or about 1 per cent of the population. Who were these "mentally ill" people? According to regulations issued in 1680, "children of artisans and other poor inhabitants of Paris up to the age of 25 . . . girls who were debauched or in evident danger of being debauched . . . [and] wayward children . . ." were among those listed as proper subjects for confinement. In addition, old people, persons with venereal diseases, epileptics, vagrants, prostitutes—in brief, all of society's *"misérables"*—were incarcerated in the Hôpital Général. Michel Foucault, a French student of psychiatric history, thus concludes: "The Hôpital Général is not a medical establishment. It is rather a sort of semijudicial structure, an administrative entity which, along with already constituted powers, and outside the courts, decides, judges and executes."

The facts I have cited are important in showing us one of the roles of the psychiatrist—indeed, his traditional role: He is a physician working in a mental hospital, employed, as a rule, by the state, and charged with the task of confining and "treating" people who are considered "insane." Although some of his methods have changed, the social role of the institutional psychiatrist has remained what it has always been.

Nor is its importance diminished. At the present time in the United States, approximately 750,000 persons are incarcerated in mental hospitals—90 per cent of them against their will. This is about three times the number of persons imprisoned in jails.

The mental hospital is also important for the psychiatrist: Of 15,200 practicing psychiatrists in the United States, approximately

50 per cent are in institutional practice, most of them in mental hospitals, or in related administrative positions.

I do not imply that the hospital psychiatrist does not try to help his patient, but rather that his interpretation of "helping" is different from the patient's. If one person has the power to confine another, and uses it, it seems inevitable that the confined person will consider the other his jailer. This point of view, often held by mental patients, was expressed by Valentine Alamazov, the protagonist of Valeriy Tarsis's autobiographical novel, "Ward 7." Finding himself incarcerated in a mental hospital, Alamazov had this to say to his psychiatrist:

"I don't regard you as a doctor. You call this a hospital, I call it a prison. . . . So, now, let's get everything straight. I am your prisoner, you are my jailer, and there isn't going to be any nonsense about my health . . . or about examination and treatment."

It was Sigmund Freud who created the second major form of contemporary American psychiatric practice—psychoanalysis.

In the eighteen-eighties, when Freud was a young physician, to be a psychiatrist was to be an alienist or hospital psychiatrist. Traditionally, the psychiatrist was called in by a "mentally healthy" member of the family to treat one of its "mentally sick" members; often this meant removing the sick member from the family and putting him in a mental hospital as a "patient."

Freud departed from this traditional approach. Instead of acting as the agent of the family—ostensibly caring for the patient, but actually protecting the family from him—Freud created a new professional role—the agent of the patient.

He did not accept the situation as it was presented to him, usually by the patient's family. Instead, he listened at length to the patient to ascertain how he perceived his problem; and he tried to help him realize his own aspirations and goals, even if these brought the patient, or Freud himself, into even greater conflict with the family or with society.

Thus, ethically, Freud acted like other physicians, but unlike other psychiatrists: He tried to help his patient, not someone else. By systematically refusing to "treat" patients who did not want to be treated by him, Freud departed from the accepted psychiatric methods of his day. Many psychoanalysts still adhere to this principle in treating patients. Most hospital psychiatrists do not.

It is important to note also that Freud characterized psychoanalytic treatment in humanistic and pedagogic terms and did not regard his work as medical. Psychoanalysis was never intended to make "sick" people "well" again. The analyst's task, in Freud's words, was "to serve the patient . . . as a teacher and educator."

Freud was emphatic that the analyst—and hence also the psychotherapist who only listens and talks and uses no "medical" methods—does not cure disease. Indeed, although the three great pioneers of psychoanalysis—Freud, Adler and Jung—had little good to say about one another's doctrines and methods in later years, they all agreed on one thing: that psychological methods of therapy are *not* medical procedures.

We are now ready to reconsider the question: What is mental illness? In order to do this, it is necessary to understand the principal uses of the concept of mental illness and their social consequences.

First, the term "mental illness" is used to refer to certain types of bodily diseases—that is, to diseases of the brain whose predominant symptoms are abnormalities of behavior (for example, neurosyphilis). According to one school of psychiatric thought, all mental diseases are of this type. Those who hold this view assume that some metabolic, genetic or neurological defect—perhaps a very subtle one—will ultimately be found to explain all disorders of thinking and behavior now called "mental illness."

No one would deny that, like any other part of the body, the brain may be injured or become diseased. Nor are there, to my knowledge, any psychiatrists who would deny that some of the people nowadays diagnosed as mentally ill (and free of demonstrable organic disease) might actually be suffering from the effects of as yet undiscovered neurologic or metabolic disease processes. But for those who regard mental illness as a type of brain disease, the concept of mental illness is unnecessary and misleading. If they mean that people labeled mentally ill suffer from diseases of the brain, it would seem better for the sake of clarity to say that and not something else.

The second major use of the term "mental illness" is to denote a "functional" or "psychological" disorder. Proponents of this view admit that patients called "mentally ill" do not suffer from bodily diseases, but they maintain that such individuals exhibit defects or deformations of their personalities so severe as to justify calling them "ill."

When physicians (or others) label people as "sick" merely because their actions differ from those of their fellows, they speak metaphorically—as poets, not scientists. To be sure, this kind of metaphoric use of the term "sick" is not limited to psychiatry: People also say that our economy is "sick," that a joke is "sick" or that someone they dislike makes them "sick." Yet only in connection with mental illness do we systematically act as if figure of speech were fact. No one believes that "sick economies" require medical help, but nearly everyone believes that "sick minds" do.

The power to name, or to classify, is the basis for the third use of the term "mental illness"—that is, to denote a deviant social role. For our purposes it is necessary only to distinguish between two types of social roles: those that are assumed voluntarily, such as husband or graduate student, and those that are ascribed to a person against his will, such as draftee or convicted criminal.

Roles are social artifacts. Role deviance, therefore, has meaning only in the context of specific social customs and laws. The criminal is deviant because he breaks the law; the homosexual because most people are heterosexuals; the atheist because most people believe—or say they believe—in God. In the same way, the so-called "potential killer" (who, however, has not yet killed anyone) is considered deviant because he appears to be more dangerous than most people; and so is the chronically withdrawn mental-hospital patient, because most people are—and are expected to be—socially more responsive. (I shall say more about the problems that such persons pose for those about them, and for society in general, later on.)

But which kinds of social deviance constitute "mental illness"? The answer is: that conduct which deviates from psychiatrically defined rules for mental health.

However obvious this may be, its implications for our understanding of mental illness seem to be vastly unappreciated. The fact is that every time psychiatrists formulate a new rule of mental health they create a new class of mentally sick individuals. For example, the proposition that prejudice against Jews or Negroes is a manifestation of psycho-pathology—one of many instances in the contemporary inflation of the concept of mental illness—is nothing but an attempt to expand the category of people who can be legitimately classified as psychologically sick.

Since the consequences of being labeled mentally ill include such penalties as personal degradation, loss of employment, loss of the right to drive a car, to vote, to make valid contracts or to stand trial—and, last but not least, incarceration in a mental hospital, possibly for life—the expansion of the category of people who can be so designated is useful for the increased employment of psychiatric methods of social control.

Labeling someone mentally ill is a special kind of name-calling. In other fields name-calling may constitute libel, but calling someone "mentally sick" does not. The main reason for this is that the psychiatrist who makes a diagnosis of mental illness (especially on an involuntary patient) has more social power than the person he diagnoses.

The role of power in the psychiatric diagnostic process becomes obvious only when the potential patient is a Very Important Person. When someone like Secretary of Defense Forrestal disturbs people by his ideas and actions, it is difficult to get a psychiatrist to label him mentally ill. The reason for this is that by casting the individual in a socially deviant role the psychiatric diagnostician imparts a negative, debased identity to that person. This he cannot do if his intended "patient" is socially more powerful than he is. When a mental-hospital superintendent in Louisiana tried to incarcerate and "treat" Gov. Earl Long, the Governor fired the doctor—and walked out of the hospital.

One of the traditional problems of legal psychiatry, as we saw at the outset, is the determination of criminal insanity. Lawyers and psychiatrists persist in trying to distinguish between "sane" and "insane" criminals, and in finding a "scientific" basis for determining which offenders ought to be "punished" with imprisonment and which "treated" with involuntary mental hospitalization.

I submit that criminal insanity is a metaphorical and strategic concept just as civil insanity is. The effort to distinguish, by psychiatric methods, among different classes of criminals is really an exercise in second-order classification: Having labeled some persons as "criminals," we have the option of labeling them also as "mentally healthy," and dealing with them by means of penal sanctions, or as "mentally ill" (that is, as "criminally insane"), and dealing with them by means of psychiatric sanctions.

I do not believe that insanity should be an "excusing condition" for crime. Lawbreakers, irrespective of their "mental health" ought to be treated as offenders.

Another classic dilemma of psychiatry is the problem of what society should do with its "insane" citizens who, while having committed no crime, lack "insight" into their "illness" and hence do not seek "treatment." Here we should distinguish between two fundamentally different types of psychiatric practice. The person who decides to consult a psychiatrist and pays him for his services is like a graduate student pursuing a course of study: he assumes the role of mental patient (if we wish so to label his role) *voluntarily* and is free to cast it off. By contrast, the person who is coerced into psychiatric treatment by his relatives or by the law, and who does not pay the psychiatrist for his services, is like a prisoner sentenced to a term of servitude; he is placed in the role of mental patient *against his will* and is not free to cast it off.

The psychiatrist thus has a choice between doing something *to* his patient and doing something *for* him. One of the things the psychiatrist can do to his patient is to prescribe certain life games, with the expectation that these will pacify the patient's family and social environment—and perhaps also "help" the patient. Since this kind of treatment is carried out against the wishes of the patient, it requires coercion.

One of the things the psychiatrist can do for his patient is to analyze his life games, with the expectation that this understanding will help the client to lead a life more free and responsible. To do this, however, requires a voluntary, cooperating client. Coercion has no place whatever in this type of psychiatric work. Such a psychiatrist aspires to be on tap, not on top.

The reader who finds this thesis persuasive might wonder about its practical application. If we look upon mental illness as a metaphor and a social role, rather than as a disease, how will this affect what we *do?*

For work with voluntary clients the consequence would be mainly professional and economic: The humanistic view of mental illness would open opportunities for training nonmedical persons (psychologists, social workers and others) in psychotherapy and psychoanalysis, and would eliminate the rationale for preventing such persons from engaging in the independent practice of these skills.

For work with involuntary clients the consequences would be mainly legal and social: The humanistic view of mental illness would remove the justification for involuntary mental hospitalization and treatment; accordingly, it would require the mobilization of fresh personal efforts and social resources to cope with problems now dealt with by means of traditional psychiatric methods.

It would be impossible suddenly to empty out our mental hospitals and to stop all commitments—though, to be sure, I consider these desirable goals. To attain them, however, we must provide suitable alternatives to the present social functions of involuntary mental hospitalization. I must limit myself here to mentioning only a few such alternatives, each directed toward ameliorating a specific type of human problem.

The usual justification for commitment is that the person whose confinement is sought is "dangerous to himself or others." My position is based on a principle enunciated more than 100 years ago by John Stuart Mill: "The only purpose for which power can be rightfully exercised over any member of a civilized community, against his will, is to prevent harm to others. His own good, either physical or moral, is not sufficient warranty."

Suicide, for example, should be recognized as a basic human right. The threat of suicide, or an attempt at suicide, should not be ground for involuntary mental hospitalization. (This does not mean that a physician should not treat a person who, say, is unconscious as a result of an overdose of barbiturates. It does mean that, after the patient has regained consciousness he should not be confined in a hospital against his will.)

While being "dangerous to oneself" should never be considered a legitimate reason for depriving a person of his liberty, being "dangerous to others"—if it involves breaking the law—is the best reason for doing so. One of the main functions of society is to prevent violence among its members. Thus, if individuals commit violence, or threaten to do so, they should be treated for what they are—law-breakers.

Judicial sentencing of lawbreakers does not deprive us of the opportunity of also trying to help them. If we truly believe that some lawbreakers are "mentally ill," we could offer them psychiatric help in prison. As always, the clients ought to be free to accept or reject such help.

The social control, by means of psychiatric sanctions, of dangerous behavior is complicated by the fact that people often disagree on what constitutes "dangerousness," and, even if they agree on it, on how such "dangerousness" is to be established. Thus, one group of persons now often committed is composed of individuals who manage their lives more or less adequately, but who break certain laws or social customs, and are therefore considered "dangerous" and treated as involuntary patients.

If we wish to avoid using coercive psychiatric measures against persons of this type, we have two basic options. Instead of constantly proliferating legislation prohibiting various kinds of personal conduct not directly injurious to others (as we now do), we might consider repealing and eschewing such legislation. We would thereby eliminate many types of "crime," and hence the need to define such criminals (as "dope addicts," "homosexuals" and so forth) as mentally sick. Or, if we wish to persist in our efforts to control private behavior by means of criminal sanctions, we might decide that it is more humane to punish persons who transgress these prohibitions by means of penal rather than psychiatric sanctions; the result would be the jailing of many individuals now committed to mental hospitals. (The desirability of confining lawbreakers in mental hospitals rather than in prisons is sometimes advocated on the allegedly humanitarian ground that conditions in mental hospitals are better than in jails. Even if this were true—and as a rule it is not—it would not justify redefining lawbreakers as patients. The proper remedy for inadequate prisons is prison reform.)

In addition to persons whose dangerousness is actual, established by what they have done, there are those whose dangerousness is potential, who are feared for what they might do. We often hear of "potential trouble-makers" who, however, have broken no laws, and hence could not be convicted of crime, but whom many would like to "diagnose" as "deranged" and restrain in mental hospitals.

We cannot eat our cake and have it, too: we cannot have a free society and imprison—in jails or mental hospitals—people who have broken no law. This does not mean that some people might not be "potentially" dangerous to others (indeed, many, like drunken drivers, are very dangerous); it means only that we cannot restrain such people through our mental-hygiene laws without gravely injuring the entire fabric of our society.

Another large group of persons confined involuntarily in mental hospitals is the aged; in some public mental hospitals as many as one-third of the inmates fall into this group. Yet, even hospital psychiatrists admit that many of these patients do not need mental-hospital care. "Only 50 per cent of the [elderly] patients . . . hospitalized required hospitalization in a mental institution," testified Dr. Dale C. Cameron, superintendent of St. Elizabeth's Hospital in Washington, before a House committee. "For many older patients," he added, "the primary need was found to be for physical rather than psychiatric care."

The fact that public mental hospitals accept geriatric patients—whose "mental illness" is so clearly a strategic concept designed to justify their forcible removal to places of custody—diminishes the pressure on society to provide suitable accommodations for them.

Still another group of involuntarily hospitalized patients is composed of individuals who present so-called psychiatric emergencies. Examples are the young man who becomes uncommunicative, does not leave his room, refuses to eat, perhaps even soils himself; or the young woman who faints and thereafter remains unresponsive and acts as if she were unconscious.

Patients of this type do not object to being hospitalized or to receiving medical care. Moreover, some of them suffer from bodily illness—brain tumor, head injury, uncontrolled diabetes. Others develop medical problems as a result of their behavior—severe dehydration because of failure to eat and drink, for example. Such patients should therefore he hospitalized in medical, not mental, hospitals, and should be treated as medical emergencies. Consent for hospitalization and treatment should be given by relatives, and confinement should last only until the patient has regained his powers.

The application of these principles to the care of chronic mental patients would help us to avoid coercion in their care as well. Regardless of the cause—subtle malfunctions of the brain, the effect of prolonged institutionalization or flight from communal existence into a world of private dreams—people who are almost completely unable to cope with their problems of living will no doubt always be with us. Such "nondangerous" but gravely disabled individuals could be dealt with by offering them care—good and attractive enough so that they would willingly accept it—while leaving them free to make other choices.

In short, the abolition of involuntary mental hospitalization and treatment would mean that psychiatric help, like medical, would (on the whole) have to be restricted to voluntary clients. Furthermore, some persons who are now cast in the role of involuntary mental patients would, if they broke laws, have to be dealt with as offenders, not as patients.

The nominal aim of psychiatry is the study and treatment of mental disorders. The consequences of subscribing to this apparently harmless, conventional definition of "mental health" work are, in our present age, momentous. Accepting the existence of a class of phenomena called "mental diseases," rather than inquiring into the conditions under which some persons may designate others as "mentally ill," has been the decisive step in embracing what I call the mental-health ethic. In so doing, the study of a large part of human behavior is subtly transferred from ethics to psychiatry, from the free marketplace of ideas to the closed wards of the mental hospital.

The psychiatrist deals with moral and social problems, not with medical diseases. Hence he cannot help being embroiled in the moral conflicts of his patient and of his society. The psychiatrist's role as moral legislator and social engineer is obscured, however, by the rhetoric of mental health and illness which makes his work appear as a species of medical therapy. This evasion of ethical judgments and choices may be reassuring to the laity and comforting to the profession. But can we, as individuals, afford it?

The individual can never escape the moral burden of his existence. He must choose between obedience to authority and responsibility to himself. Moral decisions are often hard and painful to make. The temptation to delegate this burden to others is therefore ever-present. Yet, as all history teaches us, those who would take from man his moral burdens—be they priests or warlords, politicians or psychiatrists—must also take from him his liberty and hence his very humanity.

A humanistic psychiatry must, therefore, repudiate its seemingly therapeutic mandate, the pursuit of which often results, intentionally or unwittingly, in moral tranquility gained at the expense of freedom and responsibility. Instead of trying to diminish man's moral burdens, such a psychiatry must aim at increasing his powers and so making him equal to his task.

And what is this task? No one has stated it better than Albert Camus when he wrote: "The aim of life can only be to increase the sum of freedom and responsibility to be found in every man and in the world. It cannot, under any circumstances, be to reduce or suppress that freedom, even temporarily."

# An Analysis of Szasz'
# "Myth of Mental Illness"

FREDERICK C. THORNE

*Dr. Thomas S. Szasz has stirred up a great deal of
controversy by his claims concerning "the myth of mental
illness." Dr. Thorne, Editor of the* Journal of Clinical
Psychology, *is of the opinion that public confidence in
psychiatry has been seriously undermined by Dr. Szasz'
charge that many psychiatric practices infringe on human
rights. In this paper Dr. Thorne undertakes an analysis of
Dr. Szasz' principal contentions, concluding that his
arguments are extremist and largely invalid.*

Thomas S. Szasz has recently created a great deal of public confusion concerning the concept of mental health by his contention that
mental illness is a myth and, by implication, the claim that current
psychiatric practices infringe on human rights by committing mental patients to hospitals against their will. Szasz has taken his arguments to the general public in popular articles and books, writing
in a superficially convincing style which, however, involves serious
untruths and distortions of facts.

Because Szasz's arguments might well set back the evolution of
modern psychiatry and clinical psychology at a time when a huge
national mental health program is just starting, it behooved the
author to make an ideological analysis of his latest claims.

Following is an analysis of Szasz' claims in a *New York Times
Magazine* article of June 12, 1966, entitled "The Myth of Mental
Illness" [1]

1. Mental illness is a myth because minds are not physical ob-

Reprinted from the *American Journal of Psychiatry,* CXXIII, pp. 652-656, 1966.
Copyright 1966, the American Psychiatric Association.

[1] Szasz, T.S., "The Myth of Mental Illness," *New York Times Magazine,* June 12,
1966, pp. 30–31, 90–92.

jects and consequently are not subject to physical disease in the medical sense.

*Rebuttal: While mental disorder may have different causes than physical diseases, the functional effects are comparably disabling. "Illness" as a generic term refers to disablement rather than to any specific physical or psychological cause.*

2. Insofar as men are human beings, they always have some choice in how they act—hence they are always responsible for their conduct.

*Rebuttal: Not psychiatrically true. All mental disorder involves loss of self-control in some manner. The greater the impairment of self-control, the less a man is volitionally responsible for his conduct.*

3. There is method in madness . . .

*Rebuttal: An overgeneralization implying that deliberate motives determine all symptomatology.*

4. Social situations and human behavior in them are analogous to games. Confusion over changing rules for playing games results in conflict in trying to solve problems of living—some severe enough to be diagnosed as "mental illness" or "disease." This is invalid because we are dealing with disordered human relations.

*Rebuttal: Not psychiatrically true. At best an oversimplification applicable only to limited cases. Mental disorder is more than just poor gamesmanship, as Szasz implies. There is a hen-egg problem here which Szasz does not realize. Are human relations disordered inevitably because of conflicting life or "game" styles? Or because either or all participants in a situation may be psychologically ill? Either may be true.*

5. The historical model of mental hospitals is to serve as a place for institutionalizing many types of persons not adapting to society, including many others besides the overtly mentally ill.

*Rebuttal: While it is true that the role of mental hospitals has been gradually extended to serve many clinical types other than the classically mentally disordered, the decision to admit other types of cases was made deliberately because better facilities were not available at the time and place.*

6. Even though current laws authorize the involuntary commitment of psychotic persons to mental hospitals, such deprivations of human rights are not validly applicable to the aged, epileptics, alcoholics, etc., who do not have any mental disease. In fact, since there is no such thing as mental disease, the whole commitment system is unconstitutional and undemocratic.

*Rebuttal: Practices regarding commitment of other groups besides the psychotic evolved as social expedients at a time when more specialized facilities were not economically feasible or professionally possible.*

7. Intolerable abuses have occurred when persons have been committed against their will by psychiatrists who were reacting more to the demands of third persons or social authorities than to the needs of the patient, to whom he is first obligated.

*Rebuttal: Abuses are possible in any situation involving humans. However, most civilized societies have recognized the physician as the one most able to diagnose and treat conduct disorders with an understanding, healing manner. Historically, greater abuses have occurred with nonpsychiatric case handling.*

8. The social role of the psychiatrist is determined by the nature of the institutions in which he works. This role is determined by the "disease" concept and gives the psychiatrist directive, authoritative, controlling powers over unwilling patients, who actually have no "disease" but are only maladapted.

*Rebuttal: A great step forward was taken when the old jungle-rule, "eye-for-an-eye" punitive system for discouraging conduct problems was replaced by the healing methods of the physician and hospital. In general, no widespread abuses have occurred under psychiatric management, which represents an evolutionary step forward until society develops something better.*

9. Too often, "mental patients" are institutionalized for the convenience of others, with the psychiatrist representing the interests of third parties rather than the primary interest of the patient. Too often, commitment only protects the family or society at the expense of the civil rights of the patient.

*Rebuttal: While such complaints occasionally are justified, this argument is an overstatement and overgeneralized. The ethical psychiatrist tries not to be unduly influenced by complaints of third parties against the patient. Moreover, too often third parties and society do need to be protected from the patient.*

10. Szasz admits that in the organic psychoses there do occur lesions in the central nervous system such as those which underlie classical physical diseases. However, he claims that "functional" or "psychological" disorders involve conditions manifested chiefly by the person's behaving "differently" from usual social expectations. He contends that it is semantically invalid to categorize persons as "sick" just because they are different.

*Rebuttal: Szasz minimizes the psychophysiological dysfunctions underlying all the psychoses, the severe psychoneuroses, epilepsy, alcoholism, addictions, and other conditions involving greater or lesser loss of self control. The important differentiation is not between being "different" but in being "disabled" and partially out of control.*

11. It is invalid to classify a person as "ill" because of behavior expressing deviant social roles. Roles are social artifacts, and deviance has meaning only in terms of social customs or laws.

*Rebuttal: An overgeneralization. Only when deviant behavior is dangerous or disabling does it command a psychiatric diagnosis or labeling.*

12. Psychiatric opinion concerning the criteria of mental health determines the kinds of deviance regarded as "mental illness." Psychiatric opinion may be fallible, prejudiced by irrelevant factors, or even by ulterior motivations. Constitutional protection should be given against psychiatric invasion of the human rights of freedom and privacy.

*Rebuttal: Theoretically true but practically unjustified. No type of clinical practice can be more perfect than what is scientifically known at the time and place. Well trained and competent psychiatric specialists are presumably wiser and more trustworthy in their decisions than are less qualified personnel.*

13. Psychiatry creates new classes of mental illness every time it formulates new rules for mental health . . . (constantly expanding) the category of people who can be legitimately classified as psychologically sick. Labeling people as mentally ill is a special kind of name-calling . . . by a psychiatrist who makes a diagnosis (especially of an involuntary patient) and has more social power than the person he diagnoses.

*Rebuttal: These arguments involve a cynical and perverse distortion of the whole process of diagnosis by a qualified specialist. Progress in all clinical sciences occurs by the progressive differentiation of previously unrecognized etiology and patterns of disorder. It is not name-calling to devise more refined diagnoses. Szasz provides no evidence of any widespread name-calling on the part of psychiatrists, the overwhelming majority of whom use diagnosis scientifically and not to discriminate against anybody.*

14. Criminal insanity is a metaphorical and strategic concept, just as civil insanity is. . . . Insanity should (not) be an "excusing condition" for crime. Lawbreakers, irrespective of their "mental health," ought to be treated as offenders.

*Rebuttal: This argument represents a regression to a prescientific failure to discriminate between the normal and the disabled. In general, hospitalization is more humane than penal incarceration. Penal systems do not provide adequate resources for disposing of many categories of psychiatric cases.*

15. Many patients do not seek psychiatric treatment voluntarily and are coerced by relatives or authorities into a role not of their own choosing . . . like a prisoner sentenced to a term of servitude.

Coercion has no place in psychiatric treatment, which requires a cooperative client.

*Rebuttal: A classical symptom of many mental conditions is lack of insight, i.e., the person does not recognize the degree of his disability or impairment of judgment. In general, the greater the loss of insight and of self control, the more dangerous the person becomes.*

16. The humanistic view of denying the existence of mental illness would remove the justification for involuntary hospitalization and treatment. We should empty out all our mental hospitals and provide more humane alternatives, including the use of non-medical personnel such as clinical psychologists, social workers, ministers, educators, etc.

*Rebuttal: This viewpoint does not give proper weight to the fact that psychiatry and our mental hospital and clinic resources represent the best that society has yet been able to devise. Szasz has no evidence that anything currently available would be any better.*

17. Even the usual justification for committing persons on the grounds that they are dangerous to self or others is both illogical and unconstitutional.

*Rebuttal: This argument seems to be leaning over backwards in protection of the disordered person at the expense of the rights of society, which also deserves protection.*

18. Suicide should be recognized as a basic human right. The threat or attempt at suicide should not be made the basis for involuntary hospitalization.

*Rebuttal: This view is contrary to established public mores based on Judeo-Christian morality. It disregards the fact that most suicides occur in depressive states which react well to therapy. It is logical that a completely normal person might be regarded as having the right to end his own life but not humane that a curable disordered person should be allowed to do so.*

19. The social control of dangerous behavior is complicated by the fact that people disagree as to what is dangerous and also on how such control is to be established. Many persons now committed are dangerous only by "fiat" or in terms of some purely relative standard. This is dangerous to civil liberties and should be unconstitutional.

*Rebuttal: Legal status in any era is always relative to the level of enlightenment of time and place. Legal codes and psychiatric standards are not whimsical judgments by irresponsible personnel but rather the best decisions which can be reached by the fairest and best qualified specialists in society.*

20. Szasz makes an impassioned appeal for a new humanistic psychiatry which will rethink its social obligations. The nominal aim of studying and treating mental disorders, implying the existence of a class of phenomena called "mental diseases" and embodying classical coercive methods of institutionalization and treatment, should be replaced by inquiries into the conditions under which some persons may designate others as mentally ill and by a more free-thinking consideration of the games which people (including psychiatrists) play on each other.

*Rebuttal: Szasz does not have a monopoly on humanistic wishes for the future. He portrays psychiatrists as a group as being nonperceptive of what they are actually doing, responsive to ulterior motivations secondary to the primary goal of satisfying the needs of the patient, heartless in their disregard of the need to be free and uncoerced, and slaves to an authoritarian tradition which gives them total control over the lives and destinies of other humans. While Szasz might gather instances of isolated abuses of clinical authority, he cannot marshal evidence of such an indictment of psychiatry in particular or society in general. He is simply jousting against straw men for the large part of his arguments.*

21. The psychiatrist deals with moral and social problems rather than mental disease, hence he cannot keep from becoming embroiled in the moral conflicts of his patient and of society. The individual man can never escape the moral burden of his existence, and any (including psychiatrists) who attempt to take from him his moral burden must also take from him his liberty and hence his very humanity.

*Rebuttal: Szasz is behind the times in not recognizing that many social psychiatrists have long been working in the humanistic direction which Szasz recommends. Carl R. Rogers recommended such ideals more than 25 years ago, as did many other pioneers in changing psychiatric practice and hospitals into genuinely humanistic ventures.*

22. A humanistic psychiatry must repudiate its seemingly therapeutic mandate and goals of social control, and instead of trying to diminish man's moral burdens, should attempt to increase his powers and so make him equal to his task. Szasz endorses the statement of Camus that "The aim of life can only be to increase the sum of freedom and responsibility to be found in every man and in the world. It cannot, under any circumstances, be to reduce or suppress that freedom, even temporarily."

*Rebuttal: This argument is very appealing and is valid as far as it goes. Certainly no responsible authority in society, much less psychiatrists, knowingly works to deprive anyone of civil liberties. The crucial question concerns persons who are too disabled or out of control to be able to utilize freedom responsibly. The uncontrolled, violently dangerous person requires external controls and institutionalization as long as he remains in such a state. The issue is not one of denying freedoms but of withholding them until the person is able to handle them responsibly.*

DISCUSSION

Szasz's arguments contain a modicum of truth and of deserved criticism for psychiatric practices at their worst. Undoubtedly many abuses, injustices, and clinical errors have occurred during the growing up of a young clinical science whose personnel consist of fallible humans. However, it is unfair and irresponsible to criticize or categorize the entire profession of psychiatry as inhumane on the basis of isolated examples of malpractice. The profession of clinical psychology (and psychiatry to a lesser degree) has been its own worst critic in scientifically evaluating its clinical results to determine their validity and how they can be improved.

Many of the Szasz arguments are seen to be exaggerated, biased, alarmist, impractical, and even erroneous. This is the kind of harangue which would be expected from a demagogue rather than a responsible scientist. Does Szasz really believe that such immoderate attacks on his own profession will improve public confidence in the mental health movement? To the contrary, there already exist many intemperate groups who are actively lobbying against the mental health movement and whose misguided efforts are encouraged by such specious arguments as Szasz offers.

Szasz's role as an idealistic, liberal reformer would be considerably brighter if his efforts were more constructively directed. The issues he raises should be debated within scientific and professional councils rather than being broadcast to a public which does not have the background to judge the arguments. Szasz is grandiose in depicting himself as the savior of modern psychiatry at a time when a host of devoted colleagues are working with comparably high ideals.

One practical effect of Szasz's arguments has been to confuse the outlook of students, interns, residents, and young psychiatrists who do not have the experience to judge their validity. Perhaps the most important truth in the whole field of psychiatry relates to the refractoriness and difficulty in treating serious psychiatric conditions. In spite of recent progress with drugs, many psychiatric conditions do not respond to any known kind of therapy. Such cases do not respond even to the most humanitarian case handling, including a surfeit of love, everything that money can buy, kindness, warmth, acceptance, and nonjudgmental attitudes. In fact, some very experienced psychiatrists have stated that the most curative influence of the mental hospital was the unpleasantness of the situation, which stimulated the patient to mobilize all his forces to get out. And whether we wish to call severe psychiatric disorders "diseases," "illness," "disorders," "disturbed human relations," "disabilities," or "social deviances," the fact remains that we are dealing with something more malignant than a game.

While everyone wishes to do his utmost for all types of unfortunates, the fact remains that any one group cannot command more than its share of social resources, and the law of diminishing returns limits what can be invested in any single case, no matter how piteous. I suppose if nobody had anything with higher priority to do, one half of society could devote all its time to taking care of the less fortunate. Unfortunately, the work of the world must be done before such surplus resources as are available can be allocated to underprivileged groups, of which the psychiatrically disabled are only one.

# INDEX OF SUBJECTS

# INDEX OF NAMES